Abdel Wahab Khalifa (ed.)

Translators Have Their Say?

Repräsentation – Transformation
representation – transformation
représentation – transformation

Translating across Cultures and Societies

herausgegeben von

Michaela Wolf
(Universität Graz)

This book series is designed to provide a forum for interdisciplinary approaches to the discussion of translation in its wider sense. Special emphasis is given to works which focus on the research of translation and interpreting in their role of (de-)constructing cultures and societies. Particularly welcome is the interaction with neighbouring disciplines (cultural studies, sociology, anthropology, gender studies, literary studies, comparative literature, historiography, etc.).
All texts are peer-reviewed.

Die Reihe ist ein Forum für interdisziplinäre Ansätze in der Diskussion kulturmittlerischer Phänomene im weitesten Sinn. Besonders willkommen sind Arbeiten, die das Übersetzen und Dolmetschen in ihrer Rolle als Beitrag zur (De-)Konstruktion von Kulturen und Gesellschaften untersuchen. Die interaktive Zusammenarbeit mit Nachbardisziplinen (Kulturwissenschaften, Soziologie, Anthropologie, Gender Studies, Allgemeine Literaturwissenschaft, Vergleichende Literaturwissenschaft, Geschichtswissenschaft, etc.) ist ausdrücklich erwünscht.
Alle Texte werden anonym begutachtet.

Band 10

LIT

Translators Have Their Say?

Translation and the Power of Agency

Selected Papers of the
CETRA Research Summer School 2013

edited by

Abdel Wahab Khalifa

assisted by
Elena Voellmer

LIT

Printed with the support of:
Karl-Franzens-Universität Graz
CETRA, Centre for Translation Studies

KARL-FRANZENS-UNIVERSITÄT GRAZ
UNIVERSITY OF GRAZ

CETRA
Centre for Translation Studies

Titelbild- und Umschlaggestaltung: Sigrid Querch
Satz: Guntram Titus Tockner

Bibliographic information published by the Deutsche Nationalbibliothek
The Deutsche Nationalbibliothek lists this publication in the Deutsche Nationalbibliografie; detailed bibliographic data are available in the Internet at http://dnb.d-nb.de.

ISBN 978-3-643-90551-2

A catalogue record for this book is available from the British Library

Klosbachstr. 107
CH-8032 Zürich
Tel. +41 (0) 44-251 75 05
Fax +41 (0) 44-251 75 06
E-Mail: zuerich@lit-verlag.ch
http://www.lit-verlag.ch

LIT VERLAG Dr. W. Hopf
Berlin 2014
Fresnostr. 2
D-48159 Münster
Tel. +49 (0) 2 51-62 03 20
Fax +49 (0) 2 51-23 19 72
E-Mail: lit@lit-verlag.de
http://www.lit-verlag.de

Distribution:
In the UK: Global Book Marketing, e-mail: mo@centralbooks.com
In North America: International Specialized Book Services, e-mail: orders@isbs.com
In Germany: LIT Verlag Fresnostr. 2, D-48159 Münster
Tel. +49 (0) 2 51-620 32 22, Fax +49 (0) 2 51-922 60 99,
E-mail: vertrieb@lit-verlag.de

In Austria: Medienlogistik Pichler-ÖBZ, e-mail: mlo@medien-logistik.at
e-books are available at www.litwebshop.de

For José Lambert

CONTENTS

MICHAELA WOLF

Universität Graz, Austria

Foreword

The year 2013 marked the 25th anniversary of the CETRA Research Summer School. Since its inauguration, hundreds of emerging Translation Studies scholars have congregated in Misano Adriatico and Leuven to exchange novel ideas and engage in thought-provoking discussions. For many of these scholars, CETRA has served as a springboard to a successful career. It has also helped foster lasting friendships and initiated networks of cooperation and trust. CETRA students have benefited from the guidance of internationally renowned professors who afforded valuable insights into a wide variety of themes within the discipline of Translation Studies.

I was honoured to serve as the 2013 CETRA Chair Professor. This opportunity has allowed me to work with outstanding young scholars who were seeking to enhance their research skills in Translation Studies in general and sociology of translation in particular. In doing so, they have enriched their understanding not only of the different topics but also of one another. The thoughtful discussions did not stop in the classroom, but continued during social gatherings after the presentations and tutorials. I admired the collaborative spirit and highly stimulating research environment amongst scholars and teaching staff. The presentations involved highly sophisticated discussions on the latest trends in the field of Translation Studies that have quite positively challenged my views about issues of current research. Many people did not come from Translation Studies per se but from other disciplines, which stresses the interdisciplinarity of the field and highlights the challenges lying ahead. It will be interesting to see how this mash-up between disciplines will allow the field to evolve and extend its boundaries. Overall, the 2013 CETRA Summer Research School was a unique and memorable experience and I would like to encourage similar endeavours in the field.

The intellectual outcome of CETRA 2013, *Translators Have Their Say? Translation and the Power of Agency*, is another valuable contribution to the *representation — transformation* series. All papers are intellectually stimulating and strikingly indicative of the broad array of research ideas connected to the issues of "agents" and "agency" of translation. All papers have undergone a severe peer reviewing process which has helped strengthen their overall quality and arguments, and assisted the contributors in developing and refining their research methodologies as well. Ultimately, I am quite certain that these papers will help add new and decisive impulses to the field of Translation Studies.

Both the editor, Abdel Wahab Khalifa, and I would like to dedicate this volume to José Lambert, the mastermind behind CETRA, whose enthusiasm for Translation Studies has contributed significantly to strengthening the field and continues to inspire countless students to explore their scholarly passions to this very day.

ABDEL WAHAB KHALIFA

The University of Leeds, UK/Tanta University, Egypt

Rethinking Agents and Agency in Translation Studies

Setting the scene: a background

That Translation Studies is nowadays a well-established interdisciplinary field of research whose boundaries extend beyond linguistic considerations is arguably indubitable. The twentieth century, especially its second half, has witnessed the emergence of a significant number of theoretical outputs that have indeed laid the foundations of the field. Prior to that, research in Translation Studies has mainly been concerned with assessing the "fidelity" or "faithfulness" of the translated text to the source text and making general judgments about what is "right" or "wrong", thus overlooking "all kinds of other aspects connected with the phenomenon of translation, a circumstance that could teach us many things about how cultures and literatures function" (Lefevere 1992:6).

It was during the 1990s that the concern of research in Translation Studies moved from the "textual" to the "cultural". This paradigm shift has been described by Bassnett and Lefevere (1990:1) as the "cultural turn" in Translation Studies. Thus conceived, reaching the understanding that the translation process is not only about the text, and that translation is not an isolated discipline but, rather, an interdisciplinary field with a "chameleon quality" that is "able to change its colour and shape, to translate itself into many different things", marks the paradigmatic shift from the textual to the cultural in Translation Studies (Bassnett 1998:26).

Cultural approaches to translation have managed to extend the disciplinary perspective to accommodate the historical and cultural contexts beside the text itself by subscribing to the idea that nothing exists in isolation and that the meaning of anything is always determined by its context (Asad 1986:148). By the same token, Bassnett and Lefevere (1990:11) state that "[t]here is always a context in which the translation takes place, always a history from which a text emerges and into which a text is transposed". All this seems to have helped open up new means of evaluating the process(es) of translation which focused on power relations inherent in any translation activity (Wolf, 2006:9). However, the main weakness in the cultural approaches to translation is that rather than delving into the extra-textual social contexts in which the translation process takes place, they lean to remain confined into the "hermeneutics of the text" (Inghilleri 2005:134). The need to surpass the purely cultural-oriented "hermeneutic" understanding of translation has shifted the attention of research in Translation Studies to the socio-oriented approaches.

Although James Holmes (1972/1988) called for a "function-oriented descriptive" understanding of translation and recommended placing more emphasis on the social contextualisation of translation or "translation sociology" (Holmes 1988:72), his call went unanswered until recently. A significant number of recent contributions to Translation Studies have shifted the foci of the field to what Michaela Wolf (2006) describes as the "social turn" in Translation Studies. Recognising that the social implications constituting the translation process have been scarcely, if at all, taken into consideration, and that the "social" intrinsically encompasses the "cultural", "textual" and even what is beyond that, seems to have been the stimulus behind the (re)emergence of the social trend in Translation Studies.

That is to say, since its emergence as a field in its own right, Translation Studies has branched out to encompass a multitude of research trends and interests including translation sociology: a subfield which has gained momentum since mid-1990s, spurred notably by the "endeavour to make descriptive theoretical approaches [to Translation Studies] more 'agent aware'" and to address the growing interest in exploring the role of agents of translation in relation to their agency (Inghilleri 2005:142). As such, socio-oriented research in Translation Studies has thus made "translators and interpreters more visible as social actors" by bringing the interplay of agency as well as social and power relations between agents into focus (ibid.).

In keeping up with all the developments in the field of Translation Studies and following the fast-growing interest in the sociological approaches to translation, KU Leuven's Centre for Translation Studies (CETRA) invited Michaela Wolf, a high-profile scholar in the area of translation sociology, as its CETRA Chair Professor 2013. Pursuing a long-standing tradition, CETRA hosts a Research Summer School, which is one of the most prestigious events in the field. The idea of the Summer School is to gather every year a number of young talented scholars (doctoral and post-doctoral) at CETRA for nearly three weeks, provide them with valuable insights into issues of current importance in the field of Translation Studies, and encourage them to exchange ideas amongst themselves as well as with the CETRA Chair Professor and teaching staff. CETRA 2013 was unique, for both CETRA's teaching staff and scholars, since it marked the programme's silver anniversary. Twenty-five years ago, José Lambert had this unique idea of initiating a platform/network that would facilitate strong collaborative links between emerging and established Translation Studies scholars from across the globe. The present volume is the outcome of the contribution of eight CETRA 2013 scholars. The volume concerns itself with the socio-related issue of agents and agency of translation and focuses its attention on how agency manifests itself through the agents' practices in Translation Studies.

Agents of translation revisited

The impetus need to understand the various processes involved in the act of translation has drawn the attention of Translation Studies' scholars to "the sociology of agents" (Wolf 2006) or "the sociology of translators" (Chesterman 2006). This shift in focus highlights the importance of and the key role played by agents of translation in either shaping ideologies or introducing new perspectives through translation. As such, agents of translation are perceived as social actors who are heavily involved in the dynamics of translation production and the power interplay arising at every stage throughout the translation process. The concept of agent intrinsically encompasses all actors (humans) and actants (nonhumans) involved in the process of translation: from production and distribution to consumption and critical metadiscourses. In other words, agents of translation can be humans or nonhumans (see Buzelin 2005), and they are any relatively autonomous entity able to trigger cultural innovation and change or modify a state of affairs by making a difference or manifesting a result (Milton and Bandia 2009:1).

Pierre Bourdieu's theory of practice, especially his concept of habitus, has been of particular interest in agent-oriented research in Translation Studies. This interest in Bourdieu's sociology was driven by the need "within Translation Studies to focus more attention on translators and interpreters" and "to analyse critically their role as social and cultural agents actively participating in the production and reproduction of textual and discursive practices" (Inghilleri 2005:126). Understanding human agents and their practices can thus aid our understanding of how a certain translation is produced, and how the way they exercise their agency can affect the final translation product (Pym 1998:ix).

The study of the translation activity as an agent-based social phenomenon has stepped to the front against the backdrop of the polysystem theory and Descriptive Translation Studies (DTS). The DTS paradigm has provided insights on how translated literature functions within the historical and literary "systems" of the target culture through the concepts it has introduced. This has indeed broadened the scope of research in Translation Studies. However, drawing mainly on the theoretical paradigms from literary studies, where the principal focus lies on the text, DTS seems to have overlooked the important role played by the social agents as well as social reality during the process of translation. Wolf (2007:7) states that what seems to be ignored in the polysystem theory and DTS "are the conditions of the social interactions in question [...] the nature of the political and social relationships between the groups involved in these processes" of translation, or the criteria underlying the creation of a product to be placed on a specific market. Hence, the element lacking from the polysystem theory and DTS appears to be taking account of the social agents involved in the translation process and the social functions of their cultural products (Hermans 1999; Buzelin 2005). This directs our attention to Bourdieu's concept of habitus and its importance in Translation Studies. For many translation scholars, habitus appeared capable of explaining the role played by agents of translation, how they think and communicate, and the logic behind their various discursive practices (see for example Gouanvic 1997, 1999; Simeoni 1998; Kalinowski 2002; *The Translator* 2005; Wolf 1999, 2006, 2007; Vorderobermeier 2014).

Bourdieu (1990:53-60) defines habitus as "a system of durable, transposable dispositions" of "internalised structures, common schemes of perception, conception and action" that is geared towards practical decision making(s). Thus, on the one hand, habitus is a system of long-lasting dispositions that structures the practices of agents and stays with them throughout their entire lives. On the other hand, it is exchangeable in the sense that it can transpose across time and in more than one field. As such, the interest in Bourdieu's concept of habitus in Translation Studies seems to have stemmed from its ability to account for how agents of translation can be determined and yet be acting too, and how their "behaviour can be regulated and shared without being the product of conformity to be codified, recognised rules or other casual mechanisms" (Inghilleri 2005:134-5). However, although proven fruitful in evaluating the motives of agents of translation, criticism has been levelled at the application of the concept of habitus, and Bourdieu's apparatus in general, in Translation Studies. At the crux of the argument is its disposition to reduce the agent to the translator and to only view agency from an individualistic perspective (Buzelin 2005:215; see also Sela-Sheffy 1997, 2005; Abdallah and Koskinen 2007; Buzelin and Folaron 2007; Meylaerts 2008).

While there seems to be a general inclination to equate the concept of agents with that of agency, each of them refers to rather similar but different things. The following section is an attempt to define agency and illuminate this difference.

The complex question of agency

So what is agency after all? The concept of agency appears to be a slippery one and there seems not to be an agreement of what agency is or what constitutes it in Translation Studies (for an exception see Kinnunen and Koskinsen 2010's definition which will be discussed below). This insinuates that very little extensive research has been done on the power of agency and what it means in Translation Studies hence the importance of this volume. Although the research conducted by Milton and Bandia (2009), Dam and Zethsen (2009), Kinnunen and Koskinen (2010a), Abdallah (2012) and Haddadian-Moghaddam (2012) provides excellent accounts on translatorial agency, the concept still needs closer consideration.

In their *Oxford Dictionary of Sociology*, Scott and Marshall (2009:11) define agency as being a mere "synonym for action". Similarly, Buchanan (2010:10) avers that agency is "the degree to which a subject is able to determine the course of their actions". Building on Marx's views that agents (entities who practice agency) are subjects in history rather than the subjects of it, Buchanan goes on to argue that the concept "is generally used in the context of discussions about the factors that shape everyday life and place a limit on agency" (ibid.). Buchanan's definition of agency is informative as it takes account of the limiting properties of agency that are generally associated with structure (see further Haddadian-Moghaddam 2012:16).

This leads our discussion to the interaction between agency and structure. There is a strong case for linking the concept of subjectivity with that of agency (see for example Giddens 1979 and Bauman 1973). Pierre Bourdieu's insights on the issue are relevant here. Bourdieu links between the objective and subjective aspects of social life and argues that they are inevitably bonded. This viewpoint has enabled Bourdieu to challenge and transcend the agency versus structure dichotomy. However, although the two concepts are treated as separate entities, they are still looked upon in Translation Studies as being enmeshed together. As Kinnunen and Koskinen (2010b:8) rightly state: "to understand agents, one needs to look at the structures they are located in and vice versa".

As far as Translation Studies is concerned, given the prominence of socio-oriented research in the field and the growing interest in socio-cultural mediators; that is, agents (humans and nonhumans alike), there have recently been several attempts to define and endorse the enigmatic concept of agency. Milton and Bandia (2009:15) aver that their understanding of agency is not informed by a whiggish perspective, leading to a better world, rather, they stress that translatorial agents do have the ability to make choices and seek/take options. Agency, argues Buzelin (2011:7), is "the ability to exert power in an intentional way". Further, arguably building on Kaptelinin and Nardi's (2006:33) account on agency where they defined it as "the ability and need to act", Kinnunen and Koskinen (2010b:6) defined agency as the "willingness and ability to act". This reflects the representation of agency as a *perception-decision-action* loop. That is to say, perception or "*willingness* describes a particular internal state and disposition"; decision or "*ability* relates the concept of agency to constraints and issues of power(lessness), highlighting the intrinsic relation between agency and power"; and action "or *acting*, that is, exerting an influence in the life-world" (ibid.:6-7; original emphasis). That said, translatorial agency can be thought of as being practiced in specific socio-historical conditions, as part of the interplay of power strategies and influence attributed to the agents involved, and hence it is always a site of multiple determinations and actions. To address the idea of agency in translation is thus to highlight the interplay of power and ideology: what gets translated or not and why is always (at least partly) a matter of exercising power or reflecting authority. Realising the importance of and growing interest in agents and agency of translation, and given the paucity of research done so far, has led to centring the theme of this volume on the issue of agency. It aims to serve as an attempt to understand the complex nature of agency in terms of its relation to agents of translation; the role of translatorial agents and the way they exercise their agency in (de)constructing narratives of power and identity; and the influence of translatorial agency on the various processes of translation and hence the final translation product as well.

As the title implies, it is under the concept of "agency" that I have grouped the contributions of this volume into three categories: *agency and empowerment: sociological approaches to translation* (Foglia, Talento, Tahirović-Sijerčić); *agency and choice: translation policy and practice* (Hanes, Cobelo); and *narratives of agency: translation and linguistic-cultural transposition* (Bohn, Voellmer, Veidenberga). Though diverse in perspective, the eight papers presented in this volume address the concept of translatorial agency from different viewpoints, examine the (extra)textual factors that have an impact on translation decisions and outcomes, and provide insights into the chain of power relations shaped by the agency endowed to various translation agents. Since the characteristics of translation agents may vary considerably, the articles also explore how these agents contextualise their capacities in relation to others, what constrains or enhances their agency, and how they engage and exert that agency through translation. This allows for a deeper socio-cultural understanding of the dynamics of agency, which would consequently prove fruitful in revealing how agency is exercised or agents' choices are made and reflected in the final translation product.

References

Abdallah, Kristiina (2012) *Translators in Production Networks: Reflections on Agency, Quality and Ethics.* Joensuu: University of Eastern Finland.

Abdallah, Kristiina/Kaisa Koskinen (2007) "Managing Trust: Translating and the Network Economy". *Meta* 52:4, 673-687.

Asad, Talal (1986) "The Concept of Cultural Translation". In Clifford, James/Marcus, George E. (eds.) *Writing Culture: The Poetics and Politics of Ethnography.* Berkeley: University of California Press, 141-164.

Bassnett, Susan/André Lefevere (1990) *Translation, History, and Culture.* London/New York: Pinter Publishers.

Bassnett, Susan (1998) "When is a Translation Not a Translation?" In Bassnett, Susan/ Lefevere, André. *Constructing Cultures: Essays on Literary Translation.* Clevedon/ Philadelphia/Toronto/Sydney/Johannesburg: Multilingual Matters, 25-40.

Bauman, Zygmunt (1973) *Culture as Praxis.* London: Routledge & Kegan Paul.

Bourdieu, Pierre (1990) *The Logic of Practice* (tr. by Richard Nice). Stanford, CA: Stanford University Press.

Buchanan, Ian (2010) *Oxford Dictionary of Critical Theory.* Oxford/New York: Oxford University Press.

Buzelin, Hélène (2005) "Unexpected Allies: How Latour's Network Theory Could Complement Bourdieusian Analyses in Translation Studies". *The Translator* 11:2, 193-218.

Buzelin, Hélène (2011) "Agents of Translation". In Gambier, Yves/van Doorslaer, Luc (eds.) *Handbook of Translation Studies.* Vol. 2. Amsterdam/Philadelphia: John Benjamins, 6-12.

Buzelin, Hélène/Folaron, Deborah (2007) "Introduction: Connecting Translation and Network Studies". *Meta* 52:4, 605-642.

Chesterman, Andrew (2006) "Questions in the Sociology of Translation". In Duarte, João F./Rosa Alexandra A./Seruya, Teresa *Translation Studies at the Interface of Disciplines.* Amsterdam/Philadelphia: John Benjamins, 9-28.

Dam, Helle V./Zethsen, Karen Korning (2009) "Translators and (Lack of) Power: A Study of Danish Company Translators' Occupational Status". *Languages at Work – Bridging Theory and Practice* 4:6, http://ojs.statsbiblioteket.dk/index.php/law/article/view/6189, [19 October 2014].

Giddens, Anthony (1979) *Central Problems in Social Theory: Action, Structure, and Contradiction in Social Analysis.* Berkeley: University of California Press.

Gouanvic, Jean-Marc (1997) "Translation and the Shape of Things to Come: The Emergence of American Science Fiction in Post-War France". *The Translator* 3:2, 125-152.

Gouanvic, Jean-Marc (1999) *Sociologie de la traduction: La science-fiction américaine dans l'espace culturel français des années 1950.* Arras: Artois Presses Université.

Haddadian Moghaddam, Esmaeil (2012) *Agency in the Translation and Production of Novels from English in Modern Iran.* Tarragona: Universitat Rovira i Virgili: PhD Dissertation.

Hermans, Theo (1999) *Translation in Systems: Descriptive and System-Oriented Approaches Explained.* Manchester: St Jerome.

Holmes, James S. (1972/1988) "The Name and Nature of Translation Studies". In Holmes, James S. (ed.) *Translated! Papers on Literary Translation and Translation Studies.* Amsterdam: Rodopi, 67-80.

Inghilleri, Moira (2005) "The Sociology of Bourdieu and the Construction of the 'Object' in Translation and Interpreting Studies". *The Translator* 11:2, 125-145.

Kalinowski, Isabelle (2002) "La vocation au travail de traduction". *Actes de la Recherché en Sciences Sociales* 144, 47-54.

Kaptelinin, Victor/Nardi, Bonnie A. (2006) *Acting with Technology: Activity Theory and Interaction Design.* Cambridge: MIT Press.

Kinnunen, Tuija/Koskinen, Kaisa (eds.) (2010a) *Translators' Agency.* Tampere: Tampere University Press.

Kinnunen, Tuija/Koskinen, Kaisa (2010b) "Introduction". In Kinnunen, Tuija/Koskinen, Kaisa (eds.) *Translators' Agency.* Tampere: Tampere University Press, 4-10.

Lefevere, André (1992) *Translating Literature: Practice and Theory in a Comparative Literature Context.* New York: Modern Language Association of America.

Meylaerts, Reine (2008) "Translators and (Their) Norms: Towards a Sociological Construction of the Individual". In Pym, Anthony/ Shlesinger, Miriam/Simeoni, Daniel (eds.) *Beyond Descriptive Translation Studies: Investigations in Homage to Gideon Toury*. Amsterdam/Philadelphia: John Benjamins, 91-102.

Milton, John/Bandia, Paul F. (2009) "Introduction: Agents of Translation and Translation Studies". In Milton, John/Bandia, Paul F. (eds.) *Agents of Translation*. Amsterdam/Philadelphia: John Benjamins, 1-18.

Pym, Anthony (1998) *Method in Translation History*. Manchester: St Jerome.

Scott, John/Marshall, Gordon (2009) *Oxford Dictionary of Sociology*. Oxford/New York: Oxford University Press.

Sela-Sheffy, Rakefet (1997) "Models and Habituses: Problems in the Idea of Cultural Repertoires". *Canadian Review of Comparative Literature* XXIV:l, 35-47.

Sela-Sheffy, Rakefet (2005) "How to Be a (Recognised) Translator: Rethinking Habitus, Norms, and the Field of Translation". *Target* 17:1, 1-26.

Simeoni, Daniel (1998) "The Pivotal Status of the Translator's Habitus". *Target* 10:1, 1-39.

The Translator 11:2 (2005) "Special Issue: Bourdieu and the Sociology of Translation and Interpreting". Edited by Moira Inghilleri.

Vorderobermeier, Gisella M. (2014) *Remapping Habitus in Translation Studies*. Amsterdam/New York: Rodopi.

Wolf, Michaela (1999) "Zum 'sozialen Sinn' in der Translation: Translationssoziologische Implikationen von Pierre Bourdieus Kultursoziologie". *Arcadia* 34:2, 262-275.

Wolf, Michaela. (2006) "Translating and Interpreting as a Social Practice – Introspection into a New Field". In Wolf, Michaela (ed.) *Übersetzen – Translating – Traduire: Towards a "Social Turn"?*. Münster/Hamburg/Berlin/Vienna/London: LIT, 9-19.

Wolf, Michaela (2007) "Introduction: The Emergence of a Sociology of Translation". In Wolf, Michaela/Fukari, Alexandra (eds.) *Constructing a Sociology of Translation*. Amsterdam/Philadelphia: John Benjamins, 1-36.

Agency and Empowerment: Sociological Approaches to Translation

CECILIA FOGLIA

Université de Montréal, Canada

Tracking the Socio-graphical Trajectory of Marco Micone: A Sociology of Migration by Way of Translation[1]

This article is a contribution to the sociology of translation and explores, in particular, the cultural work of the Italo-Quebecois writer and translator Marco Micone, who migrated to Montreal (Canada) after World War II. The objective of this study is twofold. First, it aims at enhancing Chesterman's notion of Translat*or* Studies by elaborating a model to conceptualise the individual translator's trajectory – especially in its variant of the migrant writer-translator. Such a model, which stems from Bourdieu's (1993) concept of "genetic sociology", is socio-graphical. This means that it focuses on the genesis and the structure of the social space where the translator's project takes shape in relation to the series of transitions and positions s/he occupies in time. Secondly, this article aims at testing the conceptualised socio-graphical model on Micone's cultural works to demonstrate that in the case of migrant writers and translators cultural texts are more revealing of the agent, the context, and the audiences when they are sociologically (and not solely subjectively) investigated. It also questions the possibility of considering Micone's translations and plays as the result of the sociology he produces as a migrant individual and of which he is the object. The basic question we shall be pursuing is the following: how can Translation Studies benefit from applying a socio-graphical approach to migrant writer-translators, and translators in general, as a way to explore their socio-personal trajectory?

Keywords: Translat*or* Studies, sociology of translation, socio-graphical approach, Marco Micone, Pierre Bourdieu

Introduction

Over the past two decades, under the influence of sociological concepts and models formulated by Pierre Bourdieu, and afterwards by Bernard Lahire,

[1] The author would like to thank Hélène Buzelin for her insightful comments on preliminary versions of this text and Sanaa Benmessaoud for her linguistic revision.

Bruno Latour and Niklas Luhmann among others, Translation Studies (TS) has witnessed a steady increase in the number of scholars who have applied sociological theories and approaches to it (see Simeoni 1998; Wolf 2007a; Gouanvic 2010; etc.). Such scholars, now perceiving translation as a social practice, have started to concentrate on the study of individuals, their observable behaviour and the products of those behaviours embedded within the phenomenological context. This sociological trend, as Lawrence Venuti recalls (2013), first appeared in francophone areas, namely Quebec and France, where the translation scholar Jean-Marc Gouanvic (1999, 2007) and the sociologist Gisèle Sapiro (2010) investigated, from two different standpoints (translatorial and sociological), the fundamental role and impact played by translations in the French literary field and in the world market of translation. The endorsement of a sociological orientation of TS has gradually brought about a change in methodology. Instead of exclusively concentrating on text-analysis to posit theories, scholars have increasingly emphasised and focused on the study of the environment of translation as a "socially regulated activity" (Hermans 1997:10). In other words, they have started to conduct extensive research on the complex interplay between "the author of the text, the transfer agencies, the text, and the public in their social interlacements" (Wolf 2007a:1).

Nonetheless, the keen interest in the study of the environment of translation (namely, the invisible hands that influence translators' decision-making like editors, market(s), publishers, etc.) has neither undermined nor eclipsed the crucial role played by translators' agency, that is, their "ability to exert power in an intentional way" (Buzelin 2011:6). In fact, as Michaela Wolf argues, "the subjectivity of the participants in this "global play" is of paramount importance" (2007a:1). Indeed, the break of the sociology of translation with exclusively text-centred approaches has allowed scholars to shift their attention from translation as a linguistic operation, to translation as the tangible product of interactive social agents and events. Certainly, translators belong to and work in a social, culture-bound environment. Accordingly, translation epitomises the result of multiple processes of mediation and negotiation of cultural differences. Therefore, "mediating agents operate […] as a sort of "web" that exists between the various cultures. They are bound up in social networks which allow them to be viewed as socially constructed and constructing subjects" (ibid.:3).

Since the "cultural turn" in TS (Bassnett and Lefevere 1998), translators have gained more visibility. Evidence is given, for example, by Venuti's

(2008/1995) inquiry into the various reasons behind translators' transparency or by Daniel Simeoni's (1995) study of the discipline and Anthony Pym's reinterpretation of history from the agent's standpoint. In his innovative work entitled *Method in Translation History* (1998), Pym calls for a translator-centred approach to TS. Indeed, the focus on individual agents as central objects of research would allow scholars "to reconstruct the domain of socially conditioned subjectivity as a basis for understanding the translators' history" (Liu 2012:1170). More recently, Pym has pointed out, "there has [...] been a development from the study of translations as texts to research on translators as people, and this has gone hand-in-hand with calls for a 'humanisation' of Translation Studies" (2010:153). It is, however, worth mentioning that despite the increasing heed scholars have paid to the social exploration of individual translators, the influence exerted by the phenomenological context at large over agents (and vice versa) remains pivotal. Translations not only reflect the socio-cultural and historical conditions under which they have been produced, but they also reveal some fundamental characteristics of both the source and target contexts and of the agents implied. Hence, a sociology of translators cannot live without a translation sociology and vice versa. According to Wolf, the study of translations in relation to their cultural environment

> opened up new methodologies which were developed to shed light on the translation process revealing the power relations underlying any translation activity [...]. Additionally, new approaches to Translation Studies were given a boost, often in a common interdisciplinary effort to widen the discipline's horizon. (Wolf 2007b:132)

In the attempt to enlarge the discipline's scope, the present contribution firstly aims to elaborate a model to conceptualise the individual translator's socio-graphical trajectory especially in its variant of the migrant writer-translator. Secondly, it aims at testing such a model by exploring the cultural works of the Italo-Quebecois writer and translator Marco Micone (b.1945). The reason why we have chosen Micone as a case study is twofold. Firstly, Micone plays a crucial and unique role in the history of the Italian migration to Quebec after World War II. Through his texts, Micone gives voice to the migrant Italian community by crafting an *ad hoc* and hybrid language. Language thus becomes a powerful instrument at the disposal of migrants to disseminate their "migrant culture", which is one of adaptation and hybridity but certainly not of acculturation. Secondly, Micone's works have been mostly analysed from the subjective viewpoint of the identity quest;

the overwhelming sense of nostalgia for the homeland alternated with the conscious impossibility of going back home (see Puccini 2013). In other words, the influence of the contingent reality over his cultural products is barely taken into account. Such a rather "romantic" textual exegesis conducted on his works has brought about a major consequence. Micone's activity as a writer-translator has largely been interpreted in a limited way, in terms of his individual need to recover his Italian origins. Accordingly, the emphasis on personal motivations has overshadowed the potential his cultural works have for understanding the social dimension within which his plays and translations have taken shape. Therefore, the basic question we shall be pursuing will be as follows: how would TS benefit from applying a socio-graphical approach to migrant writer-translators (and translators in general) as a way to explore their socio-personal trajectory? Can translations related to migration gain a new status, that is, one of sociological texts, thus turning (writer-)translators into sociologists of migration processes? And if so, are Micone's translations (and cultural works in general) the result of the sociology he produces and of which he is the object?

In what follows, we shall introduce the approach we have chosen to explore Micone's texts as well as the preliminary considerations and hypothesis it has brought to light. The approach we intend to adopt to explore Micone's cultural products and trajectory as a writer-translator is socio-graphical. When we talk about "socio-graphical trajectories" we refer to translators' individual genetic sociology; that is, "the genesis and the structure of the specific social space in which the creative project [is] formed" (Bourdieu 1993:193) in relation to the series of transitions and positions they (translators) occupy in time. As stated above, Micone's works have been mostly explored using the migration as an individual experience as main interpretative framework. Instead, the socio-graphical model we intend to conceptualise here would allow us to investigate Micone's writing-translatorial evolution not only from the subjective, but also from the objective and social viewpoints. In this trend, his works would inform us on the way Micone has evolved in the *continuum* of time, the kind of sociology he has produced and undergone, and the way he has contributed to the integration of the Italian community in Quebec. It could also enlighten readers on the way the host society has reacted and been influenced by the newcomers and vice versa, as well as on the way cultures and languages have mingled with one other, and their effects on the practice of translation, etc. In this article, we shall delve more into the first point. Ultimately, the socio-graphical approach is a translator-centred model that proves to be particularly worthwhile in the case of migrant translators whose life experiences can be viewed as a double metaphor for translation; namely, a geographical, physical dislocation/relocation followed by a linguistic, sociocultural transfer. The case study prompted by Marco Micone will serve as an opportunity to rethink writing and translation as a socio-subjective event with socio-personal consequences. On the one hand, the adoption of a socio-graphical approach to Micone's production makes it possible to touch upon questions of hybrid identities' habituses and modes of cultural integration. On the other hand, it helps analyse his writing activity in a much longer time span and in relation to his context and life.

This contribution proceeds as follows. The first part draws attention to the development of a sociology of translators, which is approached by bringing Andrew Chesterman's (2009) reflection on the steady progression of a new branch called "Translat*or* Studies" within TS to the fore. On this premise, we shall illustrate the characteristics of the conceptual methodology we intend to adopt to analyse Micone's cultural works. The second part concentrates on the case study provided by Micone. We will firstly introduce his biography and social trajectory as a migrant. Then, we will investigate and outline some of the main characteristics of the socio-graphical approach applied to his trajectory as a writer-translator. Finally, we will discuss some of the preliminary conclusions and considerations that our approach has brought to light.

The origins of the conceptual research

In 2009, Chesterman published "The Name and Nature of Translator Studies", a contribution which echoed James Holmes' article entitled "The Name and Nature of Translation Studies" (1988). The latter was based on a seminal paper presented at the Third International Conference of Applied Linguistics held in Copenhagen in 1972 where Holmes put forward a conceptual schema that described different elements of TS. This contributed to making TS an independent discipline.

According to Chesterman, recent research tendencies in TS have proved to be more focused on translators than on texts. Since the role of translators is inadequately represented in Holmes' classic map, Chesterman calls for a whole revision of it in light of the new sociological trend. He also argues that this change in perspective is particularly visible "in translation sociology, translation history and in research into the translator's decision-making process" (2009:13). It goes without saying that behind any translation lies a translator, "[b]ut not all translation research takes [the translator] as the primary and explicit focus, the starting point, the central concept of the research question" (ibid.:14). Yet, Chesterman's objective is to draw translation scholars' attention to an on-going shift in emphasis within translation research. Thus, he goes back to Holmes' map to point out that even though explicit references to translators' activities are missing, save for the mention of the "translator training" under the "applied TS" section, agents are implicitly included in some branches presented in the map. Some of these are the "process-oriented" and the "function-oriented" researches developed under Descriptive Translation Studies (DTS), and the "translator training", "policy" (i.e., norms) and "translation aids" (namely, translators' resources and technological tools) developed within the applied sub-type on the map. Process-oriented approaches are concerned with the "process or act of translation itself" (Holmes 1988:72). In other words, they correspond to "[t]he problem of what exactly takes place in the 'little black box' of the translator's 'mind' as he creates a new, more or less matching text in another language" (ibid.:72). The function-oriented approach is "not interested in the description of translations in themselves, but in the description of their function in the recipient socio-cultural situation: it is a study of contexts rather than texts" (ibid.:14). It is precisely here that Holmes prophetically foresees a future area of research he calls "translation sociology" (see Simeoni 1995; Chesterman 2009). However, whilst Holmes stresses the fundamental role played by the environment of translation, Chesterman recalls that the social context includes the power exerted by agents too.

The reason why Chesterman's article can be taken as an upgraded version of Holmes' contribution lies in Chesterman's objective to bridge the gaps detected in Holmes' map. More specifically, these gaps concern Holmes' heavily text-oriented vision of TS, his almost unique emphasis on the *skopos* (that is, on the intended effect) of a translation rather than on the analysis of the agents' *telos* too (that is, the translator's motivations behind a translation) and "the scope of research on translation sociology, history and ethics"[2] (2009:19). Also, according to Chesterman, TS consists of four main branches: textual, cultural, cognitive and sociological. On the contrary,

[2] Chesterman adds in his article that "[t]o be fair, such research topics had scarcely yet appeared in 1972" (2009:19).

Holmes' map only focuses on the textual branch, thus leaving the agent dimension out of the schema. As Holmes' map does not provide a coherent image of the new subfield (Translat*or* Studies), Chesterman suggests sketching a further schema to highlight and make explicit translators' cultural, cognitive and sociological aspects. In light of this, Chesterman's pattern is not to be taken as a substitute of Holmes' map, but as a complement to it. Based on the concept of translators as the unit of investigation, Translat*or* Studies (which comprises the sociology of translators and interpreters) covers issues like the status of agents in different cultures, translators' habitus, norms, working conditions, networks, professional organisations, gender, life trajectories, power relations, activism, etc. Furthermore, it sheds light on translators' reasons (*teloi*) for translating and the personal goals they want to achieve through translation. Chesterman concludes that in wake of the sociological trend that TS has witnessed, a new translation approach essentially centred on translators has taken shape, and this could be named the "agent model". However, Chesterman's contribution shows one critical weakness. He does not provide either an exhaustive definition or a list of approaches adopting the agent model of translation. All he provides is an overall analysis of TS scholars' research tendencies that are ultimately translator-centred.

In the next section we shall concentrate on the model to be used in our case study, which aims at enhancing Chesterman's understanding of Translat*or* Studies.

Enhancing Translat*or* Studies: outlining the socio-graphical approach

Translator-centred approaches have developed since the 1990s. As Wolf maintains, "[i]ndividual figures of translators have frequently been investigated in *historically* oriented works" (2007a:14, emphasis added). For instance (ibid.), Jean Delisle and Judith Woodsworth (1995) explored the role of translators in the dissemination of religion, the transfer of knowledge and the construction of national literatures, thus providing accurate information on their socio-cultural context. Pym (1998) opted for an agent model of translation to chart the history of translation, whereas Venuti (2008/1995) denounced the invisible, neglected status of translators and suggested strategies to overcome their ancillary position in relation to the author(s) of the source text. Other translator-centred approaches based on the exploration of translators' agency (see Tymoczko 2010, Boéri 2008) have given valuable insight into some new aspects of translational behaviour, like the potential for manipulation or the vision of the translator as an activist and engaged agent. From being a model of research in the history of translation, translator-centredness has also become a promising approach within the sociology of translation. Numerous scholars and sociologists, like Simeoni (1998), Heilbron (1999), Gouanvic (1999, 2010), Meylaerts (2008, 2010), Sapiro (2010), to name a few, have made extensive use of Bourdieu's notion of habitus to discuss translators' agency, trajectories, behaviour and tendencies. Habitus, a set of durable and transposable dispositions (Bourdieu 1990), has been and still is a ubiquitous concept in the sociology of translation and more recently, in the sociology of translators too. However, differently to what has been done so far, we suggest an agent model of translation which, following the migrant translator's trajectory, can inform us on at least two aspects of Chesterman's (2009) three-dimensional nature of Translat*or* Studies: namely, the cultural and the sociological ones, the cognitive being replaced by the socio-personal one.

Before tackling the model we aim to conceptualise within the framework of migration, some preliminary assumptions will be provided. First of all, Marco Micone's translations-adaptations and self-translations fall within the literary field. Secondly, as stated above, his works have mainly been interpreted from a subjective viewpoint, thus eclipsing its sociological potential. Thirdly, although we are dealing with one single migrant writer-translator, the model we aim to elaborate can possibly be applied to a wider range of non-migrant writer-translators, as well as translators in general.

To develop our socio-graphical model, we have started from Pierre Bourdieu's (1996) social theory (or theory of the social origin) of the work of art. By social theory, the French sociologist refers to the fact that social conditions and dynamics deeply influence and shape the way individuals and groups think and act, and vice versa. Bourdieu aims at applying his social theory to literary works and specifically tests it on Gustave Flaubert's (1869) *Sentimental Education*. Bourdieu maintains that literary writings have the capacity to

> concentrate and condense in the concrete singularity of a sensitive figure and an individual adventure, functioning both as a metaphor and as metonymy, all the complexity of a structure and a history which scientific analysis must laboriously unfold and deploy. (Bourdieu 1996:24)

Therefore, the application of the social theory to the literary field (which is for the French sociologist a fictional but emblematic representation of the complex interplay between the personal and the socio-historical context) would allow Bourdieu to achieve two aims: the reinterpretation of literary texts from a social perspective and the development of an analytical method where the notions of power, field and habitus can interact. So, the reason why we have chosen Bourdieu's social theory as a starting point for our model is threefold: its applicability to the literary field, its emphasis on the social dynamics influencing the realisation of cultural products, and its aim to outline an analytical model. In this paper, we shall concentrate more on the first two points.

According to Bourdieu, western literary criticism has, since the 1960s, excessively focused on writers' familiar and psychological aspects to interpret facts, thus neglecting their interaction with the social context. To explain his theory, he cites the example of Jean Paul Sartre who, in his critical analysis of Flaubert, simply investigates the French novelist from a psychological outlook. On the contrary, Bourdieu (1993) claims that critics' excessive interest towards writers' private lives has brought about the development of two dichotomous approaches to investigate literary texts, either through the "retrospective illusion" (*illusion biographique*) or the "genetic sociology". The former conceives of cultural works as the result of an individual's initial experience or behaviour (ibid.:193; see also Hanna 2005:167). More specifically, literary critics have the "illusion" that the interplay between the context and the individual is intelligible by way of a diachronic analysis of the subject's life experiences. Consequently, texts are simply explored by following individuals' longitudinal trajectories and biographies with no particular heed to the socio-cultural and historical context. Bourdieu adds that according to this mode, any cultural product is seen as uni-determined, i.e., as the final result of *one* social determinant motivating the individual to undertake a literary project (see Hanna 2005:167). Moreover, such a hermeneutic approach (retrospective illusion) influences critics' way of interpreting texts, as it lacks any social, objective and sometimes critical stance. As far as our case study is concerned, retrospective illusion has so far been the most widely adopted approach to explore Micone's works (see Puccini 2013). Instead, the latter – that is, genetic sociology – "problematises the social conditioning of cultural works. It locates these practices in a social universe of available positions to be occupied by agents with particular dispositions" (Hanna 2005:168). Therefore, cultural works represent the outcome of multi-directional, socio-cultural practices, which result from the encounters between agents' trajectories and the objective structure of the cultural field. Genetic sociology, therefore

> takes issue with the linearity of teleological reasoning which posits that socio-cultural practice is the mechanical response to a unitary stimulus. Instead, it conceives of this practice in terms of multiple causation[3] and as the product of the dialectical relation between objective social structures and the subjectivity of social agents. (Ibid.)

In other words, although "retrospective illusion" is a translator-centred approach that takes the subject as the starting point of analysis, it is a uni-determined and barely contextualised model of investigation, as it does not account for the multiple reasons behind writer-translators' and translators' (in general) choices. The study of Micone's trajectory entails avoiding the pitfalls of purely concentrating on his biography and personal motivations to justify his decisions. Rather, exploring his trajectory signifies investigating the multiple stimuli and causations behind his individual choices, the series of positions he occupies "in the successive states of the literary field" (Bourdieu 1993:189), in the *continuum* of subjective and collective time (i.e., history) and in relation to the phenomenological context. In this way, the model we aim to conceptualise can inform us on what Chesterman (2009) calls the cultural and sociological dimensions of Translat*or* Studies; that is, on the socio-cultural context in which Micone has produced his texts, how the context has influenced his writing-translatorial choices, how and why – from being a playwright – he becomes a translator-adaptor and self-translator. Moreover, the way he translates can inform us on the nature of the reception; that is, on the kind of audience he copes with. When discussing Chesterman's statement concerning the emergence of an agent model of translation essentially focused on translators, we have claimed that he does not provide any pragmatic example of such an approach, thus remaining on the theoretical level of the definition. In light of this, we suggest considering the socio-graphical approach as a pragmatic application of Bourdieu's concept of "genetic sociology" and, at the same time, as a concrete agent

---

[3] The notion of "multiple causality"; that is, the idea according to which "translation is a complex activity for which there must be multiple sources of explanation" (Brownlie 2003:11), was first introduced by Pym (1998) and then discussed by Brownlie (2003), too. However, we cite here Hanna's article (2005) because he has investigated the concept of "multiple causation" in relation to Bourdieu's genetic sociology.

model of looking at translations. In order for the socio-graphical approach to be a pragmatic application of Bourdieu's theory and an example of what Chesterman calls the agent model, we will look at Micone's cultural works from two angles: from the structure to the agent, and vice versa (see next section). In the structure-agent level of investigation we will observe how the socio-cultural context has influenced both Micone's craftsmanship of the language and the way of conceiving his translations-adaptations and self-translations. In the agent-structure level of observation, we shall reflect on how Micone's dispositions or habitus – which corresponds to "a durable and transposable set of principle of perception, appreciation, and action, capable of generating practices and representations that are (usually) adapted to the situation […]" (Bourdieu 1991:29) – mirror the social context he inhabits, whether they have developed, changed, weakened or reinforced, etc., in a new socio-cultural context. In a nutshell, the study of Micone's habitus could enlighten us on the sociology that Micone produces or the one of which he is the object. In conclusion, the socio-graphical approach overcomes the hierarchical relationship between agency and structure, since it is plausible and viable provided that both components are considered equally and simultaneously when examining the cultural product. What is more, it is a holistic, multi-directional and agent model approach to writing and translation, as it gives readers insight into agents' habitus, subjectivity, socio-cultural underpinnings, positions taken within the historical, political and literary influences and frameworks.

A socio-graphical reading of Marco Micone's trajectory

Attention is now drawn to the socio-graphical approach applied to Micone's literary production. This approach aims at uncovering his personal writing and translatorial dispositions within a national and social system. This model does not prioritise sociological subjects over the context or vice versa. It rather investigates them as interdependent forces that mutually influence and affect the cultural product. However, before discussing the approach, we will explore Micone's socio-graphical trajectory and intricate role of being a *no man's lan(d)guage* writer-translator (see also Micone 1985 and Puccini 2013), i.e., an individual can be understood as being hybrid (that is, evidencing simultaneous manifestations of heterogeneous elements).

Trajectory of an Italian emigrant

Marco Micone was born in 1945 in Montelongo, a small village of the Molise region, in Southern Italy. At the age of thirteen, he migrated to Montreal (in the province of Quebec, Canada) with his mother and brother to join his father. It was 1958, and Italy, one of the defeated countries of the Second World War, was experiencing a harsh economic recession. Migration was a consequence of poverty and also a political solution encouraged by the Italian government to avoid workers' insurrections and strikes. Several villages in the South of Italy emptied out, and such a diaspora inaugurated the second wave of the Italian migration to Canada (the first one having occurred between the end of the nineteenth and the beginning of the twentieth centuries).

When Micone arrived in Montreal he could speak neither French nor English. All he was familiar with was vernacular Italian (spoken at home) and standard Italian (practised at school). Nevertheless, translation had already marked his early education as an Italian pupil. In fact, his elementary school teacher had nudged him into buying a black notebook (Micone 2009) where he could translate the vernacular expressions he used into standard Italian to improve his native language (Foglia forthcoming). In Montreal, he was refused by French school institutions and received his education mostly in English. Micone blamed such a "linguistic ghettoisation", as it imposed many immigrants to study in English rather than in French.[4] Over time, this inexplicably led immigrants settled in Quebec to associate the thorough knowledge of English with higher chances of being successful and rich in life. Since his childhood, Micone had a keen interest in reading literary texts, a former pastime which later became a lifetime commitment. When he came in contact with the francophone literature and its tenets (e.g., identity quest, post-colonialism, linguistic hybridity, etc.) at McGill University, he became more conscious of his condition as an immigrant and decided to pragmatically engage with political, cultural, social and linguistic issues.

After earning a degree in 1970 with a thesis on the theatre of the Quebecois playwright Marcel Dubé, an ardent supporter of the preservation of the French language in Canada, Micone was hired as a professor at Vanier College in Montreal, where he later taught Italian literature and culture due to the significant presence of second generation Italian students. This

[4] French became the official language of Quebec in 1977.

experience was highly inspiring for Micone, whose classes were a real incubator for ideas. His thorough knowledge of theatre, along with his personal admiration for Eugène Ionesco, with whom he shared some affinities (they were both emigrants, theatre-literate and sensitive to themes like the incommunicability of mankind), encouraged Micone to undertake his project of writing for the stage. He thus crafted, in French, in less than a decade, three plays of paramount importance for the history of Italian migration to Canada, namely: *Gens du silence* (1982), *Addolorata* (1984) and *Déjà l'agonie* (1988). In 1996, he re-edited this triptych under the common title of *Trilogia*. The first play dealt with the arrival and settlement in Montreal of two generations of an emigrant Italian family; the second investigated the conflict between the emigrant heritage and the local culture, whereas the third problematised the (im)possibility of becoming a Quebecois without losing one's own origins. The success of these plays coincided with Micone's legitimisation within Canadian mainstream literature, the consecration of a sub-literary field labelled the Italo-Quebecois migration writing (Berrouët-Oriol 1986-87:20), and the possibility of being translated (into English and Italian) and translating from his native language with the purpose of enlarging the Canadian national canon and accessing new ones. In 1992, Micone devoted himself to the creation of *Le figuier enchanté* (1998/1992), an autobiographical hybrid collection of stories tackling the questions of migration and the impossibility of returning home.

The publication of his autobiographical essay concludes his first stage of literary creation. It is precisely during this phase that Micone fictionalises and dramatises the big issues and consequences of migration, such as linguistic uncertainty, identity, ghettoisation, and immigrants' search for integration by escaping acculturation (see Brisset 1990) through the promotion of plurilingualism and multiculturalism (in other words, the coexistence of various languages and cultures).

Micone chooses the theatre for various reasons. First and foremost, he thinks that writing for the stage is, from a linguistic viewpoint, a much easier task for a non-native speaker than crafting a novel. Secondly, he was academically trained as a playwright. Thirdly, playwriting has mimetic and didactic functions. It epitomises the union between language and self-expression (the body) (Conroy 2010). Indeed, *mimesis* means that the audiences identify themselves with the actors, which appeals to an emotional involvement that allows Micone and the spectators to sympathise with immigrants and reflect upon the problems of fragmentation, social exclusion, linguistic and identity loss (Foglia forthcoming). Accordingly, theatre becomes a place and a means to educate individuals towards peaceful cohabitation and mutual acceptance. Moreover, as the writer and literary critic Lise Gauvin (2007) affirms, Quebecois theatre was involved, at Micone's time, in a practice of decentralisation. This could explain his propensity to adopt a literary genre that satisfies his personal, socio-cultural and activist needs. Hence, Micone contributes to decentralising the national canon by producing (and translating) literary texts that promote a "migrant culture" (Micone 1992) written in a new, hybrid language, which is neither French, nor English or Italian, but a combination of the three. Micone's decentralisation of the domestic canon is particularly visible in his theatre translations, which mark his second stage of literary creation. From 1992 to 2008, he translated for the stage seven plays, from Italian into French, originally written by canonical Italian playwrights like Luigi Pirandello, Carlo Goldoni and Carlo Gozzi, as well as a play by William Shakespeare from English into French.

At the turn of the twenty-first century, Micone reedits the poem *Speak What* (2001/1979) which tackles Quebec's linguistic issues and marks the third stage of his literary creation. He later becomes famous in Italy. Cosmo Iannone Editore, an Italian publisher particularly concerned with the question of migration, decides to translate his autobiographical essay (commissioned for Marcella Marcelli (2005) and translated under Micone's supervision), and his theatrical trilogy (translated by Micone himself in 2004 and published in 2005) from French into Italian. The self-translation of his trilogy suffers heavy modifications due to the almost two-decade interval separating the source from the target text in Italian. When self-translating plays he had originally written in the 1980s, Micone feels he is narrating the culture of an Italian community which has drastically changed over time. Not only does he modify some stories told in the texts, but also changes his characters' language, which was originally a blend of *joual*[5], vernacular Italian and informal English. His characters' multilingual nature is kept intact. However, they now speak an international French, which is no longer tainted by vernacular inflections, but embellished with anglicisms and some Italian neologisms. This is certainly symptomatic of a community that has

[5] The Merriam-Webster Dictionary Online (2014) defines joual as a spoken Canadian French, "especially the local forms of the spoken French of Quebec that differ the most from prescribed forms".

succeeded in integrating itself to the host society without experiencing a process of acculturation. As stated above, Micone was asked to self-translate his plays, which otherwise would have never existed in his mother tongue (Italian). The very first four scenes of his trilogy are self-translated literally, then he severely modifies (or almost rewrites) the rest of the text. While self-translating into Italian, Micone feels that *that* is the right picture he wants to draw of the Italian community in Montreal. Thus, he decides to replace the old version of the trilogy published in French with a new one which corresponds to the self-translation into French of his self-translations into Italian. In a nutshell, his self-translations into Italian become the source texts of his self-translations into French. This time he opts for a more faithful self-translation. The reason why Micone undergoes a double self-translation experience is twofold. Firstly, because he thinks that when self-translating for the first time from French into Italian, and after so many years, he has gained a certain distance from his personal experiences of migration and integration in Quebec, and can thus provide texts self-translated from a more objective viewpoint. Secondly, because he thinks that his self-translations into Italian represent the most realistic portrait of the dynamics and vicissitudes the Italian migrants to Quebec after World War II have ever lived.[6] Self-translation thus marks the fourth stage of Micone's literary creation. However, the aforementioned four phases are not to be investigated separately, but analysed as a continuous evolution of an original act of writing, a trajectory to be explored through a socio-graphical approach grounded in the Bourdieusian theory of "genetic sociology".

A socio-graphical interpretation of Micone's cultural works

The application of the socio-graphical model to Micone's literary production has brought about the formulation of some preliminary conclusions. First and foremost, he does not merely embark upon writing because of his condition as a migrant. Migration is certainly a *leitmotiv* in his literary production, but not the only triggering cause. In fact, his fascination with literature and writing dates back to his pre-migration years. Writing and (self-)translation symbolise the surviving thread that binds him to his homeland, but this legacy is regenerated and nourished by the Quebecois socio-cultural

[6] This information has been gathered during a private conversation with Micone in Montreal, in July 2013.

history. For instance, despite privileging Italian scenarios and characters, his literary production strongly reflects the great ideological effects conveyed by Bill 101[7] adopted in 1977 and imposing French as the official language of Quebec, and the Quiet Revolution of the 1960s promoting the secularisation of society, political power, culture, traditions and literature. Secondly, the study of Micone's socio-graphical trajectory entails a macro-level (structure → agent) and a micro-level (agent → structure) observation. The former helps both analyse Micone's literary activity in the *continuum* of time, and accounts for his transitions, from one genre to another, in relation to socio-historical events. The outcome of such an exploration shows that Micone shifts from writing to self-translation through translation and adaptation because of socio-personal needs (he privileges translation over writing when the latter becomes too self-representative) and market requirements (he is asked to translate Italian social plays because of his origins and credibility; he has, in fact, become an authoritative voice in social issues). Yet, his texts individually introduce some specific innovations from the cultural and linguistic viewpoints (e.g., culturally hybrid dialogues and neologisms), although they share common themes and techniques. This leads us to hypothesise that the names we can use to differentiate his cultural works – that is, original texts, translations, adaptations and self-translations – are but linguistic labels designating a mutually influenced and unique act of writing. His texts, in fact, show no clear-cut divide. Instead, they are constructively conceived in the *continuum* of time, history and personal experience. In other words, the exploration of individuals' life trajectories provides information on the socio-historical evolution of writing and translating processes too.

The micro-level observation, in contrast, informs us of the positions Micone occupies in the field of writing and translation, his habitus and norms in relation to "the structure of the field and the positions it makes available at a certain historical moment, as well as the kinds of symbolic and economic capital around which a field is structured" (Bourdieu 1993:189). Micone has not been trained as a professional translator. Therefore, it is likely that his habitus, i.e., his transposable dispositions, reflects the characteristics acquired during his early socialisation process and life conditions.

[7] Bill 101 (or *La Charte de la langue française*) is an Act of State signed in 1977. The charter "aims at making French the language of work and social promotion in business, and the language normally used between speakers of different mother tongues" (Dansereau 1999:68-69).

Nonetheless, since he lives in a plurilingual society and is not educated in his mother tongue (see also Meylaerts 2010:3), his initial habitus is doomed to be modified by and modify that of others. For example, it is especially in his translations-adaptations of Goldoni's plays from Italian into French that he displays a multilingual habitus. In fact, his characters constantly shift from English to French to Italian and show no difficulty in understanding one another. Micone does not provide any translation in brackets or in footnotes; rather, he simply indicates the code switching in bold.[8] We could certainly ask ourselves whether this constant code switching jeopardises the audience's comprehension of the play. Happily, however, Micone elaborates a witty strategy to overcome this hypothetical problem. As to the introduction of English segments into his translations-adaptations, sentences are generally short, simple, and language is rather ordinary (i.e., "These Italians are crazy", Micone 2001/1979:6). Moreover, his plays address a Montrealese audience, which is supposedly bilingual (French and English) in nature (see Simon 2012). As to the Italian sentences he introduces in the plays, he selects Italian words that share the same root with French terms (see Levesque 1994), so that the audience can intuitively and easily understand the meaning by way of phonetic similarities (i.e., the Italian words "Rispetto, voglio rispetto" [Micone 2001/1979:6 translating Goldoni 1748] correspond in French to "Respect, je veux du respect" ["Respect, I want respect"] and as we can see, they share the same root). From the sociological point of view, this tells us more about the context and audience Micone works for. He deals with a public whose habitus is multilingual, cosmopolitan and accustomed to coping with various cultures and listening to different languages in the middle of the street. Undoubtedly, the social context not only influences Micone's way of translating, but also becomes an original and rich source of inspiration. Vice versa, Micone's habitus exhorts his

---

[8] The following is an example of trilingual, hybrid dialogue taken from Micone's adaptation of Goldoni's play (1748):

Robenif: Je suis tout à vous.
Rosaura: Tant que vous serez à Venise!
Robenif: **She's irresistible**.
Rosaura: **Che raffinamento**! (Micone 2001:15).

[Robenif: I am entirely at your disposal.
Rosaura: Until you are in Venise!
Robenif: **She's irresistible**.
Rosaura: **How refined!**] (my translation)

audiences to live a foreignising experience, or rather, to get out of their linguistic comfort zone in order to go through an unexplored contact zone where languages and cultures coexist. Despite being a non-professional translator, Micone makes up for his lack of training with his socio-personal experience and perceptions. Ultimately, micro and macro-level observations are to be examined synchronically in order to allow for the multi-directional influences affecting Micone's production to surface. Taken as a whole, his cultural products show his constant endeavour to construct a literary genre with its own language and tenets.

Micone paves the way for the Italo-Quebecois theatre of migration aiming at educating people in otherness. His stories reproduce the power struggle between dominant and dominated cultures whatever their nationality may be. His idea of "migrant culture" denies the existence of a cultural and linguistic hierarchy and postulates that cultures ought not annihilate but meet one other. Their encounter profoundly modifies them and leaves room for the emergence of a new, unpredictable hybrid culture where traces of constituent elements are still recognisable (Simon 1999:45). By defining the concept of "migrant culture", Micone provides a definition of himself as a writer-translator: he is an agent whose native language and culture are forever sealed within himself. They will never be totally erased by others and vice versa. Since he is depositary of a heterogeneous culture, he is a *no man's lan(d)guage* individual who composes at the "[i]ntersections of language and memory" (Simon 2012) using his own self-image. His works do not strive for monolingualism, but for the promotion of a translational writing and culture, since the French he uses "is shaped by other languages [Italian and English] – and in this way distance, absence and loss become a mode of enunciation" (ibid.:15).

Conclusion

This paper has aimed to conceptualise the socio-graphical approach, which can be viewed as a pragmatic application of Bourdieu's concept of "genetic sociology", as well as a concrete example of Chesterman's understanding of the agent model of TS. Hence, we can define the socio-graphical approach as a multiperspective and translator-centred method. It is multiperspective because it brings to light the sociological aspects influencing the nature of multicultural agents like Micone. It is translator-centred as it seeks to "turn up the volume" (Simon 2012:20) on (writer-)translators and their trajectories to disclose the potentialities for understanding both the private and social spaces they work and live in. As previously mentioned, the socio-graphical model emphasises the importance of "genetic sociology" and consequently of the socio-graphical approach over "retrospective illusion". In doing so, the method we suggest aims at providing a more exhaustive depiction of the kaleidoscopic nature of these multifaceted agents.

To sum up, the objective of the socio-graphical approach is to shed light on the possibility that (writer-)translators have to occupy a role other than that of socio-cultural mediators. In particular, the socio-graphical approach applied to migrant (writer-)translators aims at analysing the migration phenomenon from a sociological standpoint, which takes into account but does not limit itself to the subjective one. Micone is a polyvalent individual whose agency is hard to define. Hardly ever is he subservient to the source texts, either in the translations-adaptations or in his self-translations. This is most probably due to the fact that he was first a writer and later a translator. Through the study of Micone, we realise that migration is more a collective experience than a solely personal one. It is undoubtedly told by one single individual, but in a rather socio-cultural way which doubly informs us on the source and target languages, cultures, socio-political and historical dynamics. Throughout the article we have questioned the possibility of looking at Micone's translations (and cultural works in general) as the result of the sociology he produces and of which he is the object. So far, what we have inferred by analysing his trajectory and reading his plays and translations with a sociological eye (see Simeoni 2007:13), is that Micone starts writing to give voice to his *gens du silence* (voiceless people); to describe their socio-cultural sense of uprootedness; and their political, educational and economic discrimination in a culturally and linguistically divided city like Montreal (see Simon 2012:144). Nevertheless, he ends up depicting, especially in his translations-adaptations, how migration has socio-culturally contributed to transforming the city into a much more vibrant, multicultural, plurilingual and cosmopolitan outlook (see Beck 2006:3) or reality (ibid.:17). Micone's cultural works do not produce a sociological sense of "distancing" or "memorialisation" – that is, they do not "[relegate] individual works to their 'national' origins" (Simon 2012:13), – but of "furthering" – that is, they strive for a cultural and "multilingual fertilisation" (ibid.:16) and cohabitation. In conclusion, what TS would therefore gain from adopting such a holistic approach, especially in its variant of the migrant writer-translator, is the collection of some valuable, objective information on how a migrant community has linguistically, socially, culturally, etc. settled into the host country, or conversely fallen apart. Most importantly, such an approach might help the discipline to analyse the impact, as well as the effects, migration has (had) on the translatorial process, the selection of texts and topics to translate, and the reasons why multicultural and plurilingual individuals (like migrants) often experience different forms of writing (see Hokenson 2013:42) thus becoming polyvalent agents. In this way, scholars of other disciplines would not turn towards TS to (mainly) borrow its case studies to support or criticise their theories. They could adopt TS approaches and models to cooperatively develop theories from their very first premises.

References

Bassnett, Susan/Lefevere, André (1998) *Constructing Cultures: Essays on Literary Translation.* Clevendon/Philadelphia/Toronto/Sydney/Johannesburg: Multilingual Matters.

Beck, Ulrich (2006) *The Cosmopolitan Vision* (tr. by Ciaran Cronin). Cambridge: Polity Press.

Berrouët-Oriol, Robert (1986-87) "L'effet d'exil du champ littéraire québécois". *Vice Versa* 17, 20-21.

Boéri, Julie (2008) "A Narrative Account of the Babel vs. Naumann Controversy. Competing Perspectives on Activism in Conference Interpreting". *The Translator* 14:1, 21-50.

Bourdieu, Pierre (1990) *The Logic of Practice* (tr. by Richard Nice). Stanford, CA: Stanford University Press.

Bourdieu, Pierre (1991) "Questions of Method". In Ibsch, Elrud/Schram, Dick/Steen, Gerard (eds.) *Empirical Studies of Literature: Proceedings of the Second IGEL Conference, Amsterdam 1989.* Amsterdam: Rodopi, 19-36.

Bourdieu, Pierre (1993) *The Field of Cultural Production: Essays on Art and Literature* (tr. by Claud Du Verlie). Cambridge: Polity Press.

Bourdieu, Pierre (1996) *The Rules of Art. Genesis and Structure of the Literary Field* (tr. by Susan Emanuel). Stanford, CA: Stanford University Press.

Brisset, Annie (1990) *Sociocritique de la traduction. Théâtre et altérité au Québec (1968-1988).* Longueuil: Les Éditions du Préambule.

Brownlie, Shioban (2003) "Investigating Explanations of Translational Phenomena. A Case for Multiple Casuality". *Target* 15:1, 111-152.

Buzelin, Hélène (2011) "Agents of Translation". In Gambier, Yves/van Doorslaer, Luc (eds.) *Handbook of Translation Studies.* Vol. 2. Amsterdam/Philadelphia: John Benjamins, 6-12.

Chesterman, Andrew (2009) "The Name and Nature of Translator Studies". *Hermes: Journal of Language and Communication Studies* 42, 13-22.

Conroy, Colette (2010) *Theatre and the Body*. Basingstoke: Palgrave Macmillan.

Dansereau, Jean (1999) "La politique linguistique du Québec: Vérités et mensonges". *Globe: Revue Internationale d'Études Québécoises* 2, 63-82.

Foglia, Cecilia (forthcoming) "Théâtre, traduction et déracimilation. Marco Micone et l'expérience de l'écriture cathartique". In Belle, Marie-Alice/Echeverri, Álvaro (eds.) *Repenser la place de la traductologie dans les sciences humaines*. Arras: Artois Presses Université et Les Presses de l'Université d'Ottawa.

Gauvin, Lise (2007) "Filiations et filatures: Modalité et usages de la parole chez deux écrivains migrants, Micone et Pasquali". In Talahite-Moodley, Anissa (ed.) *Problématiques identitaires et discours de l'exil dans les littératures francophones*. Ottawa: Les Presses de l'Université d'Ottawa, 15-35.

Goldoni, Carlo (1748) *La veuve rusée* (tr. by Marco Micone, 2001). Manuscript. Montreal: Bibliothèque de l'École Nationale de Théâtre du Canada.

Gouanvic, Jean-Marc (1999) *Sociologie de la traduction. La science-fiction américaine dans l'espace culturel français des années 1950*. Arras: Artois Presses Université.

Gouanvic, Jean-Marc (2007) *Pratique sociale de la traduction: Le roman réaliste américain dans le champ littéraire français des années 1950*. Arras: Artois Presses Université.

Gouanvic, Jean-Marc (2010) "Outline of a Sociology of Translation Informed by the Ideas of Pierre Bourdieu". *MonTI* 2, 119-129.

Hanna, Sameh F. (2005) "Hamlet Lives Happily Ever After in Arabic: The Genesis of the Field of Drama Translation in Egypt". *The Translator* 11:2, 167-192.

Heilbron, Johan (1999) "Towards a Sociology of Translation: Book Translations as a Cultural World-System". *European Journal of Social Theory* 2:4, 429-444.

Hermans, Theo (1997) "Translation as Institution". In Snell-Hornby, Mary/Jettmarová, Zuzana/Kaindl, Klaus (eds.) *Translation as Intercultural Communication. Selected Papers from the EST Congress Prague 1995*. Amsterdam/Philadelphia: John Benjamins, 3-20.

Hokenson, Jan (2013) "History and the Self-Translator". In Cordingley, Anthony (ed.) *Self-Translation: Brokering Originality in Hybrid Culture*. London: Bloomsbury, 39-60.

Holmes, James S. (1988) "The Name and Nature of Translation Studies". In Holmes, James S. (ed.) *Translated! Papers on Literary Translation and Translation Studies*. Amsterdam: Rodopi, 67-80.

Levesque, Solange (1994) "Traduire c'est émigrer: Entretien avec Marco Micone". *Jeu* 70, 17-30.

Liu, Jinyu (2012) "Habitus of Translators as Socialised Individuals: Bourdieu's Account". *Theory and Practice in Language Studies* 2: 6, 1168-1173.

Merriam-Webster Online (2014) *Dictionary and Thesaurus*. http://www.merriam–webster.com/ [19 October 2014].

Meylaerts, Reine (2008) "Translators and (Their) Norms: Towards a Sociological Construction of the Individual". In Shlesinger, Miriam/Simeoni, Daniel/Pym, Anthony (eds.) *Beyond Descriptive Studies: Investigations in Homage to Gideon Toury*. Amsterdam/Philadlphia: John Benjamins, 91-102.

Meylaerts, Reine (2010) "Habitus and Self-image of Native Literary Author-translators in Diglossic Societies". *Translation and Interpreting Studies* 5:1, 1-19.

Micone, Marco (1982) *Gens du silence.* Montréal: Québec-Amérique.

Micone, Marco (1984) *Addolorata.* Montréal: Guernica.

Micone, Marco (1985) "La parole immigrée". In Caccia, Fulvio (ed.) *Sous le signe du Phénix. Entretiens avec 15 créateurs Italo-Québécois.* Montréal: Guernica, 264-265.

Micone, Marco (1988) *Déjà l'agonie.* Montréal: L'Hexagone.

Micone, Marco (1992) *Le palimpseste impossible.* Montréal: Leméac.

Micone, Marco (1996) *Trilogia.* Montréal: VLB éditeur.

Micone, Marco (1998/1992) *Le figuier enchanté.* Montréal: Boréal.

Micone, Marco (2001/1979) *Speak What.* Montréal: VLB Éditeur.

Micone, Marco (2005) *Il Fico Magico* (tr. by Marcella Marcelli and Marco Micone). Isernia: Cosmo Iannone Editore.

Micone, Marco (2009) "Écrire et traduire entre deux langues et deux cultures". http://molisedautore.blogspot.ca/2009/02/testo–originale–di–marco–micone.html [11 June 2014].

Puccini, Paola (2013) "L'autotraduction comme performance: *Non Era Per Noi* de Marco Micone". In Lagarde, Christian/Tanqueiro, Helena (eds.) *L'autotraduction aux frontiers de la langue et de la culture.* Limoges: Éditions Lambert-Lucas, 133-142.

Pym, Anthony (1998) *Methods in Translation History.* Manchester: St Jerome.

Pym, Anthony (2010) *Exploring Translation Theories.* London: Routledge.

Sapiro, Gisèle (2010) "French Literature in the World System of Translation" (tr. by Jody Gladding). In McDonald, Christie/Suleiman, Susan R. (eds.) *French Global: A New Approach to Literary History.* New York: Columbia University Press, 298-319.

Simeoni, Daniel (1995) "Translating and Studying Translation: The View from the Agent". *Meta* 40:3, 445-460.

Simeoni, Daniel (1998) "The Pivotal Status of the Translator's Habitus". *Target* 10:1, 1-39.

Simeoni, Daniel (2007) "Translation and Society. The Emergence of a Conceptual Relationship". In St-Pierre, Paul/Kar, Prafulla C. (eds.) *Reflections, Refractions, Transformations.* Amsterdam/Philadelphia: John Benjamins, 13-26.

Simon, Sherry (1999) *Hybridité textuelle.* Montréal: Île de la Tortue.

Simon, Sherry (2012) *Cities in Translation. Intersections of Language and Memory.* London/New York: Routledge.

Tymoczko, Maria (ed.) (2010) *Translation, Resistance, Activism.* Amherst: University of Massachusetts Press.

Venuti, Lawrence (2008/1995) *The Translator's Invisibility. A History of Translation.* London/New York: Routledge.

Venuti, Lawrence (2013) *Translation Changes Everything. Theory and Practice.* London/New York: Routledge.

Wolf, Michaela (2007a) "Introduction". In Wolf, Michaela/Fukari, Alexandra (eds.) *Constructing a Sociology of Translation.* Amsterdam/Philadelphia: John Benjamins, 1-36.

Wolf, Michaela (2007b) "Bourdieu's 'Rules of the Game': An Introspection into Methodological Questions of Translation Sociology". *Matraga* 4:29, 130-145.

Serena Talento

Universität Bayreuth, Germany

Consecration, Deconsecration, and Reconsecration: The Shifting Role of Literary Translation into Swahili

The sociological theory on the (re)production of cultural knowledge and the circulation of cultural goods has evidenced the role of translation as a symbolic resource in the pursuit of prestige and power. Literary translation can thus be said to be posited in the centre of a multi-relational space of intellectual, political, economic and cultural exchanges. This paper draws on Bourdieu's concepts of *symbolic good* and *capital*, together with the concept of translation as *consecration* from Casanova, Heilbron and Sapiro. The concepts will be used to shed light upon the use of translation into Swahili as a resource in the struggle for literary legitimacy. The investigation focuses around three different historical settings: pre-twentieth-century, colonial and post-colonial. These time frames have seen translations into Swahili being used as symbolic goods to obtain, as well as negate and relocate, symbolic capital for the writer, the language or the literary field on the whole. This article aims at contributing to the theoretical discussion of the sociology of the cultural product, by maintaining that the notion of translation as *consecration* is also preserved in cases when the text is a pseudotranslation. In addition, by taking the logic beneath the circulation of symbolic goods within the Swahili colonial and postcolonial experience as case studies, proposals are made towards the notions of translation as *deconsecration*, and *reconsecration*.

Keywords: Swahili literature, symbolic goods, symbolic capital, consecration, deconsecration, reconsecration

Introduction

In regards to the debate within Swahili academia during the 1980s and 1990s concerning the place for translated texts within Swahili literature, Alwi M. Shatry (1996:77) concluded:

> I rather suspect that to the Swahili, […] translations would belong where they are most appropriate – in the arena of translated literature – and would remain marginalised, if irrelevant, relative to Swahili-language literature.

The irrelevance alluded to has been a common theme demarcated by a number of Swahili critics who have tended to side-line literary translations into Swahili. Euphrase Kezilahabi, a Tanzanian poet, novelist and scholar, maintains that the historical epics set in Arabia, which were translated, adapted or pseudotranslated during pre-colonial times, had "very little relevancy to the people living in East Africa" (1973:62). Along similar lines, A. Magoti (1981:54) condemns the outbreak of translations into Swahili in post-colonial Tanzania, and contends that translation is a negative practice, which hinders the development of Swahili literature.

To counteract such a generally held view of irrelevance, in this paper I shall examine the utilisation of literary translations into Swahili. Translations will be scrutinised in regards to their use as symbolic resources for consecration and deconsecration of the Swahili writer, language or literary field on the whole.

Swahili is a Bantu language whose origin dates back to the ninth century (Nurse and Spear 1985:49). The language was historically associated with the urban coastal Muslim communities of the area stretching from southern Somalia to southern Mozambique, encompassing adjacent islands and archipelagos. As a written literature, Swahili boasts a tradition of both religious and secular poetry preserved in the form of manuscripts dating back to the seventeenth century (Mulokozi and Sengo 1995:1). This pre-twentieth century literature flourished in the cultural centres of Pate, Lamu and Mombasa (in Kenya), and Pemba and Tanga (in what is now Tanzania). During German, and subsequently British, colonial rule in East Africa, Swahili became the lingua franca of the region and, following the independence of Kenya and Tanganyika, Swahili was officially chosen as the national language of both.

Theoretical framework: symbolic goods, capital, and consecration

At the heart of this paper's perspective lies the Bourdieusian understanding of cultural products as resources – commodities which are selected and exchanged by social agents to access and accumulate the capital which such resources yield (Bourdieu 1977:4). According to Pierre Bourdieu's sociological outlook, the social world is composed of fields. These fields are semi-autonomous areas of production within which social agents (individuals, groups or institutions) occupy certain positions by virtue of the distribution and accumulation of capital (Bourdieu 1989:17). Bourdieu discerns different forms of capital: economic, which pertains to financial properties; social capital, which refers to the networks of relationships or affiliations to groups, institutions or organisations; cultural, which refers either to signs of distinction manifested through attitude (embodied), material possessions (objectified), or credentials and qualifications such as titles or education (institutionalised); and symbolic capital, which is not a form of capital *per se*, but rather represents the conversion of the other forms of capital into honour and prestige (Bourdieu 1997). The accumulation and distribution of capital determines the allocation of positions of power within the field. Hence, the logic of contending forces which make social agents struggle over resources and, therefore, positions (Bourdieu 1983:312-313). The field of production – and re-production – of knowledge is part of this logic. Within this background, cultural products are conceived as symbolic goods in that they can be converted to symbolic capital (Bourdieu 1977:5).

Drawing from Bourdieu's notions of field and capital, Pascale Casanova (2002) narrows the focus onto the circulation of literary goods with particular reference to the role of translation within an international context. From Casanova's perspective, the exchanges of literary goods are conceptualised as an international literary space of hierarchised literary fields in which *dominant* literary languages stand in a position of conflict against *dominated* literary languages. The positions depend on the accumulation and/or recognition of literary capital. This form of capital, introduced by Casanova, is a specific form of capital formed by a patrimony, an archive of texts, which functions as attestation of antiquity and/or prestige. In Casanova's own terms the literary capital represents "a symbolic central bank" loaded with literary credit (1999:245). In such a space of forces, translation represents an instrument to accessing symbolic capital for the writer, the language, the text or the literary field on the whole. Casanova (2002:14) identifies the recourse to the cultural good of translation as a practice of consecration when a writer from a dominated literary language is translated into another dominant one. Alternatively, when a dominated literary language imports texts from a dominant one, translation can represent a strategy of accumulation of literary capital, and thus, a gathering of resources (ibid.:10).

Along similar lines, Johan Heilbron and Gisèle Sapiro (2007:95) define translation as a "transnational transfer", which occurs in "a space of international relations". This space presupposes the existence of nation-states *and* linguistic groups whose interactions are marked by political, economic and cultural relations of power. Intra-relation, therefore, reposes on "competition, and rivalry" (ibid.).

The reliance on a national perspective, which Bourdieu, Casanova, Heilbron and Sapiro posit, may hinder the applicability of the theory to other contexts in which languages go beyond the boundaries of a nation-state or when the geographical space of a nation contains more than one language. Swahili is a case in point. Before colonialism, Swahili was a language spoken amongst the tens of city-states scattered along the East African coast. With the advent of colonialism, it became the language of education and administration in a space not yet a nation-state. Since decolonisation, Swahili has become a language used at a supra-national level. The existence of a space in which cultural goods are exchanged by social agents involved in intra-relations of political, economic, and cultural power can also be maintained when the existence of the space is not dependant on the presence of a nation state, but rather on politico-territorial formations which share a common language. Indeed, Heilbron (1999:432) identifies "language groups" as the basic unit of a world-system of translation, recognising that languages can pertain to more than one national reality.

The conceptualisation of translation as a commodity sanctioning access to symbolic and literary capital constitutes a viable analytical tool. Such concepts are therefore applied in this paper in order to investigate the logic beneath the circulation of symbolic goods within the Swahili experience. In detail, the paper illustrates the utilisation of translation into Swahili as a cultural resource to accumulate, as well as subtract, symbolic capital and, as a consequence, to access (or negate) positions of power.

The paper is divided into three parts. The first focuses on pre-twentieth-century Swahili literary space. Here, the recourse to translation by the Swahili classical poet as a strategy to access recognition and prestige is illustrated. I contend that the cultural good of translation also maintains its function of consecration in cases of pseudotranslation. The second part discusses the use of translation during colonial times as a form of deconsecration. I maintain that when the field of re-production of knowledge is infiltrated by exogenous agents connived with the field of power, translation can be a source of deconsecration of the literary and symbolic capital that a language and a literature have acquired so far. The final section addresses the use of translation in the space of post-colonial Tanzania as a form of reconsecration against former demeaning allegations.

Consecration: the classical Swahili poet as translator

As soon as Swahili emerged as a written literature, translation began to occupy a prominent role in Swahili literature, since some of the oldest Swahili manuscripts are poems presented as translations. In the eighteenth century, and particularly during the nineteenth century, the Swahili literary repertoire experienced a massive transfer of stories from or inspired by the *Qur'an*, Islamic legendary or historical accounts. These texts were imported in the form of poetry translation, namely in the form of the *utendi* (pl. *tendi*; also spelt *utenzi*, pl. *tenzi* in the southern Swahili dialects). Shariff (1991:45) describes *tendi* as a "narrative form" used for (Islamic) historical, and heroic poetry, in addition to moral fables. *Tendi* were used to give instruction on social behaviour and religious practices, as well as to explain the dogmas of Islam (Zukhov 2004:7). In this sense, *tendi* were prescriptive texts providing the audience with role models to follow and imitate (Vierke 2011:431).

Marking the text as a translation

Bourdieu (2002) argues that the circulation of texts and the transfer from one context into another is determined by a number of social operations which together comprise the operation of selection (pertaining to what is translated, and by whom) and an operation of "marquage" [marking, labelling] (ibid.:4). The process of marking operates through particular editions of the publishing house, the insertion in a collection or through the prefaces. This latter textual element constitutes an instrument through which the work of art is presented and appropriated to a specific vision of reality or connected to issues inscribed into the field of reception. In addition, prefaces function as the venue for the transfer of symbolic capital (ibid.).

Although the manuscripts in which classical Swahili poetry was preserved and transmitted do not match the format of the book Bourdieu might have in mind, a process of "marquage" is detectable in a number of Swahili *tendi*. A process which aims at marking the text as a translation in the spaces of the preamble, *dibaji*, and the epilogue, *tammati*. Here, classical

Swahili poets present a meta-discourse on translation, which provides the audience with information regarding the translation activity.[1]

The *tendi* are usually presented as acts of repetition through which the poets translate (*kufasiri*, *kutafsiri*, *kutarjumi*), explain or make clear (*kubaini*, *kueleza*) pre-existing Arabic sources. *Tendi* are put in the background of some antecedents – *Pana hadithi ajabu/yandikwa ndani kitabu/kwa lugha ya waarabu* (There is a wonderful account/written in a book/in the language of the Arabs)[2] – for which specific details about the original author and title may be provided.

The meta-narration also documents how poets engaged in the act of translation. A common *topos* depicting the assimilation of a source, and its subsequent rendering into Swahili, is the reference to the visual sense ("to see a book") and the impetus of the heart which such a sight triggers, eventually moving the translation act – *Mbwene hadithi chuoni* [...]/*moyowa ukatamani/lugha kuwagauziya* (I saw in a book an account [...]/and my heart desired/to change [its] language for you);[3] *Niyawenepo chuoni/moyo wangu hatamani/kubadili kimangani* (When I saw it in the book/my heart desired/to change the Arabic).[4] The activity of translation is connoted as something that is longed for, loved (*kuhibu*, *kupenda*) or desired (*kutamani*) and which eventually gives personal satisfaction – *Haona kunipendeza* (I found that it pleased me).[5] Translation is conceptualised as an emotional and bodily experience, which frames the poets as human beings made of flesh performing their role as translators during the narration.

Poets also expound the methods of the translation process, which, according to their comments, repose on the notions of fidelity and completeness. Classical Swahili poets assert to have followed the source text and to

1 The transition between the *dibaji*, the core text, and the *tamati*, is usually marked with clarity within the narration. The narrator either announces the transition or starts using different personal pronouns (the first-person for the introduction and the epilogue, and the third-person pronoun in the narration) (Vierke 2011:209-210). The core text could, therefore, have an autonomous existence. The *tendi* can also be considered performed texts. They were usually recited during gatherings in private houses, or in or gatherings such as weddings, and funerals, or religious celebration such as the Prophet's birth (Allen 1971:22), and therefore in socially circumscribed places where people bound together by various ties assembled.

2 *Utenzi wa Ras il-Ghuli* (Faqihi 1979:v). All translations are mine, unless otherwise indicated.

3 *Utendi wa Ngamia na Paa* (Allen 1971:86).

4 *Utendi wa Shufaka* (Bütttner 1894:6).

5 *Utenzi wa Ras il-Ghuli* (Faqihi 1979:2).

have given a full account of it – *Hayale yalipokwisa/Mikidadi na Mayasa/nami nimeufuata/hata yametimilia* (That is the end of the story/of Miqdad and Mayasa/and I have followed it/until it was completed).[6] They stress the fact that the text has been rendered in its entirety ("from the beginning", *awali*, *mwando*, "to the end", *akheri*), assuring that the possibility of a textual remainder had been avoided – *Yote katika kitabu/kabadili kiarabu/Kiswahili kawambia* (all that is in the book/I turned it from Arabic/, and I tell you in Swahili).[7] In addition, they appeal to impartiality and honesty in delivering the translated message from which nothing has been hidden from the audience – *Sitosita, thawambia* (I will not hide, I will tell you);[8] *Pasi neno kulisaza* (Without neglecting a word).[9] These devices differentiate authorship and erase ambiguities about the roles of the original author and the poet. Accordingly, the poets also refer to the act of translation by resorting to verbs such as *kudhukuri*, 'remember, repeat'; *kuhadithiya*, 'narrate, rehearse'; *kukhubiri*, 'announce, report'.

In discussing the forced invisibility to which (Anglo-American) translators were relegated – on the assumption that translation must read as original, and, therefore, be fluent – Venuti (2008/1995) views translators' prefaces as the place to counteract such self-effacement. Although the *dibaji* and *tamati* do not constitute prefaces in its strictest definition, they are the places where the presence of the Swahili poet as translator is made tangible and visible. In these occurrences, the use of "metalinguistic framing devices", which serve to identify a practice as a specific text-type or genre (Hanks 1996:245), allows *tendi* to secure the label of *translation*. The metalinguistic framing devices are, therefore, performative acts, which institutionalise a text demanding it to be recognised in a certain way.

Nevertheless, *tendi* display a range of transfer processes. For the purpose of this section of the article, twenty-three *tendi* were investigated. Form this corpus, however, only three resulted in having attested source texts translated almost literally.[10] Otherwise, the Arabic sources, with which a connection

[6] *Utendi wa Mikidadi na Mayasa* (Allen1971:368).

[7] *Utendi wa Ayubu* (Allen 1971:376-377). Allen's translation is here retained.

[8] *Utendi wa Fatuma* (Dammann 1940:95).

[9] *Utendi wa Kutawafu Nabii* (Allen et al. 1991:52-53)

[10] These are *Hamziyya* collected and translated by Knappert (1968); *U Mbali Suadu* collected and translated by Knappert (1971:145-163); and *Buruda ya Al-Busiri* collected and translated by Knappert (1971:165-225).

is established, seem to represent a partial source or a pretext to write a poem in its own right. This is the case of *Utenzi wa Ras il-Ghuli*[11] or *Utendi wa Fatuma.*[12] However, most of Swahili *tendi* can be considered pseudotranslations in the sense advocated by Andrea Rizzi (2008). While Toury (1995:143) and Rambelli (2009:208-209) base their definitions of pseudotranslation on the nonexistence of the source, Rizzi elaborates a more comprehensive definition encompassing a plurality of act(ivities) ranging from or mixing non-translational processes, adjustments, additions and adaptations. This mixed process eventually facilitates "[t]he coexistence of T [Translation], and PT [Pseudo-Translation] within the same text" (Rizzi 2008:161). This definition applies to *tendi* such as *Utendi wa Ngamia na Paa*,[13] *Utendi wa Tambuka*,[14] *Utendi wa Katirifu*,[15] *Utendi wa Ayubu*,[16] or *Utendi wa Mikidadi na Mayasa.*[17] These *tendi* are presented as translations, yet actually contain narratives common to the *maghazi* literature.[18] Nevertheless, they presently have no (direct) source texts as either the originals have not come to light, or none of the versions discovered could be appointed as the source for the Swahili poems. This is further supported by the fact that *maghazi* are mostly written in prose (Bertoncini Zúbková 2005:311).

Translation, and the accumulation of symbolic capital

The visibility of the text as a translation, coupled with the poet's visibility as a translator (which is emphasised within the *tendi*), elicit questions pertaining to what the recourse to translation allowed.

Swahili poets were not at the margins of the hierarchised Swahili society of the eighteenth and nineteenth centuries, but rather occupied high positions within it. The social order was based on opposing social constructs: *waungwana*, "cultured" or "patricians" and *washenzi*, "uncultured". Group

[11] Faqihi 1979.

[12] Collected and translated as "Fatuma" by Dammann (1940:92-140)

[13] Collected and translated as "The Camel and the Gazelle" by Allen (1971:77-129).

[14] Collected and translated as "Het epos van Heraklios" by Knappert (1958:121-233).

[15] Collected and translated as "'Utenzi wa Katirifu' or 'Ghazwa ya Sesebani'" by Knappert (1968/1969).

[16] Collected and translated as "Job" by Allen (1971:370-427).

[17] Collected and translated as "Miqdad and Mayasa" by Allen (1971:269-367).

[18] *Maghazi* are narratives popular all over the Muslim world. They combine legendary accounts with historical facts relating to the campaigns and wars of Muhammad after the Hegira (Harries 1962:25; Zhukov 2004:5).

membership depended on a number of variables among which great prominence was accorded to *nasaba*, "genealogy". Foreign genealogy was especially exalted, for origins in Arabia was considered "the 'better' origin, and associated with higher rank" (Horton and Middleton 2000:143). A role in cultivating such an idea was played by the extension of influence of the Omani sultanate over the East African coast from the end of the seventeenth century, in addition to the eventual resettlement of the capital to Zanzibar in 1832. This endorsed the perception of the Arabic Peninsula to be identified with aristocracy (ibid.).

Other factors which validated the status of *waungwana* related to occupation. For instance, being a merchant or a member of the *ulamaa*, Islamic scholars or judges, accredited patrician identity (ibid.). Indeed, Swahili poets were usually part of the professional group of the *ulamaa* (Mazrui and Shariff 1994:202).[19] In some cases, virtually no information is available on the poets, for example, Binti Sayidi Amini, the poetess of *Utendi wa Fatuma*. In other instances, the poets are anonymous as is seen from the poem *Utendi wa Ngamia na Paa*. Nevertheless, the plain fact of being conversant in the matter of poetry, and therefore representing a learned segment of society, implied the acceptance into the *waungwana* group. Aside for occupation or wealth, personal and moral qualities, such as knowledge of a refined language and composing music or poetry, represented conditions to be identified within the group of *waungwana* (Horton and Middleton 2000:152). Therefore, being a poet meant being part of an elevated class occupying positions of rank and prestige. What about being – or presenting oneself – as a translator?

Within the Swahili literary space of the eighteenth and nineteenth century, translation was contemplated as pertaining to the realm of poetic composition. This is manifest in the following example in which the poet Mgeni bin Faqihi summarises his conceptualisation of the poetic activity as being either a master poet or someone who knows the art of translation:

Haya mambo ya kutunga	For the matter of composing
Sharti uwe malenga	you have to be a bard

[19] Sheikh Mgeni bin Faqihi, the poet of *Utenzi wa Ras il-Ghuli* was an Islamic scholar (Faqihi 1979:vi), Saiyid Umar bin Amin bin Umar bin Amin bin Nasir al-Ahdal, the poet of *Utendi wa Ayubu*, was a judge (Gérard 1976:10) like Saiyid Mansabu bin Abdurrahman, the poet of *Maulidi ya Dali* (Knappert 1979:201).

Au maneno ya manga	or the Arabic words
Uyajue tafsiri	you have to know how to translate them[20]

In light of this mutual compatibility, the question arises: what could a translation provide that a *tendi* in its own right could not? The recourse to translation served the scope for poets to obtain recognition and consecration – translation enabled the conventionalised role of the poet to be reframed. In conceptualising the social conditions of the international circulation of cultural goods, Bourdieu (2002:5) posits that a cultural good can be selected by virtue of the "usages très instrumentalistes" ["instrumental uses"], which allow translators to plead for something which would otherwise be denied and refused in their own contexts.

Within classical Swahili poetry tradition, a "socially prescribed humbleness" (Vierke 2011:394) compelled the poets to disdain earthly fame and celebrity (the only aim being teaching, and propagating Islam) and to refuse any other final aim besides the blessing of God, together with the denial of any self-ability. Translation seems the place where this socially expected behaviour could be negotiated. While expressing incapacity and calling shame on themselves for their "defective talent" (Gérard 1976:19), the fact that poets present themselves as translators allows them to mention their skills and competences. It is by visibly framing the text as a translation that poets can exhibit their expertise in disclosing the obscurity of the Arabic *logos* – *Kufasiri nimeweza* (I was capable of translating).[21] Furthermore, the framework of translation allows to freely talk of the beauty and perfection of their work – *Nimetafusiri moya kwa moya/na mudda shuruti nimezitia/na mwiso ukuu kupangilia/lulu kwa dhahabu ndio hatima* (I have translated them one by one/and all the time I have observed the rules/in the end I arranged it beautifully/with pearls and gold, this is the end).[22] In addition, it is by presenting the text as a translation that poets could demand what would otherwise be forbidden: being famous – both by virtue of the service they made to God and His creatures and by virtue of approaching the authors of the pre-existing sources, as the following example illustrates:

Walo wakitunga nyuma	And those who wrote poetry in the past
Za tawafu na hekima	of the pilgrimage, and of wisdom

[20] *Ras il-Ghuli* (Faqihi 1979:245).

[21] *Utendi wa Ayubu* (Allen 1971:423).

[22] *Maulidi ya Dali (ya Mansabu)* (Knappert 1971:338). The translation of Knappert is retained here.

Mambo yao yali mema	their words were good
Yao ni muhtasiri	of theirs this is only an abridgment
Mutu atungao yeo	The person who composes today,
Ingawa thumuni yao	even if it is only one eight of their work
Muhasibuni na wao	reckon him with them
Naye kuwa mashuhuri	that he too may be famous[23]

While Casanova (2002:14) postulates that being translated was a means for writers from dominated literary fields to gain visibility and the right "à l'existence" ["to the existence"], in the case of Swahili it is translating in itself which promotes visibility while functioning as an instance of consecration of poets. Although the Swahili language had its position of prestige – in that the mastery of the Swahili language was conceived as a characteristic of the *waungwana* status (Kresse 2009:51) – the ascendancy of the Arabic language as the language of the *Qur'an* played its role. All the more so in a context in which the affiliation to Arabic ancestry was associated with high rank (Horton and Middleton 2000:142; Pouwels 1986:76). Classical Swahili poets benefitted from the symbolic capital, which was assumed from the Arabic text, granting the same aura of prestige to their works of art, which were presented as translations. Pseudotranslations were resources used by agents in the pursuit of prestige and recognition. This is the reason why, within pseudotranslated *tendi*, poets generally tended to clearly indicate their names together with details about genealogy: *isimu thaweka wazi,/mpate kunitambuwa* (The name [of the composer] I will put it clearly/so that you will recognise me).[24] Translation represented a constructed resource, which enabled Swahili classical poets to obtain and maintain higher positions of prestige within the realm of an already dominant space.

Deconsecration: translation during British colonial rule and the obscuration of literary and symbolic capital

With the arrival of missionaries and the establishment of colonial rule (first German and then British) in East Africa at the end of the nineteenth century, the space of Swahili literature was exposed to Western literature.

[23] *Utendi wa Katirifu* (Knappert 1968/1969:302).This is a slightly revised translation from Knappert.

[24] *Utendi wa Fatuma* (Dammann 1940:139).

Exposure started with the activity of Edward Steere, the English bishop in Zanzibar, who introduced Shakespeare and Greek mythology in the context of the mission. He translated Charles and Mary Lamb's *Tales from Shakespeare* in 1867, Charles Kingsley's *The Heroes, Greek fairy tales* in 1880 and *Aesop's fables* in 1889.[25]

Following decades of silence, translation activities returned again to the fore against the background of the Education Conference of 1925, which paved the way for the establishment of the Inter-Territorial Language Committee (ITLC) in 1930. The Committee was established with the main objective of standardising the Swahili language for use throughout the colony. The preparation of textbooks and the translations of foreign literature were the means through which the standardisation could have been enforced (TEC 1925). With the appearance of the Committee, exogenous agents entered the field of production and the transfer of knowledge into Swahili. The Committee consisted of colonial administrators as the Directors of Education for each of the territories encompassed by British East Africa[26], Reader and Assistant Reader, along with representatives of the mission bodies (Snoxall 1984:16). Although African membership is officially dated 1939, it was not until 1946 that Africans actively participated in the Committee meetings (Mulokozi 2006:15).

Furthermore, selective filtering limited the access for Africans into the field of literary translation and restricted selection to the select few who had access to literacy in English and who were trained to become subordinate administrative officers. This was the case of Edwin Brenn, an African working in the mission and as a senior clerk in the Education Department (Iliffe 1979:266), who assisted Frederick Johnson with some of his translations.[27] Conversely, other translators who were not approved by the colonial apparatus remained "illegal". This was the case of the Mombasa theologian Sheikh Al-Amin Al-Mazrui, who translated and circulated the anti-colonial teachings of Jamal ad-din Al-Afghani during the 1920s, at a moment in which Muslims were being alienated from politics (Lodhi 1994:90). It is only

[25] Although German colonial rule was promoting the use of Swahili at the low levels of administration, translations from German into Swahili hardly occurred (Geider 2008:70).

[26] Which comprised Kenya, Tanganyika, Uganda, and Zanzibar.

[27] Edwin Brenn collaborated in the translation of Treasure Island (Kisiwa chenye Hazina, 1927), King Solomon's Mines (Mashimo ya Mfalme Suleimani 1929), The Song of Hiawatha (Hadithi ya Hiawatha, 193?).

with the political changes of the 1950s, which partially opened the door to African political initiatives, that Swahili translators were allowed a more official involvement in translating activities – not just as "assistants" or "illegal" translators. This can be seen in the instance of Abdulla M. Abubakr who, in 1950, translated Voltaire's *Zadig, ou La destinée* as *Hadithi ya Zadig*, or Shaaban Robert who, in 1952 and the *Rubaiyat* by Omar Khayyam. However, arguably it was always civil servants (as was Shaaban) or officers connected with the Education Department (as was Abubakr) who, by virtue of their social capital, were allowed to translate. As a result of the network of connections which linked Shaaban to the Education Department, A.A.M. Isherwood, who held Head of the Department from 1924 to 1945, explicitly asked the Swahili poet to translate the *Rubaiyat* (Robert 1952:v).

With translation being part and parcel of the linguistic standardisation programme, the Committee was responsible for a massive exposure to Western literature, mostly Anglophone. Against this background, Western classics were transfused systematically into the Swahili literary scene. Ryder Haggard, Jonathan Swift, Rudyard Kipling, Robert Louis Stevenson, Lewis Caroll, Molière, among others of their kind, made their forced entrance into the gates of Swahili literature. The majority of these texts were translated by a single individual, Frederick Johnson, who was a British administrator, the first Secretary of the Inter-Territorial Language Committee and Senior Clerk in the Education Department. Between 1927 and 1935, Johnson translated Treasure Island, *King Solomon's Mines, The Jungle Book*, *Tales of Uncle Remus, Gullivers' Travels*, *Robinson Crusoe*, *The Song of Hiawatha*, and *Allan Quatermain* into Swahili.

The Committee was also in possession of the economic capital to undertake a widespread distribution of the texts through a range of means. At the outset, translations were serialised through journals such as *Mambo Leo*. However, from 1928 those serialised texts were collected as separate books published within the series *Masimulizi ya Mambo Leo*. Translations also appeared as separate books altogether. The translations issued by the Committee were inserted in the school curricula of the colony, while at the same time Swahili poems, which were circulated in translation among academic circles in the metropolis, were not allowed to enter the Swahili school syllabus. In this respect, it is important to bear in mind that, according to Bourdieu (1971:121), the educational system is an institution that works as an instance of consecration, either by conserving the capital of specific symbolic goods or by reproducing the categories of perception promoted by the goods.

An intense activity of collecting and purchasing Swahili poetry manuscripts made the English intelligentsia aware of the centuries-old poetic tradition in Swahili literature and its high position in society. However, the same could not be said for the translation of poetry from the Western hemisphere into Swahili, which was hardly undertaken by the English on African soil, instead extensively favouring the translation of novel. The only case of import of a poetic text, to my knowledge, was subject to a shift of genre. *Hadithi ya Hiawatha*, the translation of Longfellow's *The song of Hiawatha*, was in fact a summary prose translation. The silencing of a genre is relevant in foregrounding the practice of translation in the web of power relations. As Cronin (2007:254) contends, in order to understand translation practices:

> we must ask ourselves not only why so much gets translated, but also why so much does not get translated. [...] Just as a figure is defined by, and necessitates a ground, so also the figure of translation demands the figure of non-translation if we are to make any sense of the activity in our society [...].

The shortage of poetry translations into Swahili during colonial times is commented on by Omboga (2011:137) who observes that "[t]here is not so much that has been translated from European poetry inspite of its aggressive intrusion, and domineering presence during the colonial times". Omboga claims that the reason lies in the complexities of the Swahili prosodic system. From my point of view, a complete answer to why there was a shortage of translation of English poetry should take into account the following rationale: it is more likely that the reason for being silent in poetry translation, while being eloquent in the translation of prose, is linked to the notion of literary and symbolic capital. However, the linkage between translation and symbolic capital being proposed does not repose on a process of accumulation. This is because it is usually postulated in the sociology of the cultural product. In the situated colonial context I am referring to here, such relationship is anchored on a process of obscuration of capital. In this hypothesis, I would concur with Pierre Bourdieu's (1991:67) conception of genres as resources, which entail different forms of prestige and are, thus, associated with social hierarchies.

As previously mentioned, the elevated position of poetry in Swahili society made the ability to compose a socio-cultural factor means to access high rank. In addition, religious poetry also secured the privilege of survival, as it was preserved in manuscripts, while other textual types, such as secular poetry or folktales and fables, were left to the vehicle of oral transmission (Mazrui and Shariff 1994:92). Under secured colonial rule prose became a prominent genre through imposition. The insistence of prose over poetry can be seen to work as a strategy to obscure and, therefore, deprive and subtract from the literary capital accumulated by Swahili literature. Thus, Swahili literature would be promoted with a defective image, caused by the absence of a genre, which in itself constitutes a source of prestige. In this respect, the comment of Augustine Beale Hellier, a Committee member, missionary and translator, makes evident how such "shortcoming" was emphasised:

> The word *Literature* connotes art, the exercise of the imagination, dramatic ability, descriptive power, and skill in characterisation. No Novel yet exists which is the original work in Swahili of a Native of the country. (Hellier 1940:257, original emphasis)

In addition, it can be argued that the translation of prose was also a strategy to deprive the level of sophistication which Swahili language had achieved. The translations of the Committee were commonly extensively abridged. The textual manipulation was usually reported within the text, either in the translator's preface or the title page. It is interesting to note that Johnson mentions Swahili amongst the reasons put forward to justify abridging the texts. The "necessity" to present an extensively summarised text lies not in the responsibility of the translator(s), but rather in the very nature of the target language which is considered unfit for the content of the book:

> Pengine ilikuwa lazima kubadili maana kidogo na pengine kufupisha habari kwa kuwa hazikufaa kwa maneno ya Kiswahili. (Johnson 1927:572)[28]

The idea of the "inadequacy" of the Swahili language – as was being propagated by the Committee – was one of the issues discussed during the Education Conference of 1925. Amongst the conclusions reached by the Committee and formulated by its Chairman Johnson, number two clearly hints at the incapacity of Swahili, as a Bantu language, to express "high thinking":

[28] Sometimes it was necessary to alter the meaning, and sometimes to shorten the narrations because they did not suit the Swahili words.

> It was felt however, that in Swahili, as in English, and other languages, there must be literature of both simple, and more advanced composition, and that in the latter more words of Arabic, and foreign origin would naturally be employed to express *thoughts of more advanced scholars, which could not be adequately expressed in language of pure Bantu origin*". (TEC 1925:160, emphasis added)

In such a context, when translation is undertaken by exogenous agents who coincide or are connived with the field of power, translation from dominant to dominated language could be seen not so much as a strategy of consecration – as advocated by Casanova, Heilbron and Sapiro – but rather as strategy of deconsecration. In the Swahili colonised literary space, when translation was undertaken by social agents from higher positions of the social hierarchy for consumption by agents in lower positions, translation worked to impose categories of perception in order to patronise the defective position of the target language and literature on the whole – a (counterfeit) view which would have proven useful to the colonial enterprise.

Reconsecration: post-colonial translation and the (re)validation of the Swahili language

With the end of colonial rule and the independence of Kenya and Tanganyika (present day Tanzania),[29] the import of translated books as symbolic goods concerned Tanzania to a greater extent than Kenya. The reason for this dissimilar attention can be seen to emanate from the different linguistic policies enacted by the respective governments. While Kenya continued to use English, in Tanganyika Swahili was not only declared the national language in 1962, but was also affirmed as the official language of the government of Tanzania in 1967. This shows that a strong linguistic policy interested Tanzania at a critical time in its history, thus making Swahili the language of nation building (Martin 1988:241). The Tanzanian population experienced a "Swahilisation" process, which made Swahili a pan-ethnic language cementing together the newly forged Tanzania (Mazrui and Shariff 1994:44-45).

However, the 1960s and 1970s were marked by a conflict of status between English and Swahili, aimed at showing Swahili in a bad light and

[29] Kenya attained independence on December 12, 1963. Tanganyika attained independence on December 9, 1961 and became a republic on December 9, 1962. Zanzibar became independent in 1963. In April 1964 Tanganyika and Zanzibar united and gave birth to the United Republic of Tanzania (Mwakikagile 2008).

disproving the possibility that Swahili had become the national language, or, least of all, a language able to profess high culture (Klein 1986:217). In 1970, the Swahili scholar George A. Mhina denounced the victimisation of Swahili as not "being self-sufficient":

> Mara nyingi twasikia wataalam wengine wa lugha wakisema kuwa lugha ya Kiswahili haina uwezo wa kujitosheleza. (Mhina 1970:2)[30]

In post-colonial Tanzania, *kujitegemea* or self-reliance, was the fundamental dogma of *ujamaa* or Tanzanian socialism. *Ujamaa* was a political philosophy elaborated by Julius Kambarage Nyerere. As the president of TANU (Tanganyika African National Union), Nyerere led Tanganyika to independence and become its first president until 1985 (Mwakikagile 2008:20).

Nyerere imagined Tanzania as a self-reliant nation to an extent that involved liberating the nation from the language and literature of the coloniser. The very decision to make Swahili the national and the official language of Tanzania can be identified as the outcome of such a process. In addition, the Africanisation and localisation of school curricula and syllabi was promoted in order to offer Tanzanian students literary, historical and cultural contents, which would have been relevant to rebuilding the identity of the peoples after colonial rule (Mngomezulu 2012:132).

However, in spite of the Africanisation of school curricula, during the first decade following independence (1962-1972), an intense activity of translation of Western classics was undertaken by Tanzanian activists, as well as political and academic figures – Plato, Shakespeare, Molière and Conrad were amongst the works translated. Nyerere happens to be the translator who inaugurated the flow of Shakespearean translations with his first translation of *Julius Caesar* and *The Merchant of Venice.* Almost at the same time, Samuel S. Mushi translated *The* Tempest, *Macbeth* and *Oidipus Tyrannos.* Mushi held the position of "Promoter for Swahili" within the Ministry of Community Development and National Culture from March 1965 to June 1967 and was also a scholar at the University of Dar es Salaam until his departure in 2011.

Bearing in mind that "[a]nalysing the flows of translations in the light of the power relations among languages also allows us to better understand

[30] Too often we hear plenty of linguists asserting that Swahili has not the capability of being self-sufficient.

historical changes" (Heilbron and Sapiro 2007:97), I maintain that in the context of post-colonial Tanzania, and in the context of the Swahili-English conflict translations, there were cultural resources boosting the promotion and validation of the Swahili language. Casanova (2002) postulates that the translation of literary texts, which are considered to have universal value, into dominated languages is a strategy to import capital and prestige. While Casanova mentions the translation of *Julius Caesar* as an exemplification of the use of translation to acquire "l'ancienneté manquante" [the missing antiquity] (2002:10), it seems more rational to think that Nyerere's translation, as well as the translations of Western classics in a broader sense, has to do with the second rationale identified by Casanova – that is "rivaliser" (ibid.).

The field of Swahili literature was already in possession of antiquity and, therefore, literary capital which had been disavowed during colonial times. The selection and import of a Western classic piece of literature served to demonstrate that Swahili was capable of taking charge of the complexities of, and become a means of, high culture. This is exemplified by the following citation, taken from the introduction to the second translated edition of *Julius Caesar* conducted by Nyerere. The President/translator frames the translation in the background and in response to:

> watu wasiojua Kiswahili, ambao wanafikiri kuwa Kiswahili si lugha pana ya kutosha kueleza mawazo makubwa au ufasaha safi bila kuazima mno maneno mapya ya kigeni. (Nyerere 1969:vii)[31]

His translation is therefore used to appropriate the prestige or symbolic capital of the source text in order to demonstrate the legitimacy of Swahili vis-à-vis its detractors. The comment by Nyerere seems to resonate against the incapacity purported in the writings of Johnson and the Committee. In this overall context, translation was used to champion the autonomy of Swahili as a literary language, and the autonomy of the Swahili literary field on the whole, *against* the ascendancy of English language and literature. Thus, translation proved to be useful in regaining the symbolic capital of Swahili, which had previously been denied by nasty allegations against it – the defamation used as a tool of control.

---

[31] ...those who do not believe in Swahili, those who think that Swahili is not rich enough to express deep thoughts or stylistic elegance unless using foreign words.

Concluding remarks

Contrary to the irrelevance ascribed to literary translations into Swahili, this paper has shed light on the utilisation of translation by a diverse range of agents within different time spans as a resource to foster individual or institutional plans of action in order to access or negate positions of prestige and power.

Bourdieu's theory concerning the (re)production of knowledge, and Casanova, Heilbron and Sapiro's contributions to the circulation of symbolic goods within an international space of cultural, political and economic relations, have been considered in this article. The concepts of *capital* and of translation as *consecration* have been utilised in order to expose the logic underlying the circulation of translated texts into the Swahili literary and social spaces.

The first part of this paper focused on the role of pseudotranslation as a symbolic resource apt at offering the Swahili classical poet an opportunity to plead for fame and prestige, and eventually to be consecrated by virtue of the symbolic capital accumulated through the practice of translation. This section has confronted a blank space in the theorisation concerning the circulation of symbolic goods, arguing that the cultural good of translation maintains its function of consecration in cases when the translation is a pseudotranslation.

The second part of this paper concentrated on the British colonial context in which the agents of translations were exogenous connived with the field of power. Here, the process by which the use of translation can be used as a resource to obliterate the literary and symbolic capital, which a language and a literature have acquired, was analysed. In this respect, I have proposed the notion of translation as *deconsecration*. This notion will enable a viable concept to be applied in the theoretical discussion of the sociology of the cultural product in contexts beyond the Swahili experience.

The final section of this article presented the use of translation from dominant languages in the Tanzanian post-colonial context. In such a space, translation provided the power to resonate against previous categories of perception. As such, translation enabled renegotiating the terms of cultural (re)production with the objective to recuperate the literary and symbolic capital previously negated. Thus, I described translation in such a context as a strategy of *reconsecration*.

The diachronic perspective adopted in this paper was aimed at illustrating the differentiated possibilities that lie beneath the recourse to translation within the space of literary exchanges. The Swahili experience has provided a frame of reference through which one can discern practices related to the availing of symbolic capital beyond the concept of accumulation. The utilisation of translation as a deliberate operation to be invested with a consecrative force proved multi-layered and dynamic. The shifting role of translation within the diverse time frames discussed has illustrated that the consecrative performance is not a single event fixed in absolute temporal coordinates. Quite the reverse, it is something which resonates back and forth with previous and future acts of representations. Once activated, the consecrative potential inscribed within the translational act is exposed to a plurality of (re)usages. At the heart of this analysis is the idea that the kernel of consecration can be subtracted or retrieved according to social and historical contingencies and, by virtue of such inherent adjustability, it can be re-manipulated and thus reinvented.

References

Allen, John W.T. (1971) *Tendi.* London: Heinemann.

Allen, John W.T. et al. (1991) *A Poem Concerning the Death of the Prophet Muhammad: Utendi Wa Kutawafu Nabii.* Lewiston: Edwin Mellen.

Bertoncini Zúbková, Elena (2005) "Classical Swahili Poetry and its Linkage with the Arabic 'North'". In Makward, Edris/Lilleleht, Mark L./Saber, Ahmed (eds.) *North-South Linkages and Connections in Continental and Diaspora African Literatures.* Trenton/ Asmara: Africa World Press, 308-318.

Bourdieu, Pierre (1971) "Le marché des biens symbolique". *L'Année Sociologique* 22, 49-126.

Bourdieu, Pierre (1977) "La production de la croyance: Contribution à une économie des biens symboliques". *Actes de la Recherché en Sciences Sociales* 13, 3-43.

Bourdieu, Pierre (1983) "The Field of Cultural Production, or: The Economic World Reversed" (tr. Richard Niche). *Poetics*, 12:4-5, 311-356.

Bourdieu, Pierre (1989) "Social Space and Symbolic Power" (tr. Loïc J.D. Wacquant). *Sociological Theory* 7: 1, 14-25.

Bourdieu, Pierre (1991) *Language and Symbolic Power* (tr. Gino Raymond). Cambridge: Polity.

Bourdieu, P. (1997) "The Forms of Capital" (tr. Richard Niche). In Halsey, A.H./Lauder, Hugh/Brown, Phillip/Stuart Wells, Amy (eds.) *Education: Culture, Economy, and Society.* Oxford: Oxford University Press, 46-58.

Bourdieu, Pierre (2002) "Les conditions sociales de la circulation internationale des idées". *Actes de la Recherche en Sciences Sociales* 145, 3-8.

Büttner, Carl Gotthilf (1894) *Anthologie aus der Suaheli-Litteratur.* Berlin: Felber.

Casanova, Pascale (1999) *La république mondiale des lettres.* Paris: Seuil.

Casanova, Pascale (2002) "Consécration et accumulation de capital littéraire, la traduction comme échange inégal". *Actes de la Recherche en Sciences Sociales* 144, 7-20.

Cronin, Michael (2007) "Double take: Figuring the Other, and the Politics of Translation". In St-Pierre, Paul/Kar, Prafulla C. (eds.) *In Translation. Reflections, Refractions, Transformations.* Amsterdam/Philadelphia: John Benjamins, 253-262.

Dammann, Ernst (1940) *Dichtungen in der Lamu-Mundart des Suaheli.* Hamburg: Friederichsen, de Gruyter & Co.

Faqihi, Mgeni (1979) *Utenzi wa Ras 'lGhuli* [*The Poem of Ras 'lGhuli*], ed. Leo van Kessel. Dar es Salaam: Tanzania Printing House.

Geider, Thomas (2008) "A Survey of World Literature Translated into Swahili". In Reuster-Jahn, Uta/Oed, Anja (eds.) *Beyond the Language Issue: The Production, Mediation, and Reception of Creative Writing in African Languages.* Cologne: Rüdiger Köppe, 67-84.

Gérard, Albert (1976) "Structure and Values in Three Swahili Epics". *Research in African Literatures* 7:1, 7-22.

Hanks, William (1996) *Language and Communicative Practices.* Boulder: Westview.

Harries, Lyndon (1962) *Swahili Poetry.* Oxford: Oxford University Press.

Heilbron, Johan (1999) "Towards a Sociology of Translation. Book Translations as a Cultural World-System". *European Journal of Social Theory* 2:4, 429-444.

Heilbron, Johan/Sapiro, Gisele (2007) "Outline for a Sociology of Translation: Current Issues and Future Prospects". In Wolf, Michaela/Fukari, Alexandra (eds.) *Constructing a* Sociology of *Translation.* Amsterdam/Philadelphia: John Benjamins, 93-107.

Hellier, Augustine Beale (1940) "Swahili Prose Literature". *Bantu Studies* 14:3, 247-257.

Horton, Mark/Middleton, John (2000) *The Swahili: The Social Landscape of a Mercantile Society.* Oxford: Blackwell.

Iliffe, John (1979) *A Modern History of Tanganyika.* Cambridge: Cambridge University Press.

Johnson, Frederik (1927) "Editor's Introduction to *Kisiwa chenyi hazina* (*Treasure Island*)". *Mambo Leo* 50, 572.

Kezilahabi, Euphrase (1973) "The Development of Swahili Poetry: Eighteenth-Twentieth Century". *Swahili* 42:2, 62-67.

Klein, Leonard (1986) *African Literatures in the 20th Century: A Guide.* New York: Ungar.

Knappert, Jan (1958) *Het epos van Heraklios.* Leiden: Brill.

Knappert, Jan (1968) "The Hamziyya Deciphered". *African Language Studies* 9, 52-81.

Knappert, Jan (1968/1969) "The 'Utenzi wa Katirifu' or 'Ghazwa ya Sesebani'" [The 'Poem of Katirifu' or 'Ghazwa ya Sesebani']. *Afrika und Übersee* 52, 81-104; 264-313.

Knappert, Jan (1971) *Swahili Islamic Poetry.* Leiden: Brill.

Knappert, Jan (1979) *Four Centuries of Swahili Verse: A Literary History and Anthology.* London: Heinemann.

Kresse, Kai (2009) "Knowledge and Intellectual Practice in a Swahili Context: 'Wisdom' and the Social Dimensions of Knowledge". *Africa* 79:1, 148-167.

Lodhi, Abdullaziz (1994) "Muslims in Eastern Africa – Their Past and Present". *Nordic Journal of African Studies* 3:1, 88-98.

Magoti, A. (1981) "The Role of Translation in the Development of Kiswahili, and its Effects". *Studies and Documents* 2, 45-56.

Martin, Denis C. (1988) *Tanzanie: L'invention d'une culture politique.* Karthala/Paris: Presses de la Fondation Nationale des Sciences Politiques et Karthala.

Mazrui, Alamin/Shariff, Ibrahim N. (1994) *The Swahili: Idiom and Identity of an African People.* Trenton: Africa World Press.

Mhina, Georg A. (ed.) (1970) *Maendeleo ya kiswahili na mazoezi: Makusanyo ya maandishi. A Swahili Anthology [The Development of Swahili and Exercises: A Collection of Texts]*. Dar es Salaam: Nelson.

Mngomezulu, Bhekithemba R. (2012) *Politics and Higher Education in East Africa. From the 1920s to the 1970s.* Bloemfontain: Sun Media.

Mulokozi, Mugyabuso (2006) "Fasihi ya Kiswahili na Utandawazi" [Swahili literature and Globalisation]. In: Sewangi, Seleman Simon/Madumulla, Joshua (eds.) *Makala ya Kongamano la Kimataifa la Jubilei ya Tuki [Proceedings of the IKR Jubilee Symposium]*. Dar es Salaam: TUKI, 2-23.

Mulokozi, Mugyabuso/ Sengo, Tigiti S.Y. (1995) *History of Kiswahili Poetry.* Dar es Salaam: Institute of Kiswahili Research.

Mwakikagile, Godfrey (2008) *The Union of Tanganyika and Zanzibar: Product of the Cold War?* Pretoria: New Africa Press.

Nurse, Derek/Spear, Thomas (1985) *Swahili: Reconstructing the History and Language of an African Society, 800-1500.* Philadelphia: University of Pennsylvania Press.

Nyerere, Julius K. 1969. "Utangulizi wa Toleo la Pili" [Introduction to Second Edition]. In Shakespeare, William *Juliasi Kaizari [Julius Caesar]* (tr. Julius K. Nyerere). Dar es Salaam: Oxford University Press, vi-vii.

Omboga, James Zaja (2011) *Literary Translation in Kiswahili: Locating Text, Context, Culture and Pedagogy in Cultural Transfer.* Lambert: Academic Publishing.

Pouwels, Randall (1986) Horn and *Crescent: Cultural Change and Traditional Islam on the East African Coast, 800-1900.* Cambridge: Cambridge University Press.

Rambelli, Paolo (2009) "Pseudotranslation". In Baker, Mona/Saldanha, Gabriela (eds.) *Routledge Encyclopedia of Translation Studies.* London/New York: Routledge, 208-211.

Rizzi, Andrea (2008) "When a Text is Both a Pseudotranslation and a Translation: The Enlightening Case of Matteo Maria Boiardo (1441-1494)". In Pym, Anthony/ Shlesinger, Miriam/Simeoni, Daniel (eds.) *Beyond Descriptive Translation Studies: Investigations in Homage to Gideon Toury.* Amsterdam/Philadelphia: John Benjamins, 153-162.

Robert, Shaaban (1952) "Utangulizi" [Introduction]. In Khayyam, Omar. *Omar Khayyam Kwa Kiswahili [Omar Khayyam in Swahili]* (*Rub'ayyāt* tr. Shaaban Robert). London: Macmillan, v-vi.

Shariff, Ibrahim N. (1991) "Islam and Secularity in Swahili Literature: An Overview". In Harrow, Kenneth (ed.) *Faces of Islam in African Literature.* Portsmouth: Heinemann, 37-57.

Shatry, Alwy M. (1996) "Translation Reinterpreted". *Research in African Literatures* 27, 73-77.

Snoxall, Ronald (1984) "The East African Interterritorial Language (Swahili) Committee". In Maw, Joan/Parkin, David (eds.) *Swahili Language and Society*. Vienna: Afro-Pub, 15-24.

TEC (Tanganyika Educational Conference) (1925) *Report of Education Conference 1925: Together with the Report of the Committee for the Standardisation of the Swahili Language*. Dar es Salaam: Government Printer.

Toury, Gideon (1995) *Descriptive Translation Studies and Beyond*. Amsterdam/Philadelphia: John Benjamins.

Venuti, Lawrence (2008/1995) *The Translator's Invisibility: A History of Translation*. London/New York: Routledge.

Vierke, Clarissa (2011) *On the Poetics of the Utendi: A Critical Edition of the Nineteenth-Century Swahili Poem 'Utendi wa Haudaji' Together with a Stylistic Analysis*. Zurich: LIT.

Zhukov, Andrei (2004) "Old Swahili-Arabic Script and the Development of Swahili Literary Language". *Sudanic Africa* 15, 1-15.

HEDINA TAHIROVIĆ-SIJERČIĆ

Katholieke Universiteit Leuven, Belgium

Romani Secret Road Symbols: The First Written Words in Romani or the First Translation of Romani

Throughout history, Romani people have preserved their culture, tradition and language, but at the same time have depended on translation – among their own people, own community and in relation to the "other". "Translation" has been a part of their everyday lives. Historically speaking, their constant marginalisation, discrimination, and persecution have usually relegated them to the periphery, where they have attempted to stay as far away as possible from persecutors, on the road and travelling, fighting for bare life, just to survive. In order to survive, they produced and created secret road symbols. Following the trail of preliminary research started by Jean-Paul Clébert, Rajko Đurić and Dragoljub Acković on the Romani secret road symbols and their expression, this article will pay particular attention to the road symbols in the context of translation, drawing on sociologically oriented translation concepts and notions of heterogeneity, hybridity, and cultural translation. Likewise, it will hopefully serve as a first step into their investigation by asking: can the secret road symbols be considered as the first written words in Romani, or perhaps even as the first Romani translation carried out by Roma themselves?

Keywords: Gypsy, Roma, Romani, symbol, sign, *patrina*

Introduction

On the way from India, through Afghanistan, Iraq, Syria, Turkey, and to the Balkans, Romani peoples (also called Gypsy, Cigani, Zigeuner, among others) came into contact with different cultures and different languages, experiencing cultural changes during the time of their "exodus". The repercussions of constant persecution along the way influenced their cultural life and means of survival. Their language (Romani) and beliefs became the main guardians of their cultural, spiritual and literary heritage. Rom/Rrom (Roma/Rroma pl.) denominates these people as having Indian origin; the name can be found in Indian literature such as in the *Mahabharata*: "[A] view into personal and family names of Indians in New Delhi,

Hariana, Rajasthan and Uttar Pradesh have shown that names such as Rrom, Rroma, Rromali, Rromani are still very often in use" (Đurić and Acković 2010:10).[1]

Scholarship has generally shown that there is a close relationship between thought, language, and the spiritual and mental life and well-being of a people. This is of course also true for Roma. As people who have always found themselves in precarious situations only to survive, the thought, language, spiritual and mental life of Roma have adjusted and accommodated to the circumstances of their marginalised culture. This accommodation is always gauged in terms of the other's visibility and knowledge. The other's knowledge about Romani people eventually led to the creation of a formal discipline called "Romani Studies" (or Gypsiology, Ziganology, Romology), defined by Deborah Folaron on the website *Translation Romani* as

> an academic discipline of study emerged first as a specific area of research within linguistics. It has since developed into a dynamic domain that embraces perspectives and methodologies from other disciplines such as sociology, anthropology, ethnography, political science, migration studies, diaspora studies, cultural studies, music and history. (Folaron 2013)

This knowledge typifies Roma in stereotypical, prejudicial, and general ways. The tendency to generalise, along with pervasive notions such as nomadism – remarked by Marushiakova and Popov in *Roma Culture* as: "the nomadic way of life characteristic of their culture" – ultimately 'translate' into leaving Roma to themselves, or as reiterated by Ian Hancock, "in the desire to keep [Roma] to ourselves" (2007:32).

By keeping to themselves, and despite the constant migration, abandonment, marginalisation and discrimination, they preserved their way of life, language, customs, beliefs, culture and traditions. The Romani cultural spirit and way of life, valued by the Romani community from within, is denoted by the noun Romanipe(n)/Rromanipe(n). The term is derived from the name Roma/Rroma and refers to the feeling of belonging to the same people, with the same history, culture and habits. Despite the differences specific to each group, "Romanipe is the common denominator referring to the characteristics in common of all Romani people in the area of Afghani-

---

1 "[P]regled ličnih i porodičnih indijskih imena pokazuje da su, recimo, u Nju Delhiju, Harijani, Radžastanu, Utar Pradešu imena Rrom, Rroma, Rromali, Rromani relativno česta i danas". All translations are mine, unless otherwise stated.

stan, over Turkey and Europe, to Americas and Australia" (Đurić 2005:11). Also, in some Romani communities the Romani "Kris", which refers to the traditional Romani court where Roma are tried according to the principles of Rromanipe, is still preserved. Consequently, communities have kept to themselves and self-organised, imposing behaviour codes, which have always been upheld (and enforced) by men within the hierarchy of the family.

Despite its rich and heterogeneous nature, Romani culture has been routinely generalised and marginalised. Conventional and hierarchical distinctions differentiating between "higher" and "lower" cultures have consistently relegated it to the classification of "lower" culture, thus neglecting, subordinating, and deeming it worthless for others. Furthermore, Romani culture has fallen "victim" to its own wide diversity. Romani customs, beliefs, religions and habits represent a diversity of spiritual cultures among Roma, in addition to their diverse language dialects and cultural practices. The values and standards that typically determine and govern human behaviour and social life, as well as the material bases that inform habitat, trades, professions, clothing, jewellery, vehicles, products and tools, which are synonymous with human existence and progress, have generally not been viewed positively in terms of Roma "culture". Material substance is a primary biological need and if its demands are not met, then people cannot survive either as individuals or as a group. The preconditions for developing a Romani spiritual and material culture, and for developing the Romani language and Roma cultural life, have all been socially conditioned through history.

It is also worth noting that the Romani culture is an inherently oral one by tradition, and that the oral culture is necessarily linked to memory.[2] It is necessary to bear in mind that Roma in the past had to remember the secret road symbols for informational purposes, but as well as protection. The symbols conveyed messages and information to Roma on the move, and they targeted specific recipients. They could be translated only by transmission from one Roma group to another, from those departing to those

---

[2] The word "memory" in the language of the Roma is clear. It is the "conscience of man, of himself in the real world" („svest čoveka o sebi u realnom svetu") (Đurić and Miletić 2008:162). The word "oblivion" has its etymological origin in the Old Indian word meaning"re-death". The Roma saying "Bistardo e manušestar thaj e Devlestar" (Forgotten by man and by God) means that it is the most horrible fate a man can experience (ibid.).Consequently, it is also about remembering.

arriving. They were also used by those community members who stayed behind due to specific demands that obliged them to stay apart from their group. The symbols allowed the group to warn others and protect themselves. These symbols are significant as they are possibly the first written and produced representations of Romani words.

In this article I provide a brief introduction to the subject, with the hope that it may serve as a stepping-stone for future contributions and research. Without knowledge of Romani culture, Romani traditions and habits cannot be understood. Neither the symbols themselves, nor the way these symbols were created, constructed or translated by Roma. My underlying belief is that the history of Romani translation begins with the translation of these symbols by translators of Romani origin.

Methodology and conceptual bases

As noted earlier, the interdisciplinary area of Romani Studies is an academic discipline in its own right. Its object of study is a unique culture, which, despite the migration, suffering, marginalisation and discrimination, is still recognisable by its spirit and attachment to "homeland India". Specific norms and values in Romani culture are bound with Rromanipe(n). The history of Roma was my source of inspiration for thinking about the secret road symbols, as the first "newsletter" produced by Roma – not through letters and alphabets, but by the mixing of "hieroglyphic"signs, as mentioned in Clébert (1967:228) and in Đurić and Acković (2010:29): "composed of letters and characters of letters from many nations with different kinds of natural materials".[3] In this way, subconsciously and unknowingly, when they created and produced these symbols, Romani peoples initiated the earliest pages of their history of writing and translation. The road symbols survived through history and eventually transformed into a means of entertainment, fun and jokes.

Thinking about the road symbols led me to consider contextualising them within the sociological and cultural approaches used in Translation Studies, and to explore key cultural sociological concepts more specifically, in particular those theorised by Bourdieu (1986). For example, sociological notions help explain translation practices from a different angle and I

[3] "sastavljeno od slova i znakova pisama raznih naroda" sa različitim vrstama prirodnih materijala".

attempt to integrate questions related to cultural capital and habitus with my reflections on translation within the Romani community. Because of diverse dialects, habits, traditions and religions among different Romani groups, the greater Romani community almost always relies on some form of translation. The situation of multiple linguistic and cultural differences leads to considerations of translation in terms of the community's heterogeneity (Venuti 2004:477) and hybridity (Simon 2011:49). Lawrence Venuti expounds on the connection between translation and heterogeneity, noting that "[a]ny community that arises around a translation is far from homogeneous in language, identity, or social position", with "translation a linguistic 'zone of contact' between the foreign and translating cultures" (Venuti 2004:477). The Romani community is far from being homogeneous in language, identity and social position, and cultural translation is an important means by which Romani translation can be investigated.

Do the road symbols represent a form of Romani cultural capital for Roma? Does economic, social, and cultural capital(s) exist within the Romani community at large? Preliminary inquiries in my research have convinced me that the Romani people did indeed create their own cultural products and cultural capital, albeit unintentionally. It appears synonymous with capital that could only have been created and produced in the marginalised context of Romani protection and survival. The creation of road symbols was certainly an expression of a culture of survival, but it also relates to questions of nomadism and identity (Đurić 1987:229), as well as to issues related to the *imaginaire* of the Romani community as well (Kovats 2003:4). The exact translations of the symbols remain a mystery to the general public until this day (Đurić and Acković 2010:8). Questioning one of the older and more knowledgeable members of the Kalderash Romani community who resides in Canada[4] about these road symbols yielded the same response: Clébert is the source of this information, and the rest has remained a mystery.

One particularly noteworthy and relevant feature of Romani road symbols is the fact that they can have multiple meanings simultaneously. According to Đurić and Acković (2010:9), "different meanings are attribut-

---

4 Correspondence with Ronald Lee by email on 25 August 2013. Ronald Lee is a Canadian Romani writer, scholar, and activist who has published numerous publications, and who recently was awarded an Honorary Doctorate (2014) by Queen's University in Ontario, Canada.

ed to them, depending on the tribal groups, subgroups, religious groups, or small, local groups, even families".[5] The meanings of the symbols and their interpretations differ on various levels, expressing relationships to other Roma, to non-Romani communities, to various traditional arts and professions practiced (blacksmiths, tinsmiths, musicians, etc.), as well as to religion. These dissimilarities continuously reflect the diverse cultural and linguistic differences in the Romani community overall, and they invite a need for translation. The multiple meanings generated in the usage of the road symbols are indicative of a heterogeneous community at several levels; a community whose communication is both inter- and intra-linguistic/cultural.

Road symbols in-translation also reflect a special kind of hybridity, one linked to history and nomadism. As noted by Sherry Simon, one can explore questions of the marginalisation and exclusion "of certain populations" (Simon 2011:49) when investigating hybridity. Why and how does hybridity occur?

> When two different things are brought together – when plants or animals are "crossed", when two identities are fused, when literary genres are mixed, when a building combines the features of different architectural styles – something new results. This new thing is a hybrid. (Simon 2011:49)

In the case of the Romani road symbols, or "travelling papers", the hybridity occurred during the transition from nomadic to settled life. The "nomadic way of life" was abandoned in a significant way after the Second World War, when in 1952 a comprehensive program known as the "Great Halt" was implemented in Poland to force Roma to settle. Shortly afterwards, similar policies went into effect in Czechoslovakia, Bulgaria and Romania "in an effort to force assimilation upon the Romani peoples who, in fact, did not want to settle into another culture, but rather wanted to continue their own culture" (Pottanat and Khan 1997). There is no doubt that at the time the reformers believed that control and coercive measures towards Roma could "improve" Romani lives. They believed that education was the only hope for emancipating subaltern groups that lived, as they believed, "outside of history", and that Roma could receive an education only if they would settle. Forced settlements created even more prejudice

5 "'više značenja' su pripisana njima u ovisnosti od 'plemenske grupe, podgrupe, religiozne grupe, ili malih lokalnih grupa,' pa čak i familija".

and stereotypes against Romani people, making them more marginalised and excluded in relation to the majority societies.

With time, the secret road symbols lost their *raison d'être* and ceased to be used as they once had. Instead, they became a means of entertainment and fun, with the symbols being replaced by scripts used by majority societies in countries where Roma lived. The degradation of the spirit of secret road symbols by letters created a new type of hybridity. In Romani communities there was always a need to self-protect, and the most common way to do this had been to communicate through the secret road symbols. The question of why the road symbols continued to remain secret reflects the power imbalance between the Roma and the majority societies they were in contact with. As effectively noted by Simon: "Hybridity is necessarily a "timely" and temporary creation [...]. Once it enters into the expected repertory of cultural artefacts and systems, it loses its right to the title" (Simon 2011:52). For as long as Romani culture did not enter any repertory of cultural artefacts and systems, the once-travelling papers remained a hybrid form, indeed, "point[ing] to practices of translation that highlight the disjuncture between the cultures they are bridging, practices that create texts of interference and contamination" (ibid.). Although Simon's focus falls on the hybrid texts written by authors wishing to emphasise their position between cultures (i.e. as literary expression), this notion of hybridity for translation and in translation is also apt for investigating the earliest known form of Romani written expression as it acknowledges the first type of "Romani translation" practiced by translators of Romani origin.

Romani secret road symbols and their expressions

The Romani people left behind the first written Romani words, in the form of secret symbols, while they were on the road. Roma combined leaves, feathers, certain types of wood, metal, furniture, fabric, glass and leather, etc. to create signs in their secret code. In these signs, it was clearly seen that the particular material with which they were created did not matter, rather, what was important was what was symbolised. The signs became symbols once they were "accepted [as such] by the Romani community" (Đurić and Acković 2010:9).The symbols simultaneously expressed what was real and what was unreal and were proof of Romani meetings with other people of different languages, religions, habits and cultures. Some symbols contained information about historical events and places, making reference to historical persons who marked their lives and destinies in significant ways (ibid.:22).

The names or expressions denoting Romani secret road symbols in the Romani language differ according to which Romani group(s) wrote and created them, for example, *patrin, semno cikna*, *simbolo*, *manaj*, *šikajmako*, etc. The Romani word *patrin* with its Romani dialect variants *patrn, patra and pratin*, has its origin in the old-Indian word *patra* which means leaves. *Patrin* in the Romani language is the word most frequently used along with *semno* and *simbolo* for symbols. The word *semno* is of Romanian origin and in dialects of Roma, who were under the language influence of Romanian (Kalderash, Gurbeti, Lovara, Rumungore etc.), it means symbol or sign of power. *Simbolo* has its origin in the Greek language *simbolon*, which means sign of recognition, emblem, or sign. The word *cikna* has its origin in the Sanskrit word *cihna* which means symbol. *Manaj* means sign or meaning and its origin is in the old-Indian word *man*, which means to think, know, or judge. It is derived from the Sanskrit word *manas*, meaning spirit, soul, or mind. *Šikajmako* has its origin in the Romani word *sikavav*, which means to study or show – it has its origin in the old-Indian verb with the same meaning.[6]

Romani people used the symbols purposefully in order to protect themselves and inform other Romani groups about the good and bad of certain societies as they moved through them, trading or selling their goods to survive. The symbols they created and produced could be conceptualised as a type of Romani cultural capital. According to Bourdieu, cultural capital – which exists in embodied, objectified and institutionalised forms – can be acquired subconsciously and become embodied into a person's or people's habitus. Furthermore, it can exist as "simple cultural capital", (without institutional recognition), and be reinforced by the "collectively owned" social capital accrued through networks in which individuals of the group are members. Group solidarity is thus supported (Bourdieu 1986:241-258). Bourdieu's notion of cultural capital includes the symbolic elements that one acquires by being part of a particular social class, all of which creates a sense of collective identity. In the case of the Romani people, the creation of cultural and social capital is contingent on some form of inter- and intra-

6 The above information was summarised from Clébert 1967:232, and Đurić and Acković 2010:8.

linguistic/cultural translation between and among Romani groups, as well as the majority societies with which they are in contact.

Romani capital" can be viewed in several ways. For example, the centuries-old history of discrimination and marginalisation experienced by Romani peoples has yielded a capital that they have not built consciously. All their activities have been directed by the goal of survival. The cultural capital they have accumulated has always manifested as a result of marginalisation in relation to another, and through some concept of translation. Bourdieu's mention of representative agency within this context is of particular interest because:

> Every group has its more or less institutionalised forms of delegation which enable it to concentrate the totality of the social capital, which is the basis of the existence of the group (a family or a nation, of course, but also an association or a party), in the hands of a single agent or a small group of agents and to mandate this plenipotentiary, charged with *plena potestas agendi et loquendi*, to represent the group, to speak and act in its name and so, with the aid of this collectively owned capital, to exercise a power incommensurate with the agent's personal contribution. (Ibid.:23)

These words resonate with certain dynamics underlying the creation and production of Romani cultural capital at large, including for the secret road symbols or travelling papers transmitted and exchanged by Romani groups for centuries.

The way majority society has long understood Romani culture and cultural capital is through a representative agent, most often using the persona of the researcher or social scientist as "translator". Roma did not have their own researchers until 1969, when Vania de Gila Kochanowski and Ian Hancock completed their doctoral work and PhD degrees. As such, the scientific research carried out has been overwhelmingly non-Roma, and the community members chosen as "representatives" for research have often had nothing to do with the Romani way of life or with Romanipe(n). Furthermore, translation activities have always played a role. Collectively and individually authored works have been published in translation, and considerable work from and into Romani and majority society languages has been carried out at the levels of transcription, interpretation and/or translation. In the Romani context, this manner of building cultural capital, and where translation plays a major role, has not yet been researched in depth. The earliest form of written symbols for Romani peoples is an excellent place to begin. By consciously creating the road symbols consciously for their own protection and survival rather than creating cultural capital intentionally, Romani people defy the usual categorisation of cultural capital. In fact, still today Roma are unaware that the road symbols belong as cultural capital to their "nation". And, as campaigns such as the "Decade of Roma 2005-2015" and other projects for inclusion of Roma show, even while Romani cultural capital is convertible into economic capital, the capital has not tended to be generated by and for Roma. Romani cultural products have too often been subsumed into the cultural and economic capitals of majority nations.

Within the Romani community, symbols are a highly valued means to represent and express something: a function, a quality, or an abstraction of some materiality or physicality. The values associated with symbols and their uses are part of the common, collective knowledge and consciousness of Romani peoples. The power to create, produce, use, and reproduce symbols becomes a kind of symbolic capital for Roma, one that is recognised and appreciated. The use of the symbols leads to the transfer and internalisation of certain beliefs and behaviours. These internalised beliefs and preferences, i.e. dispositions, both condition and are conditioned by social structures. Bourdieu defines the "systems of durable, transposable dispositions" as habitus, i.e. "structured structures predisposed to function as structuring structures" (Bourdieu 1977:72). It is the physical embodiment of cultural capital. Habitus in relation to Romani peoples exists as part of the historic collective Romani community experience, i.e. as rooted in history – even though the historical recording of their experience has always been accounted for by others and not themselves. Romani experience and history is linked to memory and, as noted by Jinyu Liu (2012:1169), memory has its place in Bourdieu's description of habitus: "Bourdieu elaborates on the notion of habitus by explaining its dependence on history and human memory [...]".

As mentioned earlier, social structures and dispositions condition practices and embody a certain "feel" for social situations and environments. The survival of Romani traditions, despite historical discrimination, marginalisation, extermination and a specific way of life, is historically bound to migration and forced movement. This has traditionally kept them producing practices with the intention of just surviving. Habitus is not genetic and innate; it is culturally constructed:

> Habitus produces practices. These practices cannot be ascertained from the objective conditions. They cannot be discovered by looking at the context of

> the situation, but they tacitly exist as social practices. Habitus has social and cultural agency, but that agency does not exist in any one individual. It exists in tradition, practice and other forms of tacit knowledge. (St. Clair, Rodríguez and Nelson 2005:143-144)

Habitus is a product of history, of which Roma are also a part. It is also:

> a system of dispositions, a past that survives into the present and perpetuates itself into the future. Children learn not solely by means of theoretical models, but also by imitation. Concrete operational thought means that one learns by example. It is earlier in life that formal operational thought emerges in which one learns by models and other cognitive concepts. (Ibid.)

Romani children still learn by imitation and example, even if some of the former references and practices have succumbed to contemporary global practices shared with other communities. Romani habitus constructs, is culturally constructed, and participates in the creation of their social identity. Throughout history, Romani peoples have been attributed no real class status, or been positioned beneath almost every other social class that exists. Their collective habitus expresses this centuries-old relation to the multiple majority societies in which they live.

Cultural translation

Essentially, the *raison d'être* for the secret Romani road symbols was the need to inform and protect based on the need to move. The need to move was due to economic, social, and political difficulties, persecution, discrimination and attacks, as well as due to wars in countries where Romani populations lived. It is important to emphasise that when it comes to the question of "mobility" of Roma migration, majority societies attribute and recognise the practice of nomadism to Romani people.[7] Whether or not Roma migration was forced by circumstances is a question non-Roma hardly ever asks. Forced migration often meant that Roma had no opportunity to integrate within local societies or go to schools. Consequently, they did not experience the same possibility for education and emancipation as the other, due to continued marginalisation and segregation. Literacy was not considered within the realm of possibility for most Roma, however, their oral tradition

---

[7] We should not lose sight of the fact that many Roma are, in many countries – out of necessity or under pressure – settled or still in the process of settling. For example, many Romani groups are still half-settled in Central and Eastern Europe and the Balkans; they still live in villages or in suburban areas in shacks or construction dwellings through the winter.

and Romani language survived as an oral language in the form of different dialects within different tribes, communities and groups. Similarly, just as dialects differed amongst different tribes, the secret road symbols experienced similar diversity.

One of the many notions of "cultural translation" allows us not only to consider inter- and intra-linguistic transfers but also inter- and intra-cultural ones with regard to the Romani road symbols. Indeed, in the case of Romani, it is important to underscore the equal relevance of the linguistic component in cultural translation. The road symbols exist in relation both to Romani and to non-Romani communities. In both relationships they have to be approached, interpreted and translated using multiple types of cultural knowledge, through different understandings of several Romani and non-Romani communities. In this sense, cultural translation is used as a tool for distinguishing differences, both between different Romani groups and among diverse non-Roma communities. It effectively highlights identity. From a different perspective, the proximity in language and culture of Roma to non-Roma, i.e. the fact that they do encounter one another and live in some kind of relation with each other, implies a notion of cultural translation that invites contemplation of a notion of ethical encounter.

Finally, cultural translation holds the potential to investigate majority-minority power relations and dynamics in ways similar to postcolonial critique where research on race relations has brought to critical light the experiences of those living the effects of racism. Romani people, their culture and way of life, were created and constructed by the other as symbolic expression. The symbols are bound to nomadism, to romantic and exotic cultural illusions of Romani women and men, and to depictions of their "free lifestyle" by European authors, majority societies, and nobility – a depiction "of one's own wish and lifestyle", as stated in Clébert (1967:235). This could lend itself, as Conway (2012:3) wrote when thinking about sociologists, to an "investigat[ion] [of] cultural translation as a function of displacement". Romani people were primarily brought by majority societies into a stereotyped and generalised category of people who apparently liked to move and change places in life. There seems to have been no thought to investigate specific issues of cultural translation or mistranslation in relation to Romani cultural production in terms of the need to survive. In the case of Roma, nomadism is not a state of mind; it was when seeking protection that Roma were constantly moved (Đurić 1987:181). "Nomadism in the eyes of the non-Roma is a cultural value", one attributed to

Romani people in "which they could build and create an imaginary picture of their identification and identity" (Sijerčić-Tahirović 2012:73).

Road symbols translation

The secret Romani road symbols have yet to be translated. The secrecy of the symbols and their translation, at the time they were used, were a matter of survival. Although they inspired some anthropological, sociological, cultural and ethnological studies, these symbols and their role in the Romani community at large remained virtually unnoticed and untreated in the scientific research. There could be found just a few articles related to the matter of Romani symbols. As mentioned in Đurić and Acković (2010:8), "symbols of Roma and their role in the community are hardly noticed in current scientific researches".[8]

According to Clébert (1967:232), at the time the road symbols were used, Roma did not have an alphabet. They did, however, have a very rich number of conventional signs which made it possible for them "to communicate visually and on the spot". Their creation of the secret road symbols by mixing "hieroglyphic" signs with various materials from nature could be considered as a form of travellers newspaper, specifically for the purpose of survival. The *patrina* were used for everyday communication, and were expressed through translation for those who did not know what the signs meant and what the symbols represented. As Clébert (ibid.:233) states, the signs were generally very simple "hieroglyphics". Their meanings were kept confidential within the tribes. In his interpretation of the symbols he provides a few examples of Romani signs that were previously published in some newspapers and magazines. However, aware of their secrecy and confidentiality, he adds: "A long time ago I promised to keep this a secret [...]. They are not given completely accurately [here], but they portray their symbolic character" (ibid.).[9] The labels had a purely informational character. By combining various items and arranging them in a certain way, they informed the next group of Roma passing the same way about the possible difficulties or merits of a certain locality:

---

[8] "simboli Roma i njihova uloga u zajednici toga naroda jedva da su uočeni u dosadašnjim naučnim istraživanjima".

[9] "Odavno sam dao riječ da ću čuvati u tajnosti [...]. Oni nisu potpuno tačni, moći će nam dočarati njihov simbolički karakter".

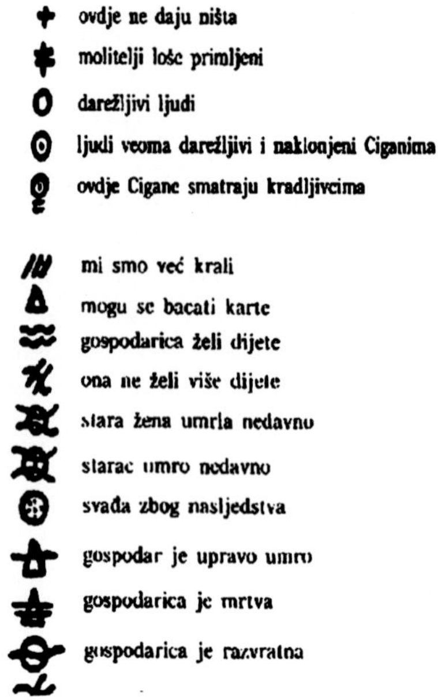

Figure 1: Romani signs/symbols (ibid.)

Meanings attributed here by Clébert (ibid.:233-234):

1: They do not give anything here.
2: Supplicants poorly received.
3: Generous people.
4: People are very generous and sympathetic to *Gypsies*.
5: Here they consider *Gypsies* as thieves.
6: We already stole here.
7: Can look into tarot.
8: Mistress wants a child.
9: She does not want a child anymore.
10: An old woman died recently.
11: An old man died recently.
12: Arguments for inheritance.
13: Master just died.
14: Mistress is dead.
15: Mistress is of poor morale.
Etc.

Translating the symbols was done by community members, since they knew and were familiar with the meaning of the "source message". The translators operated in the interest of the source culture of their own tribes. However, meanings varied and a specific tribe's symbols and signs, as well as their culture and differences in dialects, lifestyle, traditions, beliefs and habits, were not known by others. A sample of a secret road symbol message is provided by Clébert:

Figure 2: A sample of a secret road symbol message (ibid.:233)

Clébert (1967:233) "translates" it as follows: "plemenski starješina koji želi ostaviti svoja dobra-recimo osam svinja, svog konja, svoja kola i šator".[10] This message can be assumed fictitious because, as stated earlier, Clébert promised to keep it a secret. His sample translation reveals no particular meaning. The fact that the secret road symbols are visually presented in Clébert's book does not necessarily mean that he revealed their actual translation. Given the many possible interpretations for Romani words and expressions, depending on context, and given the role translation constantly plays among different communities of Roma and non-Roma alike, the need for a Romani translator or group of translators knowledgeable enough to interpret cultural meanings cannot be underestimated. Ronald Lee (personal correspondence, 25 August, 2013) underscores the fact, in the context of secret signs and symbols:

> Gypsylorists or *Gipsoloristurya,* who are non-Roma researchers who research and write about Roma, and writers of Romantic fiction refer to these *semnurya (plural in Romani language for symbols)* as "*patteran*" and think this means secret signs, and they talk about "following the Romani *Patteran".* As you can see "*Patteran*" is a *xoxamno swato* or false word and is just a misunderstanding of the word "*patrin"* meaning a "leaf" or *patrya/patrina* meaning "leaves".

The misunderstanding, the displacement of meaning that Lee talks about, is due to differences from other cultures, other traditions, and where the interests of the target culture can sometimes prevail over the source message, thereby changing the meaning in the translated target message. It also sets boundary markers. The growth of the greater Romani community's dependence on translation reflects the observation by Venuti (2004:477) that describes a community emerging around translation: "[a]ny community

10 "the head of tribe who is going to leave his goods- let's say eight pigs, his horse, his carriage and tent".

that arises around a translation is far from homogeneous in language, identity, or social position".

Communicating through road symbols was an early historical instance of Romani interpretation of representational symbols in written form and pointed to a need for translation when moving between the diverse linguistic and cultural repertories of Romani groups. Through these practices, Roma were producers of their own written words and translations –albeit unknowingly. Throughout this article, I have proposed considering these symbols as cultural products that symbolise collective thought, or which represent a collective voice belonging to a group or linguistically related groups (Gurbeti, Arlija, Lovara, Kalderash, Sinti, Kale etc.). In order to understand the symbols emitted from another Romani tribe, group or community, it was necessary to seek a translator who could interpret the "source message", i.e. someone from the same group that created and produced the symbols and who was knowledgeable of a certain tribe's culture, tradition and habits.

Migration ultimately brought some of these practices, or their remnants, to the "new world" outside of Europe. In my personal correspondence with Ronald Lee about road symbols, he wrote:

> I don't know much about the trail signs or *dromenge semnurya* that the various groups of Roma used to communicate to one another while traveling. In Canada, bunches of leaves were used to show stragglers which way the main group had gone, where they turned off to camp. If no leaves were available, rags would be tied at tree branches or fence posts. The old Roma who knew about these things have almost all passed away in Canada.

Conclusion

A Translation Studies perspective on Romani Studies opens up an enormous arena of research possibilities, one in which Romani researchers can play a critical role. This role is a critical one. Knowledge of the different aspects and approaches to Romani culture, Romanipe/Rromanipe, diverse traditions, language and a history of displacement and migration, all contribute to a more comprehensive understanding of Romani cultures in translation. This article is merely a brief introduction to the convergence of Romani Studies and Translation Studies in the early history of Romani written communication. It may well be the first instance of Romani translation created and produced by Romani peoples experiencing the need to inform and protect themselves by means of secret symbols while on the road.

References

Bourdieu, Pierre (1977) *Outline of a Theory of Practice* (tr. Richard Nice). Cambridge: Cambridge University Press.

Bourdieu, Pierre (1986) "The Forms of Capital". In Richardson, John G (ed.) *Handbook of Theory and Research for the Sociology of Education.*New York: Greenwood Press, 241-258.

Clébert, Jean-Paul (1967) *Cigani* (tr.Višnja Škrtić). Zagreb: Stvarnost.

Conway, Kyle (2012) "Cultural Translation". In Gambier, Yves/van Doorslaer, Luc (eds.) *Handbook of Translation Studies.* Vol. 3. Amsterdam/Philadelphia: John Benjamins, 21-25.

Đurić, Rajko (1987) *Seobe Roma: Krugovi Pakla i Venac Sreće [The Migration of Roma: Circles of Hell and Wreath of Happiness]*. Beograd: Beogradski izdavačko-grafički zavod.

Đurić, Rajko (2005) "Predgovor" [Foreword]. In Devis, Barbara/Đurić, Rajko/B. Đorđević, Dragoljub (eds.) *Rromanipe(n): O Kulturnom Identitetu Roma: Promovisanje i Zaštita Kulturnih Prava u Programu Javnog Zastupništva, 2003-2005 [Rromanipe(n): About Cultural Identity of Roma: Promotion and Protection of the Cultural Rights in the Programme of Public Representation, 2003-2005]*. Beograd: Care International u Srbiji i CrnojGori, 11-12.

Đurić, Rajko/Miletić, Antun (2008) *Istorija Holokausta Roma [History of the Holocaust of the Roma]*. Beograd: Politika AD.

Đurić, Rajko/Acković, Dragoljub (2010) *Rečnik Romskih Simbola [Dictionary of the Romani Symbols]*. Beograd: Rominterpress.

Folaron, Deborah (2013) "The Romani Spectrum". *Translation Romani: Exploring Ties between Romani Culture and the Field of Translation*, www.translationromani.net/en/romani [19 October 2014].

Hancock, Ian F. (2007) *We Are the Romani People = Ame Sam E Rromane Dženе.* Hatfield: University of Hertfordshire Press.

Kovats, Martin (2003) "The Politics of Roma Identity: Between Nationalism and Destitution". OpenDemocracy 30 July 2003, https://www.opendemocracy.net/people-migrationeurope/article_1399.jsp [19 October 2014].

Liu, Jinyu (2012) "Habitus of Translators as Socialised Individuals: Bourdieu's Account". *Theory and Practice in Language Studies* 2:6, 1168-1173.

Marushiakova, Elena/Popov, Veselin (2011) "Roma Culture". In Romani Project Graz *Factsheets on Roma Culture*, http://romafacts.uni-graz.at/index.php/culture/introduction/roma-culture [19 October 2014].

Pottanat, Mary/Khan, Nadia (1997) "Roma (Gypsies) and the Holocaust". *An End to Intolerance* 5, http://www.iearn.org/hgp/aeti/aeti-1997/roma-in-holocaust.html [19 October 2014].

Sijerčić-Tahirović, Hedina (2012) "Migration and its Implications for the Educational System: The Case of the Roma in Bosnia, Germany and Canada". In Bešter, Romana/ Klopčič, Vera/Medvešek, Mojca (eds.) *Formal and Informal Education for Roma, Different Models and Experience* (tr. Tom Priestly). Ljubljana: Inštitut za Narodnostna Vprašanja, 72-83.

St. Clair, Robert N./Rodríguez,Walter E./Nelson, Carma (2005) "Habitus and Communication Theory". *Intercultural Communication Studies* XIV:1, 136-150.

Simon, Sherry (2011) "Hybridity and Translation". In Gambier, Yves/van Doorslaer, Luc (eds.) *Handbook of Translation Studies.* Vol. 2. Amsterdam/Philadelphia: John Benjamins, 49-53.

Venuti, Lawrence (2004) "Translation, Community, Utopia." In Venuti, Lawrence (ed.) *The Translation Studies Reader.* London/New York: Routledge, 482-502.

Agency and Choice:
Tranlsation Policy and Practice

WILLIAM HANES

Universidade Federal de Santa Catarina, Brazil

Century of Foreign Language in *Memórias do Instituto Oswaldo Cruz*: Language Policy, Nationalism and Colonial Science[1]

The Oswaldo Cruz Institute, founded in 1900 as a public health initiative, represents the institutionalisation of empirical science in Brazil. In 1909 it launched a journal called *Memórias do Instituto Oswaldo Cruz* that now publishes only in English, but was multilingual when it began and continued to be so for much of its history, although the trajectories of the languages of publication differed greatly. If changes in language represent changes in network structure, these shifts in language policy reflect repositioning with regard to partnerships, colonialism/politics and the nature of the scientific community and the organisational development of the Institute. To better understand these changes, a diachronic, polysystemic, corpus-based approach was used to analyse the full corpus (1909-2013) of this journal. It was analysed for foreign language frequency and origin, as well as paratextual clues regarding its editorial policy. Though the journal was originally intended to promote the Institute's research, a complex dialogue with international partners was revealed. This dialogue seems to defy colonial models and threads a delicate balance between science as nationalism and the so-called *republique mondiale de la science*. The onset of English as the journal's only language of expression occurred quite late, at roughly the same time its electronic version went online. This could have been an inevitable result of a new open editorial policy set in 1980, but it also seems to be the result of the new level of interconnectivity in the scientific community precipitated by advancing communication technology, which would tend to confirm Walter Ong's theory about communication technology as a fundamental driver of society.

Keywords: sociology of science, scientific literature, tropical medicine, translation policy

[1] The author would like to express his gratitude to the Tropical Medicine Institute of Antwerp for access to their periodicals collection. This study was supported by CAPES, a division of the Brazilian Ministry of Education.

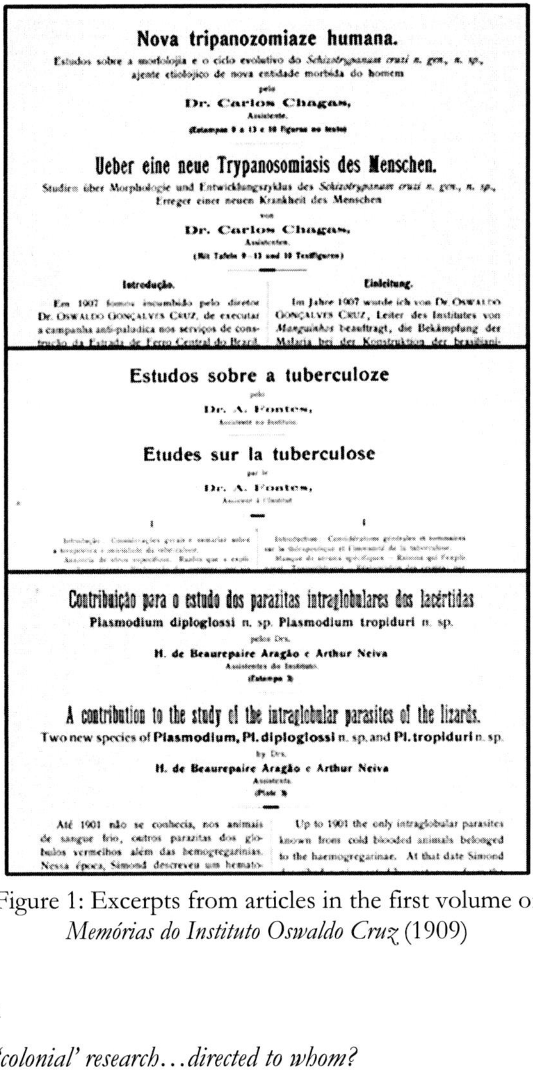

Nova tripanozomiaze humana.

Estudos sobre a morfolojia e o ciclo evolutivo do *Schizotrypanum cruzi n. gen., n. sp.*, ajente etiolojico de nova entidade morbida do homem

pelo

Dr. Carlos Chagas,

Assistente.

Ueber eine neue Trypanosomiasis des Menschen.

Studien über Morphologie und Entwicklungszyklus des *Schizotrypanum cruzi n. gen., n. sp.*, Erreger einer neuen Krankheit des Menschen

von

Dr. Carlos Chagas,

Introdução. | Einleitung.

Em 1907 fomos incumbido pelo diretor Dr. Oswaldo Gonçalves Cruz, de executar a campanha anti-paludica nos serviços de cons- | Im Jahre 1907 wurde ich von Dr. Oswaldo Gonçalves Cruz, Leiter des Institutes von *Manguinhos* beauftragt, die Bekämpfung der

Estudos sobre a tuberculoze

pelo

Dr. A. Fontes,

Etudes sur la tuberculose

par le

Dr. A. Fontes,

Contribuição para o estudo dos parazitas intraglobulares dos lacértidas

Plasmodium diploglossi n. sp. **Plasmodium tropiduri** n. sp.

pelos Drs.

H. de Beaurepaire Aragão e Arthur Neiva

A contribution to the study of the intraglobular parasites of the lizards.

Two new species of **Plasmodium, Pl. diploglossi** n. sp. and **Pl. tropiduri** n. sp.

by Drs.

H. de Beaurepaire Aragão e Arthur Neiva

Até 1901 não se conhecia, nos animais de sangue frio, outros parazitas dos glóbulos vermelhos além das hemogregarinias. Nessa época, Simond descreveu um hemato- | Up to 1901 the only intraglobular parasites known from cold blooded animals belonged to the haemogregarinae. At that date Simond

Figure 1: Excerpts from articles in the first volume of *Memórias do Instituto Oswaldo Cruz* (1909)

Introduction

A curious case: 'colonial' research…directed to whom?

The three title pages in the image above are from the first volume (1909) of a tropical medicine institute's journal, perhaps better described as a *public health* institute since it is from Brazil where the two perspectives converge. The two-column format of each article includes Portuguese and one other language – four languages in total. Finding a highly multilingual Latin

American medical research journal during the *belle époque*, when the term "colonial medicine" was still in use,[2] would already seem counterintuitive. The other languages in this volume, English, French and German, are not official languages in or anywhere in South America (with the exception of the Guyanas), so to whom, besides Lusophones, were these articles directed? The deliberate international intent (rather than regional) seems obvious, but this scattered linguistic pattern is nothing like what should be expected from a stereotypical colonial model.

This journal was not a temporary phenomenon. In fact, it still exists and currently has the highest impact factor of any journal in Latin America. It is the longest-running scientific journal in Brazil (Rocha e Silva 2010) and is among the oldest in the Southern Hemisphere (Scott 2005). The journal's publisher, the *Instituto Oswaldo Cruz* (IOC), represents the beginnings in earnest of both public health and experimental science in the country (Stepan 1981:4-5). On its website, the journal describes itself as "an international free and open-access journal publishing original research from throughout the world all over the fields of tropical medicine, medical parasitology and microbiology" (*Memórias* 2014). Although a total of five languages have been used in this journal's history, it is now completely monolingual – in a foreign language – and boasts of its increasing international connectivity (Figure 2, below).

Figure 2: Homepage of *Memórias do Instituto Oswaldo Cruz* in 2014

[2] For example, the *Instituto de Medicina Tropical* of Madrid was called the *Instituto de Medicina Colonial* until 1957.

Historical background

Oswaldo Cruz, with a mandate from the Brazilian president, established the *Instituto Soroterápico* in Rio de Janeiro in 1900 with the purpose of producing vaccines to control a number of concurrent epidemics in the capital (Coura 1994:1). This institute quickly became the foremost agency of public health in Brazil due to its radical and effective public vaccination campaigns. Oswaldo Cruz became a national figure (even occupying a chair on the *Academia Brasileira de Letras*) and, after having effectively eradicated yellow fever, the bubonic plague and smallpox from Rio, he directed the group's efforts toward the *sertão* (hinterlands) and the Amazon basin. There, a nasty disease as yet unknown to science (American trypanosomiasis) was waiting for them, the discovery of which helped launch the institute to international recognition in the area of tropical medicine.[3] This lead to a pair of nominations for the Nobel Prize in Medicine by 1921 (Coutinho, Freire and Pinto-Dias 1999:123). However, being the first laboratory of its kind in Brazil its practice was necessarily acquired from abroad, i.e., it was dependent on the use of foreign language. Different languages would open different avenues of knowledge and potential partnerships and, as shown above, the institute's research was presented multilingually. The selection and frequency of this constellation of languages remains mostly opaque and follows a curious trajectory along the history of the journal.

Theoretical setting in and beyond Translation Studies

Comparing the journal's current language policy, which has completely institutionalised English, with the original multilingual format portrayed in Figure 1 raises a number of questions. Ong (2002) and Hobsbawm (1996), for example, claim reason that communities are dependent on their language, i.e., any changes in language represent changes to the community. And since the practice of science is heavily dependent on group work and

[3] Due to the Institute's efforts Brazil won first place at the International Hygiene Exhibition at Berlin in 1907 (Memórias 89:125) and Carlos Chagas, future director of IOC, was awarded the Schaudinn Prize for Protozoology by the Hamburg Institute of Tropical Medicine in 1912, as well as "honorary degrees from the Universities of Buenos Aires, Lima, Harvard, Brussels, Hamburg, Paris and memberships in several medical societies. Additionally, he was granted the Great Prize of the Pasteur Centenary Commemorative Exposition in Strasbourg (1922)" (Wendel/Brener 1992).

intergroup communication, perennially international and interlingual in nature (see Montgomery 2000), trends in scientific language and translation policy are of both practical and theoretical importance. Moreover, given that such a move toward English has almost invariably occurred across journals of all disciplines, as well as in international government and university interfaces (see Lambert 2010; Lambert and Iliescu-Gheorghiu forthcoming), a careful examination of how and why this came about, at least in this lengthy case, may be a useful contribution especially since four other colonial languages were supplanted in this journal over the course of the twentieth century. Finally, as has been shown in the intense theoretical debate in scientific literature on issues such as the nature of authorship and intellectual property (see Hoey 2000; Hanes 2014), the so-called empirical sciences are sometimes ahead of the curve in issues common to other disciplines.

Although the topic of translation/multilingualism in science has been broached within Translation Studies, garnering a recent handbook entry (Montgomery 2010), it is still scarce in literature. This does not mean, however, that others are not studying it. Among publications from Organisation Studies, Science and Technology Studies, and from scientific literature itself, a number are pertinent to this study.

First of all, the question of the impact of language on the scientific community has been debated since the mid-1990s. Even in mainstream journals such as *Scientific American* Wayt Gibbs' 1995 article "Lost science in the Third World" indicates that high-impact scientific journals' English-only policy could effectively be cutting off sectors of the scientific community. Voices in the developing world have also addressed the effects of the scientific lingua franca, for example, Meneghini and Packer who founded the successful Brazilian-based science metapublisher *SciELO* and revisited Wyatt's question in their 2007 article "Is there science beyond English?". The panoramic work on language and translation in science by Scott Montgomery is also relevant here especially since his conclusions in his 2013 work *Does Science Need a Global Language? English and the Future of Research,* about the dating (soon after World War II) and reasons (mainly political) for English as the lingua franca of science, differ radically from the findings of the present study.

Other scientific journals have conducted bibliometric self-analysis. The *Swiss Medical Weekly* has published an account of its own linguistic evolution in Navarro's 1997 study "Die Sprache der Medizin in der Schweiz von 1920 bis 1995", contrasting citation patterns from German- and French-speaking contributors in order to trace the development of English as the main language of science in Switzerland. A study from the Oswaldo Cruz Institute's own historical society is on the citation behaviour of IOC scientists from 1909-1917, characterising them as information producers and users (Weltman 2002).

Besides the work of sociologist Bruno Latour on science as a social activity (see for example 1979, 1987, 1988), an organisational, polysystemic perspective has been used in doctoral dissertations on the dissemination of Brazilian scientific findings in Brazil and Argentina (Kropf 2006) and the interaction between the Brazilian scientific community, its institutions, and the state between 1948 and 1980 (Fernandes 1987). This demonstrated the behaviour of a community dependent on international communication in periods when foreign contact was repressed.

Research questions

Although not a complete picture, following the trail of translation and multilingual communication in the journal's published corpus is the most concrete way to begin a forensic historical reconstruction of its policies (Wagner 2008:12; Royal Society 2011:23). It represents the tip of an iceberg: its conflicts, strategies and language theory.

I would like to address four basic initial questions about the translation/non-translation and language policies of the journal over its history:

- Do the foreign language articles in *Memórias* indicate the involvement of foreigners at the IOC and, if so, does this presence indicate foreign dependence/control?
- What does the historical presence of foreign language in this journal (both at the outset and in the recent shift to English only) say about the IOC's struggle for self-positioning between identities as a nation-al(istic) agency of public health and as a member of the international scientific community, the "*république mondiale de la science*"?
- How were adverse political conditions, specifically two World Wars and two Brazilian military dictatorships (1930-1945 and 1964-1985), reflected in *Memórias*' language policy and what did such changes indicate?

- How does the selection of featured languages in *Memórias*, especially the non-use of Spanish, conform to and/or deny the colonial model from which Brazil was just emerging as the journal was established?

Methodology

The primary corpus consisted of the complete online collection (1909-2012, more than 6,000 articles), available online in PDF format, which was analysed for a number of aspects: the language of publication of the articles was determined through the end of 2012, the final complete year at the time of data compilation; author and institutional affiliation were found for all translated articles (i.e. published in both Portuguese and a foreign language); data on contributing authors from foreign institutions was compiled from 1909-1980 and, thereafter, from important special issues in 1984 and 1999[4]; the works of individual contributing authors through 1956[5] were analysed to determine the main producers of foreign language articles.

Secondary to this, paratext not available online was examined in a complete hardbound set of the journal for statements regarding language policy. All resulting data were then compiled and formatted into tables for analysis, yielding language, authorship and policy trends. In this way, these data could be compared, to a certain extent, with national and international socio-political events and then be applied to the research questions.

In order to better contextualise this research and the *Memórias*' corpus alone (articles, editorials, paratext), a small selection of other early publications by the IOC, and a broader set of historical articles and editorial pieces from external sources about the IOC, were examined. However, due to the constraints inherent in article format, the questions posed above cannot be addressed in much more than passing detail, especially given their complex political nature on institutional, national and international levels. Furthermore, certain source documentation was also produced under climates of censorship and thus remains enigmatic (especially a key editorial by Coura in 1980). Consequently, though these questions tempt entry into the realm of

---

4 1980 signalled a new editorial policy inviting outside contribution, after which the rate of articles published in the journal increased exponentially.

5 1956 is the final year in which translated articles (i.e., the same article in two languages within the same issue) were published in the journal. The next section provides more detail.

what Toury (1995) calls "explanatory research", a descriptive approach is the objective.

Results

Editorial periods and their use of foreign language

The journal's original multilingual framework was retained into the 1990s. However, as can be seen in Table 1, its composition and vigour varied widely including a virtual Portuguese-only period in the 1940s and 1970s, a sharp rise of English in the 1980s which then grinds to a halt by the mid-1990s as English became the sole channel of communication.

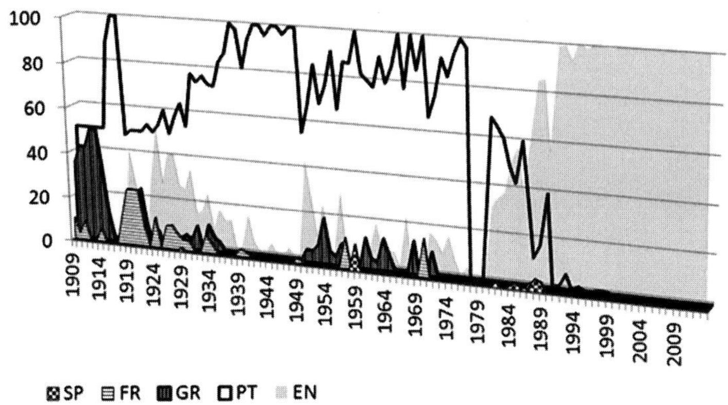

Legend: SP = Spanish; FR = French; GR = German; PT= Portuguese; EN = English

Table 1: Language trajectories as percentage of total articles in *Memórias do Instituto Oswaldo Cruz* 1909-2012

Definition of translation and non-translation eras

Over the course of *Memórias*' 105 year history there have been two distinct eras which I will label as "translation" and "non-translation". By translation, I mean that some or all articles appeared in two languages in the same issue (in either a two-column format or as separate articles in the same issue). Beginning in 1957, however, all articles appeared in a single language only (one of the previously-mentioned five), i.e. the journal remained multilingual, but no foreign language article had a Portuguese counterpart (or vice versa), so the article could only be accessed by speakers of the language in which it was originally written. It is important to clarify that the practice of providing summaries/abstracts in any language only began systematically much later – after 1980. Within these two broad eras, five distinct periods – each with a distinct approach to foreign language – can be defined.

	Translation era		**Non-translation era**		
Editorial Periods	Side-by-side translations 1909-1922 [13 years]	Separated translations 1923-1956 [34 years]	'Portuguese only' 1957-1980 [24 years]	Abstracts 1981-1989 [9 years]	'English only' 1990-2012 [23 years]
Percentage of articles published in foreign languages	**85.4%**	**21.3%**	**13.3%**	**78.8%**	**99.9%**

Table 2: *Memórias do Instituto Oswaldo Cruz*: the presence of foreign language articles in each editorial period

Breakdown of distinct editorial periods

Before proceeding to describe the individual editorial periods, the following table has been inserted to more clearly demonstrate the relative prominence of the languages in each editorial period.

From 1909-1922, in what I will call the *side-by-side period*, the vast majority of articles appeared in two languages, which were arranged in a two-column, or side-by-side, bilingual format (see Fig.1 for visual), although some articles appeared untranslated (i.e. monolingual), either in Portuguese or a foreign language. German was the predominant foreign language: 35% more frequent than English and French combined. Journal output, especially in foreign languages, declined sharply between 1915 and 1921 and remained low – dropping from 84.9% in this period to 18.5% in the next, i.e., 1923-1956.

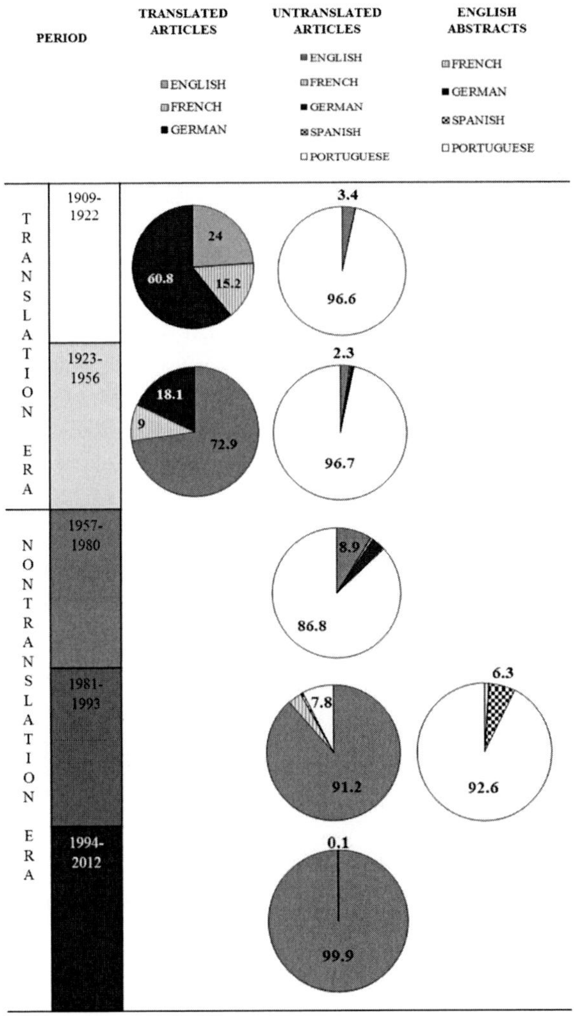

Table 3: *Memórias do Instituto Oswaldo Cruz*: relative prominence of published languages by editorial period 1909-2012

From 1923-1956, during what I will call the *separated translation period,* there was not only a drop in foreign language use (both translated and untranslated), but also a change in layout. The foreign language versions appeared as separate articles within the same issue, sometimes immediately after the

Portuguese version, and sometimes segregated in a section after the Portuguese articles. Within this period of greatly reduced foreign language presence, English was the predominant foreign language – 63% more frequent German and French combined. Moreover, there was also a notable increase in untranslated foreign language articles. The publication of untranslated articles in German was still roughly twice that of French, and a single article in Spanish – the first – appeared in 1929; the second would not appear until 1959.

Starting in 1957, in what could be called the *Portuguese only period*, translated article versions were no longer published in *Memórias*. The foreign language presence dwindled to 13.3% – the inverse of the *side-by-side period* (1909-1922). There were twice as many English articles as all other foreign languages combined. The journal shut down from 1977-1979, which will be discussed below. The last German article appeared in 1971.

After closing down for three years, *Memórias* was re-launched in 1980 with a new editorial board and policy encouraging contributions from other institutions (Coura 1980). The consolidation of English as lingua franca in the journal was underway at this point, outnumbering Portuguese articles almost 2 to 1. Beginning in 1981, abstracts, initially often one sentence long, appeared in italics without the title "Abstract" or "Summary". Due to this key characteristic, I will call it the *abstract period*. Portuguese and Spanish articles with English abstracts (always at the beginning) were found to have a same-language abstract at the end of the article before the bibliography. Keywords were not used in 1981 but were present by 1989. Although this practice was specified in the new policy (see Table 4), the fact that Portuguese, Spanish and French articles were published with and without English abstracts indicates that the practice was not strictly enforced. Spanish and French combined represented only 2% of the total output during this period. Also of note is that the first editorial in English appeared in 1984.

The final articles in French and Spanish were published in 1989, leaving only English and Portuguese. With Portuguese output at 0.5%, from that point until the final Portuguese article appeared in 1998, an almost literal *English Only Period* began in 1990. Nevertheless, the online instructions for authors still ostensibly allowed submissions in Portuguese as late as March 2012 (Internet Archive 2001), indicating that the journal's movement toward a lingua franca was not exactly policy-driven, although possibly encouraged by the requirement of English abstracts since 1980. The journal first appeared online in 1996 and joined SciELO (a Brazil-based, online metapublisher for developing countries) at its inception in 1997, which, although open-access, sets no specific language policy for member journals (SciELO 2010). Moreover, IOC became a charter member of the International Association of National Public Health Institutes (IANPHI) in 2006 (incidentally at a meeting that took place in Brazil) (IANPHI 2013).

Paratextual evidence of editorial policy

Given that only a limited amount of paratext has been made available in the online collection, the paratext of printed editions of the *Memórias* provided critical data on editorial policy. A summary of key editorial statements is provided in Table 4. Regarding extra-institutional contributors, the question was not raised in 1909, they were excluded by 1923, discouraged by 1957, encouraged by 1980 and taken for granted by 2013. It is significant that German was excluded as a language of publication by 1980. The rising importance of English can be traced from worry about the quality of English in the abstracts in 1980 to the use of international outsourcing for language editing services in 2013.

YEAR	LANGUAGE(S)	STATEMENT
1909	PT/FR*	NOTICE: The "MEMORIAS" will be published in issues which will not appear at fixed dates and which will form volumes of more or less 200 pages. There will appear at least one volume per year [...] All correspondence related to the "MEMORIAS" should be addressed to the "Director of the Oswaldo Cruz Institute [...]".
1923	PT*	THE MEMORIAS, official organ of the Oswaldo Cruz Institute, are reserved exclusively for the publication of original works carried out in it. It will appear in issues, without fixed dates, with a minimum of one volume per year. All correspondence should be directed to "Editing of the Memorias do Instituto Oswaldo Cruz [...]".
1957	PT*	The MEMÓRIAS, official organ of the Oswaldo Cruz Institute, are intended, principally, for publication of original works carried out in it. It will appear in separate issues, or in a complete volume, according to editorial conveniences. All correspondence should be addressed to: MEMÓRIAS DO INSTITUTO OSWALDO CRUZ [...].

1980	PT/EN	NOTICE TO CONTRIBUTORS The *Memórias do Instituto Oswaldo Cruz* welcomes previously unpublished scientific articles mainly in the fields of parasitology [7 more categories] and epidemiology of infectious and parasitic diseases. Papers should be sent to: Memórias do Instituto Oswaldo Cruz Caixa Postal […] Manuscripts (2 copies) in English, Spanish, Portuguese or French must be typewritten […] The English Summary (200 words maximum) […] must be written by a person who knows the language perfectly.
2013	EN	Editorial Policy The *Memórias do Instituto Oswaldo Cruz* is a multidisciplinary journal which publishes original research throughout the fields of tropical medicine […] The journal publishes eight issues constituting one volume per year. Occasionally papers presented at symposia or congresses are published as supplements […] Submitted papers must be written in English. English of low quality is a major cause of delay in publication and we strongly advise authors with English as a foreign language to have their manuscripts checked by someone with English as a first language, preferably a scientist. INSTRUCTIONS TO AUTHORS Papers submitted to Memórias will undergo the Premium Editing of English language review made by American Journal Experts, further suggestions will enhance non-native English writing style.

*My translation

Table 4: Historical progression of editorial policy in *Memórias do Instituto Oswaldo Cruz*

Discussion

Based on the abundance of data that the *Memórias* corpus has provided, the discussion will now return to the four initial study questions posed in section 1.4.

Foreign language articles in Memórias and foreign dependence/control

Foreign language articles by Institute scientists

The paratext in Table 4 revealed that studies not carried out by or with Institute fellows were proscribed from the journal in 1923 and still discouraged by 1957. Although this does not demonstrate the absence or presence of foreign participation at the Institute, it does indicate strict self-determination over the content it published. This is borne out by authorship data. For example, a group of 19 authors contributed 266 (i.e., 71%) of the 377 total foreign language articles published in the journal during the "translation era" (1909-1956). Individual contributions were in some cases quite weighty: Swiss-educated IOC researcher Adolpho Lutz, for example, authored 24% of all articles published in German until 1956, while Lauro Travassos produced 32% of all French articles during the same period.

At least a small core of fellows from the Institute did indeed spend time abroad. First and foremost, Oswaldo Cruz himself, who had just returned from study at the *Institut Pasteur* in Paris when initiating his *Instituto Soroterápico* in Rio de Janeiro, certainly stimulated a multilingual corporate culture. In 1930, Lauro Travassos produced a series of eight articles for the *Memórias* (in Portuguese) while at the *Institute for Maritime and Tropical Diseases* (now the *Bernhard Nocht Institute for Tropical Medicine*) in Hamburg, indicating that although German was beginning to disappear in the journal, longstanding ties with German Tropical Medicine institutions were not. Also of note from the authorship data is that by the end of the 1940s, there was a new generation of authors producing foreign language articles only and only in a single foreign language. This could indicate a general climate conducive to the non-translated format that began in 1957, which could have come about via habitus rather than top-down policy.

<u>Input by authors from foreign institutions</u>

After winning the grand prize at the Berlin Hygiene and Demographics exhibit in 1907, the IOC quickly attracted foreign attention. Eminent Czech parasitologist Stanislaus von Prowazek, who went on to discover the pathogen of epidemic typhus, together with IOC-trained pathologist Henrique de Rocha Lima (Marcolin 2011:9) conducted research at the Institute between 1909-1912 (Scott 1939:1025), contributing three articles to the second issue of *Memórias* in 1909.

Apart from von Prowazek and other early visiting scientists, there was a sporadic, low level of external participation in authorship (19 articles in total) never rising above three articles in any one year prior to 1980. No consistent input was seen from any one location (i.e. no on-going partnerships are evident from the author institutions). Foreign-based articles were almost unanimously in English, including those from Argentina (e.g., Mazza 1949).

However, this should not be taken to mean that the Institute was unaware of other work or did not interact with other institutions, which would appear to have been the main purpose of publishing in so many languages. In fact, Cruz' hygiene crusade in Rio de Janeiro was accused of being "of secondary importance" for "following the example of the Americans in Havana" (Scott 1939:1025). Although I will not stray from the journal *Memórias* as the main focus, I will briefly mention two other IOC publications that demonstrate its extensive interaction with other institutions. The first, a rare undated (1911 or 1912) promotional volume entitled *Institut Oswaldo Cruz*, entirely in German, details the history, techniques, publications and library holdings of the Institute, which included over 600 mostly foreign journal subscriptions. A 1929 IOC volume entitled *Leprosy: a Survey Made in 40 Countries (1924-1927)* details Heraclides de Souza-Araujo's worldwide tour of all major leprosy treatment facilities and subsequent foundation of the International Society of Leprology, including a section reproducing his extensive correspondence with these institutions in an effort to organise the expedition.

Much later, after opening its doors to outside contributors, two important special issues of *Memórias* further demonstrate the rapid, though not immediate, upward climb of the journal's foreign authorship. A 1984 special issue (*Memórias* 79 suppl.) described the proceedings of a symposium commemorating the 50th anniversary of the death of IOC director Carlos Chagas (coincidentally, this was the same year that the journal's first editorial in English appeared). The author affiliations from the 27 papers include 12 from IOC and 17 from elsewhere in Brazil. Only two co-authors (i.e., 2.8% of the total 71 authors) were from foreign institutions (Venezuela, USA).

Compared to this are the affiliations of a 1999 special issue, *The proceedings of the 26th Annual Meeting on Basic Research on Chagas Disease/The 16th Meeting of Brazilian Society of Protozoology*. An index of 1502 authors are listed for the more than 500 abstracts and 71 papers presented at 38 roundtables. Counting only the members of the roundtables, the following distribution of institutions was found: 20 from North America (2 countries, 14 different institutions), 12 from Europe (7 countries, 10 institutions), 6 from South America (3 countries, 5 institutions), and 2 from elsewhere (1 country, 1 institution). From this it is clear that as the volume of participants increased, so did their geographic distribution (as did the tendency toward an English-only language policy). Outside contributorship has only increased since then; it was reported of the *Memórias* in 2009 that "one hundred years after its founding, about 45% of articles submitted to it are from abroad" (Marcolin 2009:7).

Foreign language and self-positioning: national(istic) public health and the international scientific community

The side-by-side format is a clue

That over 85% of all articles between 1909 and 1922 appeared in a two-column translated format (illustrated in Figure 1) could have been strategically important for the Institute's students, facilitating the acquisition of terminology to better read and understand important journals published in other languages. This is corroborated by the fact that it maintained subscriptions to more than 420 scientific journals during this period (Araújo-Jorge/Santos-Barbosa/Lourenço de Oliveira 2012:33). The above-mentioned 1911 or 1912 document in German lists titles in the following languages: German (206), English (179), French (114), Portuguese (48), Italian (42), Spanish (25), indicating, in all probability, that the 15 listed staff "ate and drank" other languages and must have encouraged their students and colleagues to do the same. So the link between broad foreign language consumption thus described and the broad foreign language production under the same circumstances should be clear.

Multilingualism and monolingualism in the service of nationalism

The above indicates that substantial participation in international Tropical Medicine was necessarily a multilingual task for the IOC. The purpose for such participation in the first place, however, also leaves room for the idea of competition over community, i.e., the concept of scientific nationalism. That scientific endeavour, whether local or international, is in the end subservient to – or rather an arm of – the state (think Manhattan Project) has been a constant counterpoint to the idea of the lone scientist working in his lab, blissfully unaware of his socio-political context. Such rhetoric is still quite common today (e.g. Royal Society 2011:24, 36) and has been grafted onto universities through ranking schemes. It has also accompanied the Institute throughout the twentieth century. The Brazilian writer Monteiro Lobato perhaps summed it up best in 1918 when he stated: "Manguinhos[6], in its few years of existence [...] has done more for the country than a whole century of rhetorical omnipotence. The salvation is there" (Lobato

6 A metonymy for the Institute based on its original location in Rio de Janeiro.

1918; qtd. in Gadelha 2009). This gives the idea that the success (both practical and iconic) of the Institute was a chance to even the playing field, and monolingualism and multilingualism were just tactics for getting there. Linguistic *Realpolitik* is certainly in the repertoire of Meneghini and Packer, the founders of the Brazil-based science database SciELO, who asserted "the ability of scientists to communicate in the scientific lingua franca is part of a country's scientific capabilities" (2007:114).

Such was also at the forefront of *Memórias* editor José Coura's mind when drafting the opening statement for the journal's re-launch, even after the severe repression suffered under the military dictatorship:

> How strange that *Memórias* went from a small group of Brazilians publishing in a number of languages to a highly international organisation publishing in one.

To underscore this point, Table 5 is presented, tracing the trajectories of total production vs. production in English.

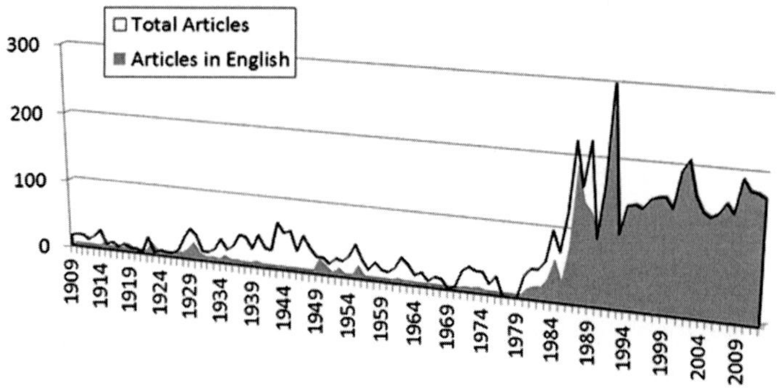

Table 5: Total article output vs. English language output in *Memórias do Instituto Oswaldo Cruz*, 1909-2012

The data above indicate that the total convergence of production in English occurs in 1998, the same time the final article in Portuguese was published. Curiously enough, this is almost identical to the point at which the journal goes online (1996), which aligns nicely with the theoretical line of Walter Ong (2002). And just a few years later (by 2013) the entire language editing process, i.e., final control over expression, was outsourced to an American firm.[7]

Although the current mythology is that English took off as a general lingua franca in the post-World War II era by virtue of worldwide US political, cultural and economic influence (e.g. Schiller 1991:18; Montgomery 2013:11), which may be the case in some places (see for example Navarro 1997), it certainly was not the case in *Memórias*. Albeit high in comparison to other languages appearing in *Memórias* and with isolated spikes (e.g. 1949, 1955) the presence of English articles remained relatively insignificant compared to, for example, the presence of German before World War I. In fact, compared to the journal's other periods, the most characteristic name for the one parallel to the Cold War would be "Portuguese only". Thus, despite considerable U.S. economic and political influence in Brazil, English was not employed as the language of scientific production until much later. Thus, the role of technology here is undeniable in the fact that opening channels of increased communication involved the increasing use of a common language, i.e., English, which, according to de Swaan's "world language system" (2002:1-4), became the language of production (and of consumption, as well) with the advent of the internet.

So does such a spectacular language movement, i.e. the worldwide asymptote toward English as the standard of (scientific) communication, indicate a new or different chapter in this story? It might be similar to the stories of other far-reaching networks such as the EU or the university. The relationship between globalisation/technology and the unchallenged global scientific lingua franca appears under-investigated in both the humanities and the scientific, technical and medical literature. Consensus seems to take it as a given, as something that "just happened", something to deal with rather than understand.

And yet SciELO founders, Meneghini and Packer, bemoan the loss of bi- or multilingualism in online publishing and lay out plans for its return:

> Of course, only visionaries or ambitious or well-funded researchers would be inclined to do so initially. Conversely, both international and national journals should consider offering two versions of every article: one in the author's native language and one in English. (2007:116)

[7] American Journal Experts (Lourenço de Oliveira 2013).

This brings us back to 1909. So when they ask "Is there science beyond English?", are they certain that this is the right question?

Adverse political conditions and language policy in the Memórias

The case of German

It is interesting to see how German dominated *Memórias* as a foreign language at the beginning. Aside from social trends such as the urban reform of Rio being based on the layout of Paris (Pinho 2010:3), Brazil was in virtual thrall to France with respect to literary culture with French (and thus French norms) used as an intermediary language for translations (Wyler 2003:56). As previously mentioned, Oswaldo Cruz, upon returning from the *Institut Pasteur*, followed the "Pasteur model" that was spreading throughout the world at the time (Carvalheiro and Gadelha 2008:701).

German, however, disappeared from the journal during the First World War, dropping from 18 articles in 1914 to one in 1915 and none between 1916 and 1919. An association between this and reported German attacks on Brazilian merchant ships, which led to Brazil's eventual entrance on the side of the Allies in 1917, is most likely beyond dispute, although it may not be the only factor. However, it should also be noted that no foreign language articles were published in either 1916 or 1917. While English and French both returned to pre-war levels in 1918, German, however, never did return, rising above three articles only in 1922 and 1953, with a final appearance in 1971. The post-war decline of German is further highlighted by the fact that no English or French had appeared in the journal in either 1912 or 1913, i.e., 100% of the articles appeared in German and that the number of German articles from 1909 to 1914 had been between two to five times that of English and French articles combined. The supposition that the language's shunning was influenced by the political climate is also supported by the fact that it again disappeared completely between 1936 and 1948. The loss is further highlighted in that, as previously mentioned, four renowned German scientists had come to help set up the Institute's protozoology area, after it won the gold medal at the Berlin International Congress of Hygiene and Demography in 1907 (Weltman 2002:179; Araújo-Jorge, Santos-Barbosa and Lourenço de Oliveira 2012:34), having authored or co-authored seven articles in the initial two years of the journal.

A further point should be made here about *Memórias*' translation behaviour: with only one translated article published between 1915 and 1917, a trend of linguistic isolation during political turmoil was established. This reappeared over the course of its history.

Dictatorship, censorship

Translations dropped to under 40% of total annual production beginning in 1930, which coincides with the beginning of the Vargas dictatorship (1930-1945). They then fell to less than 5% in three of the following years and to 0% in six more by the time the regime ended in 1945. It is important to point out the domestic dimension to the journal's linguistic isolation. Censorship in Vargas' *Estado Novo* was serious; a number of authors were imprisoned, including a woman for translating *Tom Sawyer* (Milton 2002:29), thus it is reasonable to assume that reluctance to introduce foreign material or the production of material for foreign consumption would have been high. However, relatively speaking, the Institute prospered under this regime due to the Second World War, i.e., the high demand for commodities such as plasma and the development of antibiotics (Araújo-Jorge, Santos-Barbosa and Lourenço de Oliveira 2012:36). Nevertheless, closer alignment with the government also steered the Institute toward developmentalism and away from areas such as Medical Entomology and Zoology (ibid.). Amid the drop in translation under Vargas, the relative presence of English grew. The number of monolingual English articles was four times that of German and more than eight times that of French.

The second twentieth century dictatorship (the military regime that began with a 1964 coup d'état and ended in 1985 with the current constitution), was much more difficult for IOC. With the enactment of *Ato Institucional nº* 5 (or AI-5) under the military regime, in force from 1968 to 1978, all means of communication came under rigorous censorship. What was called the *Massacre de Manguinhos* followed the selection of a new Minister of Health who expelled ten scientists from IOC (full account given in Lent 1978), closed laboratories, courses and lines of research, as well as dismantling and removing the Institute's vast Entomological Collection (Costa 2008:402). The shutting down of the journal from 1977-1979 – with only the most enigmatic of explanations offered in a brief editorial[8] – would seem to indicate the regime's catastrophic impact on the Institute, as well as

---

[8] From Coura 1980 the text consists of one unnumbered page: "The *Memórias do Instituto Oswaldo Cruz* return to regular circulation beginning with the current year 1980, after a brief interruption for reasons beyond the current administration of the Oswaldo Cruz Foundation" (my translation).

its continued fear of openly criticising the regime. Only 26 foreign language articles appeared between 1964 and 1977, the year the journal shut down, 19 of those in English. Thus, it is clear from this brief analysis that the general political climate (the case of German language), government influence (Vargas) or direct government interference (*Regime Militar*), can negatively change the course of communication partnerships, the focus or direction of scientific institutions or simply preclude their autonomy or existence. Of course, there is one complicating factor: between the journal re-launch and the official end of the regime five years later, English article output totalled 80.7% of that in Portuguese. This indicates that with the end of AI-5, considerable liberty regarding the 'foreign' was allowed. Of course, this 'foreign' factored out to English, i.e., the language of the regime's anti-communist 'benefactor' (see Green and Jones 2009).

The selection of published languages in Memórias, especially the non-use of Spanish and the colonial model

Institutional ties have already been demonstrated in the *Memórias* corpus between IOC and European centres such as the *Institut Pasteur* in Paris and the *Bernhard Nocht Institute for Tropical Medicine* in Hamburg, with staff exchanges (for example, von Prowazek and Travassos) and mutual research projects (von Prowazek and Rocha Lima) taking place. Thus, active language skills, especially in French and German, were a requirement for the Institute's interaction with its partners. Moreover, the IOC's expansive periodical holdings have also been demonstrated, indicating that multilingual communication, at least in the form of reading comprehension, was an *a prioi* assumption in IOC's concept of research.

Although there is evidence that IOC researchers did participate in events in Portugal, no textual evidence could be found for sponsorship, exchange or joint projects with medical, scientific or governmental institutions there. Thus, it appears safe to rule out that the IOC came into being or was sustained in any way through Portuguese (post)colonial effort,[9] but rather was a fully Brazilian initiative that drew its mandate and funding from Federal sources, developed a methodology inspired by certain European centres, involved European-educated researchers (for example, Cruz and Lutz) and participated in the then-budding international Tropical Medicine

9 Brazil had only become fully politically independent from Portugal in 1889 and Cruz' Institute was founded in1900.

community as an independent collaborator. However, overlying or underlying this is that Europe was widely and unreservedly seen as the *civilised* world, particularly so before the World Wars (Pinho 2010:3). Partnership with Europe conferred, beyond any technical benefits, both status and authority. The then modern techniques of science had been developed and mastered in Europe making it the "home office" of science where "serious" science was happening.

Although this covers the IOC's relations with Europe, it does not shed much light on the situation in Latin or South America. The first article in Spanish in the corpus appeared in 1929 and there would not be a second for another thirty years. At first glance, the void of Spanish language articles (3 articles in the journal's first 70 years) seems astounding, given that Brazil is surrounded by Spanish-speaking countries and that communication with neighbours, especially about common regional epidemics and other public health issues and strategies, would seem vital. The relative paucity of Spanish-language articles published in the journal over its history (30 total articles compared to 55 in French) could be explained away by the linguistic proximity of the two languages, which could allow such a level of cognate-based reading that directly addressing Spanish-speaking audiences would be rendered "unnecessary" (hence no Spanish/Portuguese translated articles).

However, there may also be evidence to suggest a certain antipathy between neighbouring countries, i.e., that they, in true colonial fashion, might have been held more as rivals than as potential allies while the colonial "other" beckoned in the distance. Such an idea, though impossible to demonstrate from the corpus (the argument from silence), is nevertheless present historically in the case of Carlos Chagas' two "foiled" Nobel Prize nominations (1913,1921) in which internal institutional conflicts were broadened to national (Brazilian Academy of Medicine) and international scales (Pan-American Medical Congress in Argentina, Argentina's Bacteriological Institute and finally the Nobel Prize Committee), complete with "industrial espionage" and public arguments, resulting in the Prize not being awarded in 1921 and even the very existence of American trypanosomiasis (i.e. Chagas' disease) being effectively discredited until after Chagas' death (all detailed in Coutinho, Freire and Pinto-Dias 1999). There is also, moreover, textual evidence to the contrary, at least in later decades: it was an Argentinian scientist, Salvador Mazza, who effectively revalidated Chagas' findings about American trypanosomiasis in an important article published in *Memórias* in 1949.

It is beyond the scope of this corpus to prove whether the absence of Spanish-language articles indicates an actual lack of regional solidarity, and whether any such non-solidarity was due to the effects of colonial models of power (i.e., in which the centre typically communicates with the periphery and not the periphery with the periphery). That being said, the discourse of colonialism has been quite evident with respect to science in Latin America – from both the colonisers and the colonised. Nearly 10 years ago, an editor-in-chief of the *New England Journal of Medicine* was quoted as saying, "Very poor countries have much more to worry about than doing high-quality research…There is no science there" (Gibbs 1995:97). More subtle, positive-sounding characterisations have also been made:

> [Chagas'] achievement was a clear demonstration that scientific and technological development is possible outside the central hub of countries with strong science, by local researchers acting … independently. (Goldbaum and Barreto 2008:698)

The opening speech from the 1984 Chagas symposium demonstrates the perceived inferiority of local science in Brazil (see also Hanes 2013:238):

> However, without doubt it was the great discovery of American Trypanosomiasis which placed him at the top of biomedical research in Brazil; more than that, it had the great merit of changing a pattern of colonial science, done in an underdeveloped country, into a pattern of science with international quality, drawing attention and curiosity from Europe and the United States. (Alves 1984:1)

Chagas himself was well-aware of his position with respect to the colonial system and, at the same time, like Cruz, was an unashamed patriot. The following statement from his inaugural lecture as chair of Tropical Medicine at the Faculdade de Medicina de Rio de Janeiro in 1926 perhaps clarifies this:

> The European nations, zealous of their colonies in the tropics, created in the universities or in major research institutes a specialisation: the study and teaching of the pathology of warm climates. Here […] duties of the most exalted and provident nationalism demand us to forcefully study and research Brazilian nosology with the purpose of promoting the improvement of our nation, of rare native traits, and to achieve by prophylactic methods, the sanitary redemption of our vast territory. (Chagas 1926; qtd. in Gadelha 2009)

An additional facet of the colonisation issue, which I will not go into in detail, is that the IOC's work was seen as an instrument of intra-territorial colonisation (i.e., the "order and progress" emblasoned on the flag), clearly acknowledged as such by Chagas himself in 1911, [The new trypanosomiasis] "creates, in vast regions of Minas Gerais and other Brazilian states, a population of degenerates, utterly unfit for the progressive evolution of our country" (Gadelha 2009; see also Kropf 2006:193).

Conclusions

This broad diachronic corpus has allowed a number of complex questions on language and identity within a pioneering, developing-world scientific institution to be approached, if only superficially. What is clear is the presence of tense interplay between issues of scientific professionalism, scientific nationalism, globalisation and technology, multilingualism vs. a "universal" lingua franca and systems of ranking and international credibility within the world of research. Meanwhile, in the practical sphere, challenges to public health continue. Although the results are preliminary, it can be said that Ong's thesis (2002) on the format of human communication and its effects on society would seem to weigh in heavily on the *Memórias*' shift to a monolingual (albeit foreign language) culture.

In addition, this shift is linked with an increasing interconnectivity and collaboration of the scientific community, despite nationalistic rhetoric to the contrary. Thirdly, the Institute pragmatically pursued different language strategies at different points to resolve its fundamental needs, to survive, pursue and expand its mission.

References

Araújo-Jorge,Tania/Santos-Barbosa, Helene/Lourenço de Oliveira, Ricardo (2012) *Uma escola para a ciência e a saúde: 111 anos de ensino no Instituto Oswaldo Cruz*. Rio de Janeiro: Fundação Oswaldo Cruz.

Carvalheiro, José/Gadelha, Paulo (2008) "Commentary: Carlos Chagas – Predecessor of Epidemiology in Brazil". *International Journal of Epidemiology* 37:4, 701-703.

Costa, Jane et al. (2008) "The Entomology Collection at Instituto Oswaldo Cruz: Restoring a Historical Scientific Collection Scattered by the Manguinhos Massacre". *História, Ciências, Saúde-Manguinhos* 15:2, 401-410.

De Swaan, Abram (2001) *Words of the World: The Global Language System*. Cambridge: Polity Press.

Fernandes, Ana Maria (1987) *The Scientific Community and the State in Brazil: The Role of the Brazilian Society for the Advancement of Science, 1948-1980*. Oxford: The University of Oxford: PhD Dissertation.

Gadelha, Paulo (2009) "International Centennial Symposium on the Discovery of Chagas Disease". Plenary speech presented at the International Centennial Symposium on the Discovery of Chagas Disease, July 2009. Rio de Janeiro: Instituto Oswaldo Cruz.

Gibbs, Wayt (1995) "Lost Science in the Third World." *Scientific American* 273:2, 92-99.

Goldbaum, Moisés/Barreto, Maurício (2008) "The Contribution and Example of Carlos Chagas". *International Journal of Epidemiology* 34:4, 697-698.

Green, James/Jones, Abigail(2009) "Reinventando a história: Lincoln Gordon e as suas múltiplas versões de 1964". *Revista Brasileira de História* 29:57, 67-89.

Hanes, William F (2013) "Examining the Impact of English on Brazilian Scientific Publishing: An Initial Exploration". *Mutatis Mutandis* 6:1, 235-251.

Hanes, William F (2014) "Authorship under the Microscope: Interdisciplinary Consensus on Translational Authorship in Light of the Multiple Authorship Trend". In Lambert, José/Iliescu-Gheorghiu, Catalina (eds.) *Universe-cities as Problematic Global Villages: Continuities and Shifts in our Academic Worlds*. Florianópolis: Copiart, 237-256.

Hobsbawm, Eric (1996) "Language, Culture and National Identity". *Social Research* 63:4, 1065-1080.

Hoey, John. 2000. "Who Wrote this Paper Anyway? The New Vancouver Group Statement Refines the Definition of Authorship". *The Canadian Medical Association Journal* 163:6, 716-717.

IANPHI (2013) "History", http://www.ianphi.org/whoweare/history.html [19 October 2014].

Kropf, Simone (2006) *Doença de chagas, doença do Brasil: Ciência, saúde e nação (1909-1962)*. Niterói: Universidade Federal Fluminense: PhD Dissertation.

Lambert, José (2010) "The Languages of Translation: Keys to the Dynamics of Culture". In Muñoz-Alvo, Micaela/Buesa-Gomez, Carmen (eds.) *Translation and Cultural Identity: Selected Essays on Translation and Cross-Cultural Communication*. Newcastle: Cambridge Scholars Publishing, 33-60.

Lambert, José/Iliescu-Gheorghiu, Catalina (eds.) (2014) *Universe-cities as Problematic Global Villages: Continuities and Shifts in our Academic Worlds*. Florianópolis: EDUFSC.

Latour, Bruno (1987) *Science in Action: How to Follow Scientists and Engineers through Society*. Cambridge/Massachusetts: Harvard University Press.

Latour, Bruno (1988) *The Pasteurisation of France*. Cambridge/Massachusetts/London: Harvard University Press.

Latour, Bruno/Woolgar, Steve (1979) *Laboratory Life*. Princeton: Princeton University Press.

Lent, Herman (1978) *O massacre de Manguinhos*. Rio de Janeiro: Avenir Editora.

Marcolin, Neldson (2009) "Vigor aos 100 anos: *Memórias do Instituto Oswaldo Cruz*, de 1909, é a revista científica brasileira de maior impacto". *Pesquisa FAPESP* 165:11, 6-7.

Marcolin, Neldson (2011) "No *front* da infecção: Há 95 anos o médico Rocha Lima descobria a origem do tifo exantemático na Alemahna". *Pesquisa FAPESP* 190:12, 8-9.

Meneghini, Rogerio/Packer, Abel (2007) "Is there Science Beyond English?". *EMBO Reports* 8, 112-116.

Milton, John (2002) *O Clube do Livro e a Tradução.* Bauru: EDUSC.

Montgomery, Scott (2000) *Science in Translation: Movements of Knowledge through Cultures and Time.* Chicago: University of Chicago Press.

Montgomery, Scott (2010) "Scientific Translation". In Gambier, Yves/van Doorslaer, Luc (eds.) *Handbook of Translation Studies.* Vol. 1. Amsterdam/Philadelphia: John Benjamins, 299-305.

Montgomery, Scott (2013) *Does Science Need a Global Language? English and the Future of Research.* Chicago/London: University of Chicago Press.

Navarro, Fernando A. (1997) "Die Sprache der Medizin in der Schweiz von 1920 bis 1995". *Swiss Medical Weekly* 127:38, 1565-1573.

Ong, Walter (2002) *Orality and Literacy: The Technologising of the Word.* London/New York: Routledge.

Pinho, Fernando (2010) "Paris, Rio de Janeiro, Belém: Circulação de idéias e práticas na modernização das cidades brasileiras na virada do século XX". Paper presented at the Conference XVI Semana de Planejamento Urbano e Regional, September 2010. Rio de Janeiro: Universidade Federal do Rio de Janeiro.

Rocha e Silva, Mauricio (2010) "Clinics has an Impact Factor". *Clinics* 65:6, 567-568.

Royal Society (2011) *Knowledge, Networks and Nations: Global Scientific Collaboration in the 21st Century.* London: The Royal Society.

Schiller, Herbert (1991) "Not yet the Post-Imperialist Era". *Critical Studies in Mass Communication* 8, 13-28.

SciELO (2010) "Criteria, Policies and Procedures for Site Classification and Certification in the SciELO Network: Version October 2010", http://www.scielo.org/php/level.php?lang=en&component=42&item=3 [19 October 2014].

Scott, Christina (2005) "The Hemisphere's Oldest Science Journal is 100", http://www.scidev.net/global/communication/news/southern-hemispheres-oldest-science-journal-is-10.html [19 October 2014].

Scott, H. Harold (1939) *A History of Tropical Medicine: Based on the Fitzpatrick Lectures Delivered Before the Royal College of Physicians of London, 1937-38.* Baltimore: The Williams and Wilkins Co.

Stepan, Nancy (1981) *Beginnings of Brazilian Science: Oswaldo Cruz, Medical Research and Policy 1890-1920.* New York: Science History Publications.

Toury, Gideon (1995) *Descriptive Translation Studies and Beyond.* Amsterdam/Philadelphia: John Benjamins.

Wagner, Carol (2008) *The New Invisible College: Science for Development.* Washington: Brookings Institution.

Weltman, Wanda (2002) "A produção científica publicada pelo Instituto Oswaldo Cruz no período 1900-1917: Um estudo exploratório". *História, Ciências, Saúde-Manguinhos* 9, 159-186.

Wendel, Silvano/Brener, Zigman (1992) "Historical Aspects". In Wendel, Silvano et al. (eds.) *Chagas Disease - American Trypanosomiasis: Its Impact on Transfusion and Clinical Medicine*, http://www.dbbm.fiocruz.br/tropical/chagas/chapter.html [19 October 2014].

Wyler, Lia (2003) *Crônicas, poetas e bacharéis: Uma crônica da tradução no Brasil.* Rio de Janeiro: Rocco.

Corpus

Alves, Guilardo Martins. 1984. "Opening Speech". *Memórias do Instituto Oswaldo Cruz* 79 (suppl.),1.

Coura, José R. (1980) "Editorial". *Memórias do Instituto Oswaldo Cruz* 75:1-2, 5.

Coura, José R. (1994) "Great Lives at Manguinhos: Oswaldo Gonçalves Cruz". *Memórias do Instituto Oswaldo Cruz* 89:1, 120-125.

Coutinho, Marilia/Freire, Olival/Pinto-Dias, João Carlos (1999) "The Noble Enigma: Chagas and Nominations for the Nobel Prize". *Memórias do Instituto Oswaldo Cruz* 94 (suppl.1), 123-129.

De Souza-Araujo, Heraclides (1929) *Leprosy: Survey Made in Fourty Countries (1924-1927).* Rio de Janeiro: Instituto Oswaldo Cruz.

Instituto Oswaldo Cruz (1909-2012) *Memórias do Instituto Oswaldo Cruz* 1-107. Rio de Janeiro: Fundação Oswaldo Cruz.

Instituto Oswaldo Cruz (1911 or 1912) *Institut Oswaldo Cruz.* Rio de Janeiro: Manguinhos.

Internet Archive Wayback Machine (2001) "Memórias do Instituto Oswaldo Cruz Online", http://web.archive.org/web/20011108160415/http://memorias.ioc.fiocruz.br/ [19 October 2014].

Lourenço de Oliveira, Ricardo (2013) "Editorial Policy", http://memorias.ioc.fiocruz.br/editorial-policy [22 January 2014].

Mazza, Salvador (1949) "Chagas Disease in the Argentine Republic". *Memórias do Instituto Oswaldo Cruz* 47:1-2, 289-302

Memórias do Instituto Oswaldo Cruz (2014) "Homepage", http://memorias.ioc.fiocruz.br/ [19 October 2014].

SILVIA COBELO

Universidade de São Paulo, Brazil

Adaptations of *Don Quijote*: Discussing Adults' Retranslations of the Classics for Children

This article provides a short yet detailed overview of the history of adaptations[1] of *Don Quijote* in Brazil (1886-2013), focusing on the ten most published adaptations, and covering historiographical issues and their agents, including the biographies of adapters. The aim of this article is to initiate an examination of the controversial relationship between re-adaptations, republications and the literary fame of a work, and test the "Retranslation Hypothesis" (the argument that first translations are more domesticating than retranslations) to verify not only if this case fits the hypothesis, but also if the re-adaptation phenomenon enhances both the manipulation undertaken by agents, and a range of translation norms. In carrying out such an examination, reference will be made to Adaptation Studies and studies of the Manipulation School. The analysis will also take into account the peculiarities of the children's literature system (including translated works) and examples from *Don Quijote* itself, using some of the studies undertaken by Cervantes' critics.

Keywords: *Don Quijote* in Brazil, retranslation, re-adaptation, translation history, children's literature, literary fame, paratexts

Introduction

Cervantes' *Don Quijote* celebrated its fourth centenary in 2005. The second book, written ten years later, commemorates 400 years in 2015. In Brazil today, there is a wide variety of versions of the Spanish classic *Dom Quixote* in Brazilian Portuguese.[2] Going through the children's section of a bookstore in São Paolo, Brazil, one does not have an easy job in choosing

[1] This article uses the term *adaptation* following Hutcheon's (2006:8) definition: "An acknowledged transposition of a recognisable other work; a creative *and* an interpretive act of appropriation/salvaging; an extended intertextual engagement with the adapted work".

[2] In this study, Cervantes' work appears in three different forms: *Don Quijote* (the Spanish book), *Don Quixote* (the English title) and the one used to discuss the Brazilian adaptations, *Dom Quixote* (the Portuguese title).

which to purchase, since there are 19 versions in prose, seven in comic form and three adaptations to *cordel* verses.[3]

This article discusses adult classics that have been adapted for children and the related retranslation and republishing phenomenon.[4] Republished works, also called *recycled* translations by Tahir Gürçağlar (2011:235), are usually presented in different formats with new illustrations, covers, and special paratexts available in certain formats, such as e-book, and with an orthography update. The same scenario can be found with an adaptation; it can be a source text, become a classic and can be rewritten. A good example is Lobato's book, *Dom Quixote das crianças,* which was adapted into comic form and, as part of the children's literature canon, has been reprinted and/or republished almost every year since 1936, while coexisting harmoniously with brand new adaptations on the publishing market. His book became a source text, was translated twice into Spanish, adapted to comic format in 2007 and has been appropriated by other media – first taking the form of a radio show and later adapted for multiple television series.[5]

The most published adapters

From the historical catalogue of 81 different versions, eleven comics, seven *cordel* adaptations, three theatre plays and 60 prose versions (thirteen are translated works) are made in Brazil. In order to have a good representative sample and a more valid claim, one of the corpus criterions for inclusion was that the adaptation had undergone more than three reissues, or more than five where the work was concluded before the twenty-first century. The other two criteria were that the work had to be in prose and originally

---

3 Candance Slater defines *cordel* as follows: "The term *literatura de cordel* was for centuries a Portuguese expression, rather than a Brazilian expression. The name refers to the way booklets were often suspended from lines (*cordel* means 'cord' or 'string') stretched between two posts" (1982:xiv).

4 In this article, *retranslation* means a new translation from a source already translated in the same language; *republishing* is a translated target text re-edited or reprinted by the same or other publishing houses. With the same logic, in this paper the term *re-adaptation* means a new version from a work previously adapted in the same target culture and language.

5 The most important are the two adaptations made by TV Globo, both exported worldwide with the title *Sítio do Picapau Amarelo* [*The Yellow Woodpecker Ranch*]. With an opening song composed by Gilberto Gil episodes were aired daily from 1977 up to 1986. From 2001 to 2007, the same channel aired a new adaptation also shown daily, with high production value. In this last show, *Don Quixote* is present twice, in 2002 and of course in 2005, but with new casting.

written in Brazil, thus excluding comics, *cordels*, theatre and translated works (first abridged outside Brazil and then translated into Portuguese). This section provides information about the ten most published authors in prose, and the trajectory of their *Don Quijote* adaptations within the Brazilian literary system over the last 127 years.

Carlos Jansen

The history of Cervantes' rewritings in Brazil began in 1886 with a publication containing a triple German genetic, *D. Quixote de la Mancha*, republished by *Laemmert & C*, a publishing house founded by a German family in Rio de Janeiro, in 1921 with illustrations by Adolph Wald.[6] On the first page there is an inscription, declaring that the book follows Franz Hoffmann's abridgement (1844), written for the Brazilian youth by Carlos Jansen (1829-1889). Born in Cologne, he arrived in Brazil in 1851 as one of the 1,800 German mercenaries hired by Dom Pedro II to fight in the Cisplatine War (1825-1828). Like many *Brummers*, Jansen chose to stay in Rio Grande do Sul.[7] At 25 years of age, he debuted as a journalist writing in Portuguese, drawing on his knowledge of Latin (Hohlfeldt 2003:69). After a short time in Argentina in 1878, he moved to the former capital, Rio de Janeiro, where he stayed until his death. During this period, he held Chair of German Language and Literature at the prestigious *Colégio Pedro II.*

The history of the Brazilian children's literature system essentially starts with Jansen who is considered a pioneer not only for the very first translations of children's classics, but also for being aware of the necessity to have these books available in Brazilian Portuguese at a time when all these titles were only found in versions written in Portugal.[8] The century was ending

---

6 Eduard Laemmert (1806-1880) and his brother Heinrich (1812-1884), born in Rosenberg, (Baden, Germany) founded the company (publishing house and bookstore) in 1838 in the imperial capital, Rio de Janeiro (Hallewell 2005/1985:232). After 1909, the copyrights were transferred to Francisco Alves, another publishing house and bookstore in Rio de Janeiro.

7 *Brummer* is a German word; it means grumbling. It seems that many German immigrants already living in Brazil complained of poor living conditions, low wages and spoke a strange dialect. Among those who choose to stay, many received land. Others, just by having a better education than those settlers have, became merchants, doctors, teachers and even politicians. (Hohlfeldt 2003:68).

8 Jansen also adapted other classic works, always following Hoffman's plans: *Arabian Nights* (1882), *Robinson Crusoe* (1885), *Gulliver's Travels* (1888), *and Adventures of Baron Munchausen* (1891). Hohlfeldt (2003:70-71) provides a complete bibliography with titles covering German grammar, geometry, geography, geology, astronomy, chemistry and French grammar.

and the young country was changing fast. Zilberman and Lajolo (1986:15) believe that it is no coincidence that the birth of Brazilian children's literature happened during a very turbulent period marked by the abolition of slavery (1888) and the proclamation of the Republic (1889). Moreover, the nation was starting a modernisation process characterised by a growing urban population composed of free slaves and immigrants and thus, in such a milieu, a newer and larger reading public emerged. *Editora Minerva* reedited the book in 1944 and republished at least six times before the early sixties. This edition was mutilated by Terra de Senna (pseudonym of the writer, journalist, playwright, poet and humourist Lauro Nunes (1896-1972) and is practically another text; the latter issues do not name Carlos Jansen as the original adapter. In 1982, the same disfigured version was published for the last time by the inconsequential *MCA* in Rio de Janeiro who had already published the previous version.

D. QUIXOTE DE LA MANCHA.

CARLOS JANSEN

LAEMMERT & C.

©Laemmert & C., 1901

©MCA Editorial e Gráfica, 1982

Monteiro Lobato

The children's literature public had to wait 50 years to read a new adaptation of *Don Quijote,* adapted by José Bento Monteiro Lobato (1882-1948). By then, Brazil (and the world in general) was completely different; the children from the pre-second World War era wanted something new, not an old fashion version from the remote nineteenth century. Lobato – publisher, editor, translator, writer and central figure in the development of the Brazilian publishing industry – realised this need and changed Brazilian children's literature forever by creating a *Lobatian heritage*, as referred to by several critics mentioned in this paper. He always sought to bring the text closer to the reader, even remarking on his desire to Brazilianise the language (Lobato 1957:274). His famous quote was originally found in a letter written in 1925 to his friend Rangel when referring to his project to adapt *Don Quijote* for a young audience. His own publishing house, *Companhia Editora Nacional* (1925-1970) released the work eleven years later, in 1936, and reissued in 1940, inserting *Dom Quixote das Crianças* within the collection *Sítio do Picapau Amarelo*. The adaptation was published by *Brasiliense* from 1944 to 2005, and is currently published by *Editora Globo*, with electronic and comic versions (2013).

©Acervo Cia. da Memória, 1936

©Editora Globo, 2013

Orígenes Lessa

The next adaptation took another 35 years to be issued. *Ediouro* (formerly *Tecnoprint*), one of the first to publish pocket books in Brazil, commissioned a new version of Cervantes' masterpiece to the writer Orígenes Lessa (1903-1986). Lessa wrote over forty titles for young people, including translations, adaptations and his own fiction.[9] After working as a teacher and translator, he was imprisoned for participating in the Constitutional Revolution of 1932. He moved to New York during World War II and was the editor of NBC programmes sent to Brazil. When he returned to Brazil, he alternated his advertising activities with his writings, being awarded a chair at the Brazilian Academy of Letters in 1981 (Guedes 2007:14-24). This adaptation is still published today by *Ediouro*, and has been available in e-book format since 2005.

[9] Lessa adapted other classics in the same period such as *Adventures of Baron Munchausen* and *The Adventures of Tom Sawyer*, among others.

©Editora Tecnoprint [Ediouro], 1971 ©Leonard de Selva/CORBIS, 2013

José Angeli

The writer José Angeli Sobrinho (1944-2012) was commissioned by the editorial *Scipione* to readapt *Don Quijote,* which was issued by the new brand series in 1985 at the collection *Série Reencontro,* in which classics were rewritten in no more than 140 pages.[10] According to the journalist Miecoanski (2012), Angeli spent his childhood reading books brought from Argentina by his father. Before reaching adulthood, he was already multilingual and had read the classics of world literature in French, Italian, Spanish and Portuguese. He attended the Faculty of Economics until the coup of 1964, after which, in 1970, he joined a tiny revolutionary group, *Communist Revolutionary Movement* [*Movimento Comunista Revolucionário – MCR*], spending time in prison between 1971 and 1973 after having been brutally tortured. He wrote some fiction and scripts for erotic comics until he turned to children's adaptations, beginning with *Dom Quixote* in 1985, still republished today by *Scipione.* As with Lessa, the same publishing house also commissioned him for adaptations of other literary classics.[11] The title, *Don Quixote – The Knight of the Sad Countenance* [*Dom Quixote – O Cavaleiro da Triste Figura*], crystallises the epithet much appreciated in the nineteenth century by the Romantics. The first change in the original edition only occurred in 2000 when the

[10] See Milton (2001a, 2001b, 2002) for details on "factory translation", or translation of mass fiction, where different forms of standardisation can be found, such as page limitations, in order to cut printing and delivery costs.

[11] *The Three Musketeers, Les Miserables, The Count of Monte Cristo, Iliad, Martin Fierro and Don Casmurro.* The last title is an abridgement from Machado de Assis, a Brazilian classic and so an intralinguistic adaptation.

cover was altered. However, the same layout and internal figures were maintained up to 2007 when everything was finally updated.

Angeli adapted his own work for a younger age range in 2003, a very successful intralinguistic adaptation that is still in print as part of the series *Reencontro infantil.* This collection served to provide the school market with different versions.[12]

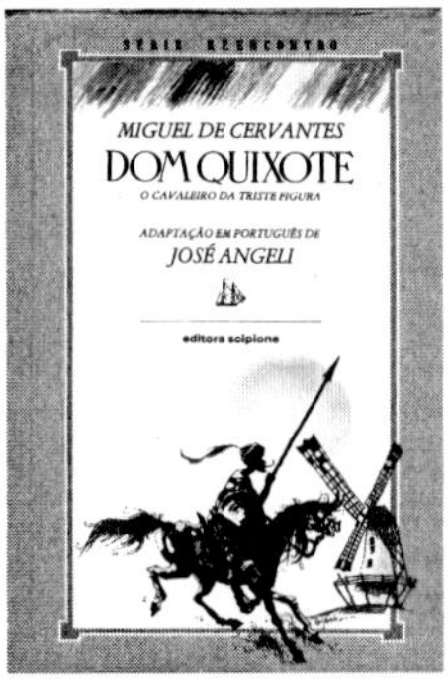

©Scipione, 1985

©Scipione, 2007

©Scipione, 2003

Ferreira Gullar

Since the beginning of this century, *Don Quijote's* 400th anniversary celebrations were marked by a number of important editions. One of the highlights was the version signed by the famous poet, translator and essayist José Ferreira Ribamar, born in São Luís, Maranhão in 1930. He moved to Rio de Janeiro in 1951 and worked as a reviser for magazines and newspapers. Imprisoned by the military government in 1968, he fled to Moscow, later to Santiago, and finally to Buenos Aires where he would live until his return to Rio in 1977. He wrote television scripts, received several literary awards and in 2002 was nominated to receive the Nobel Prize – the same year he released his *Dom Quixote* (2002) with illustrations by Doré. The book is in its fifth edition and appears on its website as a *translation*, along with versions of *Arabian Nights* and *Fables de la Fontaine*, all published by *Revan*, a thirty year old medium sized company located in Rio de Janeiro. This is the first edition analysed with footnotes (very few), and is the most expensive one.

[12] In 2000, they also issued *Don Quijote de la Mancha,* "a didactic adaptation" in Spanish by Margarita Barberá Quiles for the school system, with at least 12 reprints. In 2005, the federal government sanctioned the law 11.161, making Spanish mandatory in secondary schools (Lisboa 2009).

©Revan, 2002

Walcyr Carrasco

Walcyr Carrasco was born in São Paulo in 1951. He graduated as a journalist from São Paulo University and worked for the main national magazines and São Paulo's most important newspapers before becoming a well-known telenovela writer. Carrasco started writing for children during the 1970s, collaborating with the former children's magazine *Recreio*. He published more than thirty books, translations and adaptations of several classic works of children's literature, including *Dom Quixote*, which was published by the FTD in 2002 (reprinted five times until 2012) and illustrated by Alexander Camanho. As Carrasco was the first author after Lobato to own the copyrights to his version of *Dom Quixote*, he revised his *translation and adaptation* and it was recently re-edited by *Moderna* in 2012 (four times reprinted, also in digital format). It is practically another book with substantial text modifications, larger fonts and spacing, fewer illustrations, and plenty of paratexts. As in the first edition, there are very few footnotes.

©Editora FTD, 2002

©Editora Moderna, 2012

Leonardo Chianca

In 2005, several rewrites of *Dom Quixote* were published. The most reedited (or reprinted: this data is often omitted) are the works by Chianca, Rios and Machado. Born in São Paulo in 1960, Leonardo Chianca combines the activities of an editor with those of a writer of children's literature. He owns *Edições Jogo de Amarelinha*, a company that produces and publishes educational books for publishers across the country. After adapting various classics for both adults and children, he adapted *Dom Quixote* (2005) – a book illustrated by the Chilean Gonzalo Cárcamo (both own the copyrights), published three times by Difusão Cultural do Livro (DCL), and is also available as an audiobook. It can be contemplated as different adaptation, with eight actors who interpret the voices of the more than thirty characters in addition to the narrator of the story. DCL is a small to medium sized company, started in 1967 and mainly edits children's books.

©Gonzalo Cárcamo, 2005

©Gonzalo Cárcamo, 2010 (audiobook)

Rosana Rios

Rosana Rios was born in 1955 in São Paulo. She has been an author of children's books since 1988, with over a hundred titles with several different publishers. Rios has received literary prizes and was a *Jabuti Award*[13] finalist both in 2008 and 2011. Along with Eliana Martins, she co-authored the play *Um certo Dom Quixote* (2009). Her adaptation of *Don Quijote* was published by *Editora Escala Educational* in 2005, reprinted six times until 2012 and, like the previous version, illustrated by Cárcamo. Founded in 2004, this publishing

[13] Created in 1959, it is the most important literary award in Brazil.

company specialises in producing a range of textbooks aimed at nursery, primary and secondary education sectors. They have several series, 33 for young children and 26 for older children and teenagers. The series *Recontar Juvenil* (former *Reviver*) *is composed of* 31 books, most with 88-96 pages, and includes classic titles such as *Dom Quixote*, which was commissioned through a third party company, *Jogo da Amarelinha.* This fact produced a curious situation, a *Don Quijote* adapter (Chianca) editing another *Dom Quixote* version.

©Escala Educational, 2005

Ana Maria Machado

Ana Maria Machado was born in Rio de Janeiro in 1941 and has been compared to Lobato for her large production of books of exceptional literary quality for children and young people. She has received many important prizes, including *Hans Christian Andersen*, the highest award in children's literature, as well as being considered an author *hors concours* by the *National Book Foundation for Children and Youth* [*Fundação Nacional do Livro Infantil e Juvenil –FNLIJ*] since 1993. Machado has more than one hundred titles published in Brazil and in over twenty other countries. She was a university literature professor until 1969 when she was forced into exile after being arrested by the military regime. While in Europe, she worked as a journalist for *Elle Magazine* and the *BBC*, and in addition to teaching Portuguese classes at the Sorbonne, she wrote a thesis on the works of Guimarães Rosa under the supervision of Roland Barthes.

As Machado relates, while presenting Michael Harrison's *Dom Quixote* in 1995, her relationship with *Don Quijote* goes back to her childhood when she heard the knight's adventures as told by her father (Machado 2004:5). In 1996, she transformed the comic duo into characters in one of her books, *Secret Friends* (*Amigos Secretos*). Ana Maria Machado, former president of the Brazilian Academy of Letters and great defender of adaptations, released her book in 2005, through Mercuryo Jovem, with a long and romantic title: *O cavaleiro do sonho: As aventuras de Dom Quixote de la Mancha*, supplemented by the illustrations of the famous Brazilian painter Portinari (1903-1962).[14] The short book (54 pages) received an award, *hors concours*, for the best-readapted book issued by *FNLIJ* in 2006, and is currently in its 13th reprint (2013). Machado holds the rights of the text, and as expected, Portinari's family owns the rights for his works.

©João Candido Portinari, 2005

Fábio Bortolazzo Pinto

Fabio Bortolazzo Pinto (1974), the youngest among the ten adapters, wrote the latest adaptation of the corpus when he was only 31 years old (the average age of the other nine authors is around 55). He received his Master's degree in Arts (UFRGS) in 2006 and is a literary scholar. In the same edition in which he adapted *Don Quijote* (*LP&M editores*), Bortolazzo Pinto wrote the introduction, afterword, and notes about various works, however,

[14] The illustrations were originally made to illustrate the first Brazilian translation of *Don Quijote*, written by Almir de Andrade (first book) and Milton Amado (second book and all poems), edited by José Olympio in 1952 (see Cobelo, 2010). Unfortunately, the artist died before completing the work, leaving only 21 drawings done with coloured pencils. The edition was issued with illustrations by Doré. In 1973, these drawings were published by Diagraphis with 21 glosses signed by Drummond de Andrade.

he does not receive any copyrights. The book has been published every year since 2008 with illustrations by Gilmar Fraga, an award-winning illustrator of comics and an art director for the Porto Alegre newspaper *Zero Hora.* At the top, as in the first pages of the book and credits, there is a subtitle under *Dom Quixote*: *Version adapted for neoreaders* [sic], which suggests a wider reading public than the previous adaptations, which were intended for children.

©Newtec Editores, 2008

The retranslation peculiarities of adults' classics for children

After this short historical panorama in which retranslation and republication have played such an important role, it is important to review some concepts. Retranslations have been discussed in Translation Studies for a long time and there has always been concern with the reasons for systematically retranslating certain books, especially the ones labelled as classics.[15] Essays on retranslation usually raise the same questions that emerged at the beginning of this research: why adapt a book that has already been adapted, and how do these new works differ from previous ones? In opening her chapter on retranslations, Gillian Lathey (2010:161) displays a degree of cynicism regarding so many new translations:

---

[15] There is a resumed story about it in the *Routledge Encyclopaedia of Translation Studies*, which since its second edition has an entry for "Retranslation" (Tahir Gürçağlar 2011:233-236). For *Retranslation Hypothesis* see Berman (1990), Gambier (1994), Foz (2005) and the same above entry. The entry "Retranslation" (Koskinen and Paloposki (2013:294-298) is another source of the present discussions about it.

> The phrase new translation has become a publisher's marketing strategy, since fresh versions of old favourites always hold great promise. New translations do not necessarily represent an improvement on earlier ones, however, nor is it always the case that an early translation is no longer read.

Lathey clearly disagrees with the quality linear "progression" postulate in the Retranslation Hypothesis, an issue that has also been raised by others such as Tahir Gürçağlar (2008). The results discussed in this article confirm that the hypothesis is not an S-Universal,[16] as suggested by Chesterman (2004:40). In other words, in this study, later translations are *not* closer to the source text, since more recent *Don Quijote* adaptations are not all close to the Spanish book, as a range of varying modifications and changes are found. The first one, adapted by Jansen, is closer to the text than the second by Lobato, the latter representing the most domesticated and adapted version. Gullar presented his proclaimed "translation" in 2002, but three years later Machado inserted Portinari in her story. There are also adaptations presenting a balanced mix such as Lessa, Angeli and Bortolazzo Pinto.

Anthony Pym (1998:81-82) discusses the difference between diachronic and synchronic retranslations. Diachronic retranslations are easier to explain, since language and culture change with time and we can always blame the aging effect. In this case study, we identified this phenomenon and it illuminates understanding of the first six editions. However, it is not applicable to the subsequent four from the same decade (principally because of the existence of two adaptations made simultaneously in 2002 and three in 2005), or to the continuous republishing of some of the older ones (i.e.: Lobato, Lessa and Angeli), which seem to be unaffected by generation gaps and are still being published in the same format as their original. Although these editions have undergone minor orthographic revisions, the old-fashioned lexicon has been preserved with the result that it might sometimes appear as mere gibberish to the young reader of this century. This has been noted by Hallewell (2005/1985:661) and confirmed by the textual analysis, as at least forty terms that are certainly unknown by the current reading audience were found. Venuti (2013:100) also comments on readability, an advantage linked to sales, where a fresh translation can attract new readers and at low cost since a "publisher may decide to issue retranslations

[16] "Some hypotheses claim to capture universal differences between translations and their source texts, i.e. characteristics of the way in which translators process the source text. I call these S-universals (S for source)" (Chesterman 2004:39).

of canonical texts that have fallen into the public domain – simply because their canonicity ensures a market demand, and they are cheaper than copyrighted texts".[17] However, in this study, there are the same diachronic works assuming both a synchronic and *active* role. Active retranslation is a term adopted by Pym to name retranslations sharing the same period and cultural environment such as the adaptations from this corpus, nine of which are published today and share the same reading public.

Retranslations, argues Pym (1998:83), are "a subtle index of historical importance". As such, they are associated with a certain *marked negativity* in relation to republished material. However, in the case of *Quixote's* adaptations, re-editions and reprints, this would also reinforce the validity of the previous works. In contrast to full retranslations, the re-adaptations do not always openly challenge this validity; often, a new version of a canonical work simply complements a collection of re-rewritings from the book without intending to substitute previous adaptations. Venuti (2013) also mentions translator awareness regarding previous translations, which can be seen as competing interpretations. Those works would be designed to "make an appreciable difference" (ibid.:100), "to challenge a previous version" (ibid.:104) and "call attention to their competing interpretation" (ibid.), something not found in explicit form in this particular research.

In contrast to the full translations, the paratexts from the *Don Quijote* versions presented above do not try to convince the readers they are reading an improved adaptation, if compared with the older ones. This was something the publishers could insinuate, since three bestsellers from the last century are still on sale, challenging the present new versions, especially Gullar's *adapted translation.* Gullar's self-termed adapted translation contains episodes usually cut from other children's versions, as is the case in the existence of a first text in Arabic, written by the historian Moor Cide Hamete Benengeli and then translated into Spanish by a "moro aljamiado" [Morisco who knew Castilian],[18] or the apocryphal book from Avellaneda.[19]

[17] "An indication of the rapid evolution of the Portuguese language in Brazil is the fact that the popularity of Lobato is starting to decline because, among children, his language is becoming out of fashion!" [Um indício da rápida evolução da língua portuguesa no Brasil é o fato de a popularidade de Lobato estar começando a diminuir porque, entre a criançada, sua linguagem está ficando fora de moda!], says Hallewell (2005/1985:661) in 1985 (1st edition).

[18] As translated by Edith Grossman in her version of Don Quixote, with note: "A Moor who had been converted to Christianity" (Cervantes 2003:67).

André Lefevere (1992) leads us to rethink the so-called intrinsic value of a literary work, which he believes has less importance than it is granted. He thus emphasises the importance of rewritings that he contends have been mainly responsible for the image of a writer, a work, a period, a genre, and quite often an entire literature. Every writer from our corpus, with the exception of Bortolazzo Pinto (and to a lesser extent, Angeli), is famous, a veteran and well experienced in adaptations. The same can also be said about the publishing companies, several of them being large and well known in the editorial world. Some of the illustrators are also well recognised, for example Doré and Portinari, and we found some renowned paratext authors such as Lobato's curator. This data confirms the *celebrity status*, mentioned by Hutcheon (2006:143), as an important element of the adaptation reception context. Fame works as a sort of feedback. Thus, being involved in a *Don Quixote* edition brings notoriety, and the work's literary fame attracts renowned names. This could provide an explanation for the interest of many publishers in *Don Quixote* and the release of different editions.

Koskinen and Paloposki include the concept of the *supplementary* between retranslations which constitutes a further argument that can be used for re-adaptations:

> The supplementary nature of retranslations suggests a positive attitude towards difference: variation is a facet of supplementary. Different, varying interpretations need not be locked into a continuum of assimilation – source-text orientedness (or any other binary division: free/literal, domesticated/foreignised, etc.), where the researchers' particular viewpoint is seen as that of determining faithfulness or assimilation. Instead, texts and their interpretations function simultaneously on several layers, denying easy classification into assimilative first and source-text oriented new translations. (Koskinen and Paloposki 2003:23)

[19] Just to corroborate the fluctuation movement, from 2012 two new *translations/adaptations* were issued, which was very close to the source (more than all the other ten works analysed here). The first one is from the English professional translator Eduardo Rado, issued in 2012 by Editora Nova Cultural (collection *O Prazer da Leitura*). With 294 pages, the adaptation seems to be very complete, with several episodes never adapted for children. The subsequent version carries the signature of the Academic Lígia Cardemartori and was published by FTD in 2013 (also long, 232 pages), who had lost its version by Carrasco to Moderna, confirming the idea of *pots & pans* found in Tahir Gürçağlar (2008): "These classics were indispensable for publishers as pots and pans are in a kitchen".

For these scholars, retranslation, as well as adaptation, is the result of the changing needs and perceptions of readers. This additional quality of retranslation alludes to the fact that it serves the purpose of engendering variety. After all, texts and their interpretations exist simultaneously in multiple layers, as can be seen in the Brazilian adaptations of *Don Quijote* where many of the writers seem to supplement and not replace the previous rewritings. One good example is *Dom Quixote das Crianças,* the Lobatian version read by every subsequent adaptor and all avowed fans of Lobato. As Koskinen (2012:23) noticed, the affect memory[20] induces an emotional approach and plays a fundamental part in retranslated works, especially regarding children's classics, something that can explain Lobato's 1936 version still being in print, available in digital format and transformed into comics. It is also noteworthy that all the six authors interviewed had read Lobato's adaptation during their childhood.

Lefevere is categorical in this regard. He argues that "if a writer is no longer rewritten, his or her work will be forgotten" (1992:110). If we consider rewritings and refractions as a great collection of work derived from a given text through translations, adaptations (and their retranslations/re-adaptations and republications), reviews, essays, critical studies, and if for some reason a narrative ceases to be read, commented on, reinterpreted, rewritten, adapted – in short, loses its literary fame – it is probable that this book would disappear as a living text within a society. In addition, this literary fame is extended to the agents involved in its survival; publishing *Dom Quixote* brings prestige and translators or adapters and editors (especially the most republished) usually benefit from having a classic work such as Cervantes' masterpiece among their works or collections.

Returning to our first questions: which texts are chosen? Why is a book adapted more than once? In the case of *Dom Quixote*, it is quite safe to say it is *because it is a classic.* These books have to be seen as a belonging to a different category – this applies to their retranslations and republications as well. They are categorised as *must read* books and are considered part of the cultural capital expected of a fairly educated person; titles which are usually found on school reading lists. That said, these works have to be treated and analysed differently (from adult literature, and works written specifically for children) because of their uniqueness. Several of these books are adapted,

---

[20] Koskinen (2012:24) explains the term as "an emotionally expressed feeling that recurs when recalling a significant experience".

and although in many studies it is unnecessary to distinguish adaptations from translations, the findings in this research reveal differences between re-adaptations of classics for children and their retranslations for adults. Hence, this study proposes a new category which could be referred to as *re-adaptations of the classics for children.* Below are some of the peculiarities of this proposed category:

- very few titles: "Some 30 to 50 texts are regarded by the general public and the book trade as children's classics" (O'Sullivan 2005:132);
- double disqualification: Adaptations and children's literature are not regarded as part of high literature and receive less academic attention, as has been previously mentioned;
- fidelity issues: Translations of classics for adults are more open to "strange, disruptive and contradictory elements [...] and try to preserve them" (ibid.:138), but adaptations tend to radically intervene and "tame anything provocatively alien, making the unacceptable more acceptable or entertaining, and removing disturbing ambiguities" (ibid.). Even when a translation has undergone many adaptation procedures, it is usually closer to the source text than an assumed adaptation – the differences become wider as these are narratives in which readers expect modifications. In this sense, it is not coherent to speak of incompatible freedom, or to complain about missing/condensed passages, caricatured characters, or different endings. After all, it is an adaptation;
- manipulation: According to O'Sullivan (ibid.:145), as adaptations have different forms of transmission arising out of the necessity to make old works available to younger generations or readers who historically cannot read them, the objective can justify and legitimate the manipulation by the agents, thereby allowing major changes, unnecessary interventions and arbitrary alterations to make the text suitable and more entertaining. This situation is very different when the target text is a translation of an adult classic "where the first commandment is the inviolability of the original wording" (ibid:146);
- authorship: Frequently, foreign classic adaptations are treated equally as texts written in the source language (ibid.:147). Consequently, some scholars do not understand them as translations. This situation makes research even harder as catalogues would indicate the adapted foreign

work as a national text. This discussion also involves the issue of adapters' copyrights as previously discussed.

Concluding remarks

According to O'Sullivan (2005:132) and Soriano (1995:25), *Don Quixote* was one of the first books "stolen" from adult libraries by young readers, together with *Gulliver's Travels* and *Robinson Crusoe*. These classic titles are still popular contemporaneously, given that it is very common to find them in the same publisher collection or series. Nevertheless, despite their honourable origin, these adapted works are usually received with some negative reserve, as we can see by the following observations: "Generally speaking, many historians and scholars of translation continue to take a negative view of adaptation, dismissing the phenomenon as a distortion, falsification or censorship" (Bastin 2011:5).

Linda Hutcheon addresses infidelity claims stating that: "For a long time, 'fidelity criticism', as it can be known, was the critical orthodoxy in adaptation studies, especially when dealing with canonical works" (2006:6-7). For Hutcheon, a successful adaptation is not about fidelity to a prior text, but is achieved in relation to creativity and the "skill to make the text one's own and thus autonomous" (ibid.20). After all, these are children's books, adapted from classic works and mostly retranslations. These books have desacralised the untouchable titles from our occidental literature and dare to cut, resume and paraphrase, with the result that these original giants are appropriated, adapted, and brought closer to the common public and young readers alike.

Lathey (2010:174) states that retranslated children's fiction classics are a multifunctional aspect of the publishing industry, with commercial interests determining the constant retranslations, repackaging, as well as new illustration and publication of anniversary editions. O'Sullivan (2005:133) claims, "classics are a safe bet for publishers: they sell well, copyright has usually run out so that no royalties are payable and, as they have no immediate topical relevance, their shelf life is not limited". As can be deducted from this quote, O'Sullivan views the role of agents, and the way the exercise their agency, as omnipresent. That is to say, children's books are regarded by publishing agents as "classics" when they are listed amongst bestselling titles for a long period of time. For these publishing agents, as O'Sullivan goes on to argue, "classics are not, in the main, original texts or literary translations, but are more likely to be arbitrarily adapted editions of *well-known works*" (ibid.:148; emphasis added). Nevertheless, she also cites "factors immanent in the text" (ibid.:136) among the deciding reasons for selection and reception of classics of children's literature. Tahir Gürçağlar (2011:236) also diminishes the matrix of literary work when presenting several studies on retranslation. For her, retranslation is "a function of the dynamics of the target context, rather than a response to any inherent properties of the source text".

The object of this study and the data presented prevents us from fully accepting the above view, that 81 *Don Quijote* re-adaptations function merely as a marketing ploy, since according to Edward Riley (2002:38), one of the reasons for the acclaimed perennial success of *Dom Quixote* is in the text itself. Anthony Close (2010) – a critic who provides an excellent overview of the authors who have influenced the reading of *Don Quijote* in all its versions and adaptations since its publication in 1605 – explains that by allowing different interpretations, often resulting in opposite readings, the book has absorbed a wide variety of readers and admirers during the last four centuries.

So the question remains: Do we really need so many versions of *Dom Quixote*? A glance at the findings would seem to suggest that the answer is *yes*, at least from the point of view of the publishing industry, since Cervantes' book always sells. In today's business parlance it is a *cash cow*, an old and well-known product, dear to the public, with a steady and predictable demand and low publishing costs. In this case study, our results match Tahir Gürçağlar's findings (2008) that demonstrate that *Don Quijote* adaptations have performed, since the beginning, the role described previously as that performed by "pots & pans". These have always been seen as an indispensable item in any serious children's classic collection. Moreover, in the Brazilian case, one peculiarity to note is that every element of the corpus is linked to the educational system. This tendency first started with Jansen, who rewrote the piece when noticing the lack of good adaptations that he could recommend to his students at the imperial high school *Dom Pedro II*. This was further continued by Lobato who sold huge quantities of books to public schools. Subsequently, for those completely immersed in the learning process, special supplements for students (and teachers) with exercises, crosswords, etc. were provided; whilst targeting government recommendations increased, future sales were guaranteed.

The presence of so many different versions of this masterpiece continues to encourage and stress the demand for more research and attention – especially with the coexistence between the three authors of the last century and the many new contemporary ones, all of whom serve to renew the great work of Cervantes and introduce a variety of readings that do justice to his literary fame. It is a pleasure to see kids quite comfortable moving among books, *cordels*, comics and tablets, for ultimately, to put it in Koskinen and Paloposki (2003:33) words, the readers "would not want to be without any of the" famous knight's story.[21] For this reason it is essential to continue to study the phenomenon of re-adaptation of children's classics and differentiate them from full retranslations to better understand the complex mechanisms behind the so many *Don Quixotes.*

References

Bastin, Georges L. (2011) "Adaptation". In Baker, Mona/Saldanha, Gabriela (eds.) *Routledge Encyclopaedia of Translation Studies.* London/New York: Routledge, 5-8.

Berman, Antoine (1990). "La retraduction comme espace de la traduction". *Palimpsestes* 4, 1-8.

Chesterman, Andrew (2004) "Beyond the Particular". In Mauranen, Anna/Kujamäki, Pekka (eds.) *Translation Universals: Do They Exist?* Amsterdam/Philadelphia: John Benjamins, 33-49.

Close, Anthony (2010/1978) *The Romantic Approach to "Don Quixote": A Critical History of the Romantic Tradition in "Quixote" Criticism.* Cambridge: Cambridge University Press.

Cobelo, Silvia (2010) "Os tradutores do *Quixote* publicados no Brasil". *Tradução em Revista* 8, 1-36, http://www.maxwell.lambda.ele.puc-rio.br/trad_em_revista.php?strSecao=input0 [7 December 2013].

Foz, Clara (2005) "Retraducción del *Quijote* al francés (1614-2001): Recorrido histórico y crítico". In Vega Cernuda, Miguel Á. (ed.) *¿Qué Quijote leen los europeos?* Madrid: Universidad Complutense.

Gambier, Yves (1994) "La retraduction, retour et détour". *Meta: Journal des traducteurs* 39:3, 413-417.

Guedes, Sandra (2007) *Orígenes Lessa e a propaganda brasileira.* São Paulo: Universidade Metodista de São Paulo: MA Dissertation.

Hallewell, Laurence (2005/1985) *O livro no Brasil: Sua história* (tr. Maria da Penha Villalobos/Lólio Lourenço de Oliveira/Geraldo Gérson de Souza). São Paulo: EDUSP.

[21] In their article, the phrase refers to the rewritings of Lewis Carroll's *Alice in Wonderland* in Finland. The authors underline that in some cases (i.e. *Robinson Crusoe* or *Alice in Wonderland*), the classic status is rarely disputed and even emphasised in reviews – as seen in the case under study.

Hohlfeldt, Antônio (2003) *Deus escreve direito por linhas tortas: O romance-folhetim dos jornais de Porto Alegre entre 1850 e 1900*. Porto Alegre: EDIPUCRS.

Hutcheon, Linda (2006) *A Theory of Adaptation*. London/New York: Routledge.

Koskinen, Kaisa/Paloposki, Outi (2003) "Retranslations in the Age of Digital Reproduction". *Cadernos de Tradução* 11:1, 19-38.

Koskinen, Kaisa/Paloposki, Outi (2013) "Retranslation". In Gambier, Yves/van Doorslaer, Luc (eds.) *Handbook of Translation Studies*. Vol. 1. Amsterdam/ Philadelphia: John Benjamins, 294-298.

Koskinen, Kaisa (2012) "Domestication, Foreignisation and the Modulation of Affect". In Kemppanen, Hannu/Jänis, Marja/Belikova, Alexandra (eds.) *Domestication and Foreignisation in Translation Studies*. Berlin: Frank & Timme, 13-32.

Lathey, Gillian (2010) *The Role of Translators in Children's Literature: Invisible Storytellers*. New York/London: Routledge.

Lefevere, André (1992) *Translation, Rewriting and the Manipulation of Literary Fame*. London/New York: Routledge.

Lisboa, Maria F. G. (2009) "A obrigatoriedade do ensino de espanhol no Brasil: Implicações e desdobramentos". *Sínteses* 14, http://www.iel.unicamp.br/ojs-234/ index.php/sinteses/article/download/1227/911 [19 October 2014].

Lobato, Monteiro (1957) *A Barca de Gleyre*. São Paulo: Editora Brasiliense.

Machado, Ana M. (2004) "Presentation". In Harrisson, Michael *Dom Quixote*. Ed. by Michael Harrisson, Illustrations Victor Ambrus (tr. Luciano Vieira Machado). São Paulo: Ática.

Milton, John (2001a) "The Figure of the Factory Translator". In Hansen, Gyde/ Malmkjaer, Kirsten/Gile, Daniel (eds.) *Claims, Changes and Challenges in Translation Studies*. Amsterdam/Philadelphia: John Benjamins, 169-180.

Milton, John (2001b) "Translating Classic Fiction for Mass Markets. The Brazilian Clube do Livro". *The Translator* 7:1, 43-70.

Milton, John (2002) *O Clube do Livro e a Tradução*. Bauru, SP: EDUSC.

Miecoanski, Ellen (2012) "Trilha de livros". *Gazeta do Povo* 13 December 2012, http://www.gazetadopovo.com.br/falecimentos/conteudo.phtml?id=1327545&tit =Trilha-de-livros [19 October 2014].

O'Sullivan, Emer (2005) *Comparative Children's Literature*. London/New York: Routledge.

Pym, Anthony (1998) *Method in Translation History*. Manchester: St Jerome.

Riley, Edward C. (2002) "La singularidad de la fama de Don Quijote". *Cervantes: Bulletin of the Cervantes Society of America* 22:1, 27-41.

Slater, Candance (1982) *Stories on a String: The Brazilian "Literatura de Cordel"*. Berkeley: University of California Press.

Soriano, Marc (1995) *La literatura para niños y jóvenes: Guía de exploración de sus grandes temas* (tr. Graciela Montes). Buenos Aires: Ediciones Colihue.

Tahir Gürçağlar, Şehnaz (2006) "The Uses of Paratexts in Translation Research". In Hermans, Theo (ed.) *Crosscultural Transgression: Research Models in Translation Studies II: Historical and Ideological Issues*. Manchester: St Jerome, 44-60.

Tahir Gürçağlar, Şehnaz (2008) *The Politics and Poetics of Translation in Turkey, 1923-1960*. Amsterdam/New York: Rodopi.

Tahir Gürçağlar, Şehnaz (2011) "Retranslation". In Baker, Mona/Saldanha, Gabriela (eds.) *Routledge Encyclopaedia of Translation* Studies. London/New York: Routledge, 233-236.

Venuti, Lawrence (2013) *Translation Changes Everything: Theory and Practice*. London/New York: Routledge.

Zilberman, Regina/Lajolo, Marisa (1986) *Um Brasil para crianças: Para conhecer a literaturailnfantilbBrasileira: História, autores e textos*. São Paulo: Global.

Literary Works

Angeli, José (1985, 2002, 2007, 2013) *Dom Quixote: O cavaleiro da triste figura*. São Paulo: Scipione.

Angeli, José (2003) *Dom Quixote*. São Paulo: Scipione.

Bortolazzo Pinto (2008, 2010) *Dom Quixote*. São Paulo: LP&M.

Carrasco, Walcyr (2002) *Dom Quixote*. São Paulo: FTD.

Carrasco, Walcyr (2012) *Dom Quixote*. São Paulo: Moderna.

Cervantes, Miguel/Portinari, Cândido/Drummond de Andrade, Carlos (1973) *D. Quixote*. São Paulo: Diagraphis Editora.

Cervantes, Miguel (2001) *Don Quijote*. Barcelona: Editorial Crítica.

Cervantes, Miguel (2003) *Don Quixote* (tr. Edith Grossman). New York: HarperCollins Publishers.

Chianca, Leonardo (2005, 2012) *Dom Quixote*. São Paulo: Difusão Cultural do Livro.

Gullar, Ferreira (2002) *Dom Quixote de la Mancha*. Rio de Janeiro: Revan.

Jansen, Carlos (1901) *D.Quixote de la Mancha*. Rio de Janeiro: Laemmert & C.

Jansen, Carlos/Terra de Senna (1956, 1982) *Dom Quixote de la Mancha*. Rio de Janeiro: Minerva and MCA.

Lessa, Orígenes (1971, 2001, 2005) *Dom Quixote*. São Paulo: Ediouro.

Lessa, Orígenes (1972, 1980) *Dom Quixote*. São Paulo: Abril Cultural.

Lobato, Monteiro (1936) *Dom Quixote das crianças*. São Paulo: Cia Editora Nacional.

Lobato, Monteiro (1944-2005) *Dom Quixote das crianças*. São Paulo: Brasiliense.

Lobato, Monteiro (2013) *Dom Quixote das crianças*. São Paulo: Editora Globo.

Machado, Ana M./ Portinari, Candido (2005) *O cavaleiro do sonho: As aventuras e desventuras de Dom Quixote de la Mancha*. São Paulo: Mercuryo Jovem.

Quiles, Margarita B. (2006) *Don Quijote de la Mancha*. São Paulo: Scipione. [with CD].

Rado, Eduardo (2012) *Dom Quixote*. São Paulo: Nova Cultural.

Rios, Rosana (2005) *Dom Quixote*. São Paulo: Escala Educacional.

Narratives of Agency: Translation and Linguistic-Cultural Transposition

VÉRONIQUE BOHN

Université de Genève, Switzerland

Towards a Typology of Interlinguistic Strategies in Political Communication: The Swiss Political Parties as Case in Point

This paper discusses how political actors in multilingual settings can use language in their communication work and what kind of path they follow in order to coordinate a message in several languages. In particular, the paper aims to give a first insight into the different interlinguistic strategies that are actually implemented and to propose a general typology. To do so, the exploratory research applies an empirical approach and focuses on a corpus of periodicals published by Swiss political parties. Five interlinguistic strategies have been revealed: asymmetry, parallelism, separation, bilingual edition and hybridity. A closer look at the strategy distribution for each language pair shows that, while all five strategies can be found for the pair German-French, the pairs German-Italian and French-Italian display a variety of strategies far more restricted; the range is even smaller for the pairs that involve Romansch. However, in each case, not to communicate in one language (asymmetry) is a strategy used by a significant number of political parties.

Keywords: political communication, multilingual systems, Switzerland, political parties, interlinguistic strategies, political periodicals

Framework of a multilingual political communication

It is generally acknowledged that language plays a crucial role in politics and the link between the two has been investigated at length, especially by linguists. However, most studies have focused on messages given in only one language. When they do deal with two or more messages in different languages, they usually adopt a comparative approach and treat them as two completely separate items (see, e.g., Geser 1992; Nørholm Just 2009). Unfortunately, such studies leave aside a range of cases wherein political messages in different languages are related to each other in one way or another. Indeed, political messages nowadays often contain an important intertextual component across languages. While Translation Studies has been busier with the politics or politicisation of translation than with the actual translation of political texts (Schäffner 2007), the field is increasingly becoming interested in the way political texts are translated. In this context, two kinds of research can be identified. A first group of studies deals with messages that are linked together through international exchanges, i.e., that are largely produced by globalisation. It is in this perspective that Schäffner (2004:120) should be interpreted when she says:

> It is through translation that information is made available to addressees beyond national borders; and it is very frequently the case that reactions in one country to statements that were made in another country are actually reactions to the information as it was provided in translation.

The second trend examines multilingual systems, which are environments fully marked by lingual interdependency, as they entail the necessary coordination of a political message in several languages by the same actor.[1] For instance, Gagnon (2006) analyses how the political speeches of the Canadian government are produced in French and English.

The research carried out in this paper relates to this second type. In particular, it focuses on Switzerland and employs an empirical approach based on periodicals published by political parties and intends to give an overview of how political actors can deal with the multilingualism of the system under study. Multilingual systems are interesting instances for Translation Studies because, by definition, their public sphere is composed of many languages. As a result, members of the system have no other choice but to deal with the variety of languages. As Meylaerts (2011:744) suggests, "there is no *language* policy without a *translation* policy". The question is, considering the various languages, when and how is translation used?

I suggest that political actors' reaction to multilingualism can be schematised in the form of three questions:

(1) What do they want to communicate in each language?

(2) How do they want to communicate in each language?

(3) What relationship do they want to establish between the languages?

Question 3 is particularly interesting, as it is the one that properly gives the interlinguistic dimension to the reaction and thus allows actors to cope with the multilingualism, while questions 1 and 2 would also apply to unilingual systems. It should be stressed here that, although they represent different

[1] The term "multilingual systems" refers here to those systems where multilingualism is institutionalised, e.g., through the recognition of several official languages. The symbolic stakes in such systems are quite different from those in systems that are *de facto* multilingual.

aspects of the reaction, the questions are interrelated and the order of the questions, as presented here, does not reflect a real step-by-step procedure – the decomposition only aims to emphasise the different dimensions of the reaction.

I propose to use the expression "interlinguistic strategy" to refer to the answers given to these questions by political actors and thus to their reaction to the multilingualism. The adjective "interlinguistic" should be a direct reference to the necessity for political actors to take a variety of languages into account and to coordinate them, i.e., a direct reference to question 3 specific to multilingual systems. The word "strategy" reflects a characteristic of political communication. Indeed, it must not be forgotten that political communication does not solely aim to reproduce an ideology, but its nature is deeply persuasive (Bazil 2010:5). As Tresch observed (2008:269) that political communication is not an end in itself but a strategic choice. It follows that common decisions are taken that correspond to what one views as necessary or desirable. In the context of multilingual settings, it could mean that political actors will weigh the effort necessary to communicate in another language against the benefits (i.e., the support of the other language community) that would be obtained (Ernst 1998:228). Therefore, the term "interlinguistic strategy" will describe the way a political actor coordinates a message in different languages while striking a balance between the resources spent and the support gained.[2]

This paper presents the results of the first stage of a broader research project, the purpose of which is to analyse these "interlinguistic strategies". The exploratory study should help us to identify general trends in the coordination work of the Swiss political parties as realised through their periodicals, to establish a first typology of interlinguistic strategies and to determine how these strategies are distributed. To do so, a corpus of 39 publications has been selected.[3] Before moving on to methodological considerations and results, a few words should be said about the channel of communication, the multilingual system and the political actor chosen.

---

[2] Interestingly, there is no absolute threshold for the balance itself. The level at which implementing a particular strategy is too costly is a subjective matter, i.e., the level at which the amount of resources spent is considered too important depends on the political actor. In this respect, the political actor's ideological stance towards the language diversity (i.e., the perception of and the value given to the language diversity) can play a key role.

[3] The selection of periodicals will be dealt with in more detail in the methodological section.

A channel of communication: the political parties' periodicals

Political parties employ different kinds of communication channels. They can run a website, distribute leaflets, deliver speeches, etc. All the channels used in a certain context by a certain actor form a communication repertoire (Kriesi, Bernhard and Hänggli 2009:350). In this study, considering that a communication repertoire can be quite vast, only a part of it is analysed, i.e., the periodicals published by political parties. In this paper, a periodical is understood to be a publication that comes out regularly (temporal dimension), thus made of a series of units (issues) that assembles several texts (articles) within a unit. It can be identified by a title. The temporal dimension is especially interesting, as it can underline a certain logic of publication and thus a certain publishing policy, particularly regarding the interlinguistic strategies.

Political parties themselves use different names to refer to these periodicals: newspaper (*Zeitung*, *journal*, e.g., by the Swiss People's Party or the Socialist Democratic Party), magazine (e.g., by the Christian Democratic People's Party), bulletin (e.g., by the Green Party), etc. The umbrella term of "periodical" has been chosen, as it is quite neutral while reflecting the temporal dimension that is important for this research. Furthermore, it should help distinguishing this sort of publication from the "traditional" newspapers, such as *The Times*, *Le Monde* or *Die Süddeutsche Zeitung*. These two kinds of text function quite differently. In the case of traditional newspapers, texts are expected to meet objectivity criteria (whether this reflects the reality is another story). On the contrary, as their political allegiance is clearly stated, periodicals issued by political parties will be perceived as mostly persuasive (i.e., as a tool for political propaganda) rather than informative. Another interesting aspect is that this type of channel falls into the category of communication managed by the organisation itself; that is, not mediated by another actor (such as traditional newspapers, radio, television, etc.) (Kriesi, Bernhard and Hänggli 2009:351). Indeed, according to clues given in some periodicals, this may be the very reason why political parties actually use this kind of text; because they reckon that their messages are twisted and reported in a biased way by independent media. Interestingly, this stance is held by the Swiss People's Party (right-wing), as well as the Socialist Democratic Party (left-wing). Thus, the former writes in one of its issues: "We, the UDC, are under the impression that we are often painted in a distorted and unilateral way" (Brunner 2012:1).[4] Similarly, the latter complains that "the public and the party members get a selective, partial and deformed depiction [of the party] [through mass media]" (Fehr 2001:3).[5]

It should be outlined that publication frequency varies according to the political parties. It ranges from three to 36 times a year. Furthermore, the periodicals bring together articles of different natures. Some texts are directly related to current affairs and allow political parties to put their arguments forward at strategic moments in political life and to prompt citizens to elect a certain politician or to vote on a factual issue in a certain way. Other articles offer spaces where broader, more general topics (or concepts) can be discussed (e.g., an article about innovation and Swiss economics can be found in the April 2013 issue of the Christian Democratic People's Party's periodical in German). This is not to be underestimated, as having power in a political system includes, among other things, the capacity to introduce and impose particular topics. Besides, periodicals may contain articles that do not seem to have a direct influence on the politics of the system but are linked to the party's life. Such articles play a significant role in the image of and the identification with a political party. A typical example for this type of article is the accounts of the yearly cards tournament organised by the Swiss People's Party.

A multilingual system: Switzerland

According to Widmer (2004b:1), Switzerland has the particularity to be a state that was constituted as a multilingual state.[6] Indeed, article 4 of the Constitution recognises four national languages (German, French, Italian and Romansch), which have to cohabit with each other. It is true that tensions between the linguistic communities are not completely inexistent. For instance, the vote on Swiss adhesion to the European Economic Area (EEA) in 1992 revealed a substantial gap between the French-speaking community and the German-speaking one. This sparked a debate so the government commissioned a study on the linguistic cleavage in Switzerland (Kriesi et al. 1996:5). More recently, there has been an argument about the

[4] "Wir als SVP haben doch das Gefühl, dass wir öfter verzerrt und auch einseitig dargestellt werden" (my translation. All translations are my own unless otherwise stated).

[5] "Sie [die Partei] wird der Öffentlichkeit und der Mitgliedschaft gefiltert, gestückelt und gedreht präsentiert".

[6] "Sa spécificité [de la Suisse] réside dans le fait qu'elle s'est constituée comme État plurilingue".

first foreign language to be taught at school. The Federal Act on Languages of 2007 only states that students should know another national language plus a foreign language before the end of compulsory schooling (article 15, paragraph 3). However, it says nothing about the choice of languages and does not indicate whether the national language should be taught before the other foreign language. These "details" are to be determined by the cantons.[7] Now, certain cantons, especially German-speaking ones, have decided to teach the foreign language (usually English) before the second national language (typically French), which was seen by some people as a threat to national cohesion. However, despite these instances of tension, conflicts around languages are quite rare and political issues seldom crystallise around them, at least when compared to other countries, for example, to Belgium. Therefore, Switzerland is often considered to be a model of multilingualism and a natural laboratory for the management of language diversity (see, e.g., Widmer 2004a:159).

The linguistic regime of Switzerland is based on two main principles. First, article 18 of the Constitution establishes the freedom to use any language as a fundamental right. Second, the linguistic relationships are governed by the principle of territoriality in which a territory is linked to one or more languages. According to article 70, paragraph 2 of the Constitution, the cantons determine their official languages and, when doing so, they have to respect the traditional territorial distribution of languages. This leads to a quite static system, with a juxtaposition of spaces characterised by a particular language or set of languages. However, interestingly, the canton's borders do not entirely follow the language lines: out of the 26 cantons, four of them are (officially) bi- or trilingual.

Späti argues (2012:152) that language law in Switzerland is little codified compared to other countries, which prompts her to say that it is rather of a symbolic nature. Indeed, the legislation (Constitution and Act on Languages) establishes few obligations. While the Act does determine which official documents must be provided by the Confederation and in which national languages, many of its articles stipulate what may be done rather than what must be done, particularly concerning the promotion of multilin-

---

[7] Switzerland has a federal structure. The term "canton" refers to an independent region, which is free to pass laws in particular domains (e.g., education, police…) and thus has some leeway in managing its territory.

gualism. Interestingly, the legislation applies to the federal authorities and does not constrain external actors such as political parties.

An actor: the political parties

Political parties are chosen because of their position in society. Indeed, they constantly allow for restructuring of political life and do not have to observe as many strong formal or informal rules as, for example, the government.[8] Furthermore, their financial means allow them to put in a sustained effort towards communication (e.g., compared to individuals). At the same time, they are still very limited (e.g., compared to interest associations) and political parties must make decisions about their forms of communication.

The political parties' landscape is strongly shaped by the federal structure of the Swiss polity. Thus, the cantonal chapters play a larger role than is the case in other countries. For example, this is illustrated by the fact that, "in general, it is not possible to join a national party directly; instead, membership begins in the local section of one's place of residence" (Ladner 2007:326). This means that communication is not exclusively piloted by the national party – cantonal chapters can take the initiative and develop their own strategies.

An empirical study: identifying interlinguistic strategies

This section aims to describe the study that was carried out and it presents the results obtained. After the methodology is explained, a typology of interlinguistic strategies (identified with help of the corpus) will be suggested and their distribution will be exposed.

Applying a corpus-based approach

In order to provide a first general overview of the different kinds of periodicals published by Swiss political parties (and of the interlinguistic strategies that are implemented through them), a vast corpus has been selected. The twelve political parties that appear on the Federal Chancellery's register of

[8] From a symbolic point of view, the government is supposed to represent the country as a whole and has to respect some principles concerning the minimum quantity of information to be provided in each official language. On the contrary, political parties can decide who they want to represent and the choice of languages they want to communicate in amounts to a strategic move.

political parties (as of August 2013) have been used as the basis, apart from the *Lega dei Ticinesi* – this party defends the interests of the only Italian-speaking Swiss canton (Ticino) and does not aim to reach all language communities. For each of these parties, the "general" and the youth branches have been taken into account. Finally, the corpus includes five multilingual territories: Switzerland as a whole (federal level) and the four multilingual cantons (Bern, with French and German; Freiburg, with French and German; Graubünden, with German, Italian and Romansch; and Wallis, with French and German). This makes a total of 11 × 2 × 5 = 110 chapters. However, this number is merely a theoretical one, as not every political party is represented in every multilingual territory by both "general" and youth branches. In fact, there are 91 chapters, out of which 24 publish one or more periodicals.[9] This amounts to 39 publications.

First, publications have been examined at a macro-level. Six criteria have been taken into account: the layout (the "look" of the publication, including colours, logos, font and so on), the publication frequency and timing, the number of pages, the columns (i.e. the structure), the articles in general and, obviously, the languages. The period of time considered runs from August 2010 to September 2013.[10] After analysing half of the publications, the same trends have showed up repeatedly; five different kinds of periodicals have been identified. Subsequently, all of the periodicals have been classified according to the typology thus formulated.

Proposing a typology

As already stated, the corpus has revealed five different strategies.

Asymmetry

This label refers to cases in which a political party publishes a periodical in language A, but not in language B. Of course, this does not necessarily mean that the actor does not communicate in the second language at all, as

---

9 The publications were qualified as newspapers if they contained at least four pages and were available in print versions (and not merely in electronic versions), principally so that they could be distinguished from newsletters. Furthermore, political parties' websites were used in order to determine whether the party does have a periodical (questionnaires, for example, were not sent to political parties). This presupposes that anything that is not on the Web does not exist, which, of course, could give a distorted insight into the reality.

10 For some political parties the period was more limited as their records, as presented on the Internet, do not go back to 2010.

the periodicals are only a part of the communication repertoire or can exist at a different level (e.g., cantonal and not federal). However, this does mean that the communication structure is different between the languages. A striking example for this is the case of the PLR, the liberal party in Switzerland. The party has no periodical in French at the national level. Yet, the chapters in the French-speaking cantons do have their own periodicals (except for the canton of Jura).[11]

Parallelism

Political parties that have adopted a parallelism approach publish periodicals in each language. Moreover, the layout and the choice of articles and texts as a whole are the same, or at least are similar. Of course, the similarity is seen at a macro-level; texts can show marks of adaptation at a micro-level or appear in a slightly different order. The publications of the UDC, the Swiss People's Party, fall into this category. While the French-speaking readers have a periodical called *Franc-parler*, their German-speaking fellow-countrymen can read the *Klartext*. Both "newspapers" (as the party itself labels them) are issued simultaneously (the same month) and offer the same page numbers. The layout is strictly the same; if one disregards the language, it is not possible to distinguish one edition from the other (for example, the smiley sun of the party with the name of the periodical below can be found on the upper left side of both front pages). The periodicals are structured by the same columns and each article in one language has a counterpart in the other.

Separation

In this case, the political party publishes a periodical for each language, but the publications are quite autonomous from each other. The layout is not necessarily the same and it is not possible to find a strict match between the articles, even though some topics can be common (in particular, voting-related topics). Even the number of pages and the frequency of publication can differ strongly. This type of strategy is well illustrated by the periodicals issued in German and Italian by the PS, the Socialist Democratic Party. The periodical in German, called *links*, is published nine times per year, while the frequency for the Italian publication, called *ps.ch*, is published four times per year. The timing itself differs. For instance, in 2012, an issue of *ps.ch* came

[11] Most German-speaking cantonal chapters have their own newspapers, in addition to the national one.

out in March while *links* did not. Furthermore, there is a substantial gap between the mean number of pages, with 20 pages for the German edition and 4 for the Italian one. Similarly, the layout shows divergences; the title *ps.ch* is situated in the upper right on the front page while the mention *links* can be found on the upper left side and follows a red cube in which the name of the party (PS) is presented. Another example for the divergent layout is the position of the page number; *links* displays it on the top of the pages while, in *ps.ch*, it is printed in a black square at the bottom. Finally, the articles are completely different (even regarding the subjects).

Bilingual edition

As can be inferred from its name, this strategy consists of printing a periodical that mixes different languages and is thus hypothetically intended for any language community of the territory. It comes in two subtypes: duplication and simple mix.

In the duplication form, the "same" articles are available or "repeated" in language A and in language B. The periodical of the Bern chapter of the UDC is one example of this type. The periodical's name itself brings together French and German: *Berner Journal Bernois*. Typically, one page is composed of a text in German with a French version of this text in a green box. Therefore, the reader can decide to read the article in the language that suits him/her best (or read both versions).

In the simple mix form, the periodical shows a row of original articles that are either in language A or language B. The articles are not the "same" as they are not "repeated". For instance, the national youth chapter of the Socialist Democratic Party produces a periodical that mixes articles that are either in French or in German but that appears only once.[12] Thus, in the June 2013 issue, an article in French about housing shortage is surrounded by articles in German about completely different subjects (education, wages, meeting between cantonal chapters, etc.).

Hybridity

In this last case, the periodical is characterised by a combination of two or more of the aforementioned strategies. Depending on the combination chosen, different forms can be found. For example, the periodical of the

[12] Interestingly, the periodical name exists in the four national languages: *Infrarot*, *Infrarouge*, *Infrarosso* and *Infracotschen*. However, only articles in French and German can be found. Indeed, on the webpage of the party, the publication is described as being "bilingual".

Christian Democratic People's Party (federal level) is based on parallelism, separation and bilingual edition, with the simple mix subtype. Meanwhile, the periodical of the Green Party (federal level) "only" mixes parallelism and separation.

From this typology, one can wonder about which strategies are used the most and by which party – or in other words, how the strategies are distributed. The second part of the results attempts to give insight into this question.

To do so, one has no other choice but to consider the distribution by language pairs. Indeed, the typology proposed here works well for binary systems, i.e., for settings with two languages. However, it is more difficult to apply when more languages are involved, because a political party may not implement a homogenous strategy for all languages, i.e., it can establish links of different natures between the languages. For example, the Green Party (federal level) publishes periodicals in French and German that are linked together by a hybridity strategy, but the Italian-speaking people do not have their own periodical (asymmetry). This means that, if this typology is to be applied, the situations should be examined by language pairs. Regarding the corpus, this implies that the number of periodicals to be considered at the federal level and the relevant multilingual territories will vary according to the language pair.

The discussion will begin with German and French, which means that the number of periodicals to be considered at the federal level will be reduced and that Graubünden will no longer be taken into account as a multilingual territory. Doing so narrows down the theoretical number of chapters to 88, with a real number of 74. Twenty-two chapters publish one or more periodicals, for a total of 33 publications.

	Chapters number	Percentage	Chapters*
Asymmetry	7	30 %	PS VS, PS BE, PLR CH, PLR VS, PST CH, PST BE, JCS CH
Parallelism	4	17 %	PS CH en., PS FR, UDC CH, UDF BE

Separation	2	9 %	PS CH gen., JUDC CH
Bilingual edition – duplication	2	9 %	UDC BE, PEV BE
Bilingual edition – simple mix	4	17 %	JUSO CH, PLR BE, PLR FR, Green BE
Hybridity	4	17 %	PDC CH, Green CH, PEV CH, UDF CH

*A list of abbreviations can be found in the appendix

Table 1: Strategy distribution for German-French

The reader will notice that the total number of chapters is 23, while there were 22 chapters mentioned above. This is because the Socialist Democratic Party at the federal level (code PS CH in the table) publishes two periodicals for each language: one that deals with general topics (code PS CH gen.) and that is based on the separation strategy, and another that is limited to energy-related issues (code PS CH en.) and that falls into the parallelism category. Therefore, the party has been coded twice.

According to these results, the most employed strategy is asymmetry, which is quite surprising as it corresponds to a non-communication strategy in one language. Of course, this lack of communication should be nuanced with a reminder that periodicals are only a portion of a party's communication work. This could be explained by various factors including ideological grounds, lack of financial means or resources, etc. The specific reason cannot be given here, because this would require other methods, in particular ethnomethodological ones. The second most used strategies are parallelism, bilingual edition – simple mix and hybridity. Separation and bilingual edition – duplication are at the bottom. However, if we do not distinguish between the two subtypes, bilingual edition ranks second, after asymmetry and before parallelism and hybridity.

The distribution does not seem to follow partisan lines. For example, as stated above, the Socialist Democratic Party (left-wing) uses two different strategies, parallelism and separation, which can also (parallelism by the "general" branch and separation by the youth one at the federal level) be found in the Swiss People's Party (right-wing). Similarly, it is striking that hybridity is used in all political trends (Greens in the left-wing, PDC and PEV in the centre, and UDF in the right-wing). This could mean that the party's ideological view on language diversity does not strictly follow the ideology as a whole and/or that the external constraints (financial means, other resources, etc.) outweigh the general ideological stakes.

Finally, hybridity is monopolised by the "general" parties at the federal level. Simultaneously, a slight trend can be observed for the bilingual forms, which are adopted more often by cantonal chapters (except for the youth branch of the Social Democratic Party, code JUSO CH).

Consider now the strategy distribution for German-Italian. These languages are brought together on two multilingual territories only (the federal level and the canton of Graubünden). Thus, the theoretical number of chapters is 44, for a real number of 37 chapters. Thirteen chapters publish one or more periodicals, which amounts to 18 publications.

Results for this language pair are presented in Table 2.

	Chapters number	Percentage	Chapters*
Asymmetry	8	57 %	PS CH en, JS CH, UDC CH, JUDC CH, PDC GR, Verts CH, PEV CH, JCS CH
Parallelism	0	0 %	---
Separation	4	29 %	PS CH gen, PLR CH, PDC CH, PST CH
Bilingual edition – duplication	0	0 %	---
Bilingual edition – simple mix	2	14 %	PS GR, UDF CH
Hybridity	0	0 %	---

*A list of abbreviations can be found in the appendix

Table 2: Strategy distribution for German-Italian

It is striking that the range of strategies is far less wide than is the case for the pair German-French: only three strategies are used out of the six forms possible. Again, the most implemented strategy is asymmetry. It is followed by separation and then by bilingual edition subtype simple mix. Interestingly, while the pair German-French tends to give preference to parallelism over separation (4 chapters for the former to 2 for the latter), the chapters completely put aside forms of parallelism when it comes to the relationship between German and Italian and turn to establishing a separation-based link between the languages (i.e., a more autonomous link).

As can be observed with the pair German-French, there does not seem to be a correlation between the partisan lines and the strategies. Furthermore, nothing can be said about the differences between national and cantonal chapters, as the number of cantonal chapters is too small to allow any conclusion on this matter.

The analysis for the pair French-Italian shows similar patterns, as can be elicited from Table 3.

	Chapters number	Percentage	Chapters*
Asymmetry	8	73 %	PS CH en, JS CH, UDC CH, JUDC CH, PLR CH, Verts CH, PEV CH, PST CH
Parallelism	0	0 %	---
Separation	2	18 %	PS CH gen, PDC CH
Bilingual edition – duplication	0	0 %	---
Bilingual edition – simple mix	1	9 %	UDF CH
Hybridity	0	0 %	---

*A list of abbreviations can be found in the appendix

Table 3: Strategy distribution for French-Italian

For this pair, only the federal level has been taken into account, as no canton has both French and Italian as official languages. This narrows down the theoretical number of chapters to 22 and the real number to 21. Ten chapters publish one or more periodicals, which amounts to 13 publications.

In comparison to the distribution for German-Italian, the same strategies are implemented and broadly in the same proportion, though the asymmetry is reinforced from a relative point of view (73% to 57% for German-Italian).

Asymmetry is even more present if one looks at the distribution for the language pair German-Romansch. For this pair, the theoretical number is 44, with a real number of 37. Thirteen chapters publish one or more periodicals, which amounts to 14 publications.

	Chapters number	Percentage	Chapters*
Asymmetry	14	100 %	PS CH gen, PS CH en, PS GR, JS CH, UDC CH, JUDC CH, PLR CH, PDC CH, PDC GR, Verts CH, PEV CH, UDF CH, PST CH, JCS CH
Parallelism	0	0 %	---
Separation	0	0 %	---
Bilingual edition – duplication	0	0 %	---
Bilingual edition – simple mix	0	0 %	---
Hybridity	0	0 %	---

*A list of abbreviations can be found in the appendix

Table 4: Strategy distribution for German-Romansch

Table 4 shows that the relationship between German and Romansch is based solely on asymmetry. Besides, in the framework of the asymmetry, communication is always realised in German. Tables for the pairs French-Romansch and Italian-Romansch present the exact same distribution and will not be reproduced here.

The predominance of asymmetry concerning Romansch, in any combination that it may be (German, French or Italian), means that this language is not used in the periodicals, aside from a few "outbursts" that are incidental and do not form a systematic logic. Therefore, it can be assumed that political parties communicate with the Romansch-speaking people either through another communication channel or in another language, or do not intend to communicate with them at all.

Conclusion

The exploratory study has shown that political parties can implement a full range of interlinguistic strategies in order to deal with the multilingualism of the Swiss context. However, the distribution and the range itself seem to vary according to the language pair under scrutiny. For instance, the more a language involved in the pair has a minority position in Switzerland (typically, Italian and Romansch), the narrower the range will be. Another intriguing finding from our empirical study is the fact that bilingual editions tend to be primarily used at a cantonal level. Such a trend could be explained by identity mechanisms in the sense that citizens living in a bilingual canton are more directly exposed to multilingualism and that the coexistence of several languages forms part of their everyday life.[13] Further investigation will hopefully shed additional light on this intriguing possibility in the data.

More broadly, the next step in the research will be to analyse how and why a strategy is used when compared to the other possibilities. In this sense, one should wonder what factors determine the strategy used, such as the financial means of the political party, its other resources (e.g., the number of partisans, sympathisers or employees ready to participate in the party's work), its ideology – which hypothetically includes how it perceives the language diversity – or the anticipated social expectations toward the party. To do so, a field investigation would be most appropriate.

---

[13] Given the territoriality principle discussed above, it is actually quite easy to lead a monolingual life if one lives in a monolingual canton.

Such method would also allow the researcher to investigate the real writing-process of these periodicals. Indeed, the typology proposed here has been formulated on the basis of the products. It does not reveal what truly happens behind them, within the editing team. Rather, it only hints to the text production and does not provide any real insight into it. This aspect, however, is crucial, because, for example, it is not easy to distinguish a practice of joint writing from translation if one looks solely at the product, especially if one does this only on a macro-level.

In this context, the issue of resources is an avenue worth exploring. In particular, a separation strategy does not automatically imply that periodicals are completely isolated from each other. For example, the generalist periodicals of the Socialist Democratic Party are separation-based, yet they sometimes contain the same pictures (used for different articles). This suggests a common ground between the editing teams. Similarly, editors who have access to shared resources may be free to select the elements they want to use. This is quite obvious in the case of the hybridity strategy. Therefore, one can wonder what kinds of resources are common, how they are defined and what rules govern them.

References

Bazil, Vazrik (2010) "Politische Sprache: Zeichen und Zunge der Macht". *Aus Politik und Zeitgeschichte* 8, 3-6.

Brunner, Toni (2012) "Wieso ein SVP Extra-Blatt?". *Extrablatt der Schweizerischen Volkspartei*, November, 1.

Ernst, Andreas (1998) "Vielsprachigkeit, Öffentlichkeit und politische Integration: Schweizerische Erfahrungen und europäische Perspektiven". *Swiss Political Science Review* 4:4, 225-240.

Fehr, Hans-Jürg (2001) "Der direkte Draht". *Links.ch*, 20 June, 3.

Gagnon, Chantal (2006) "Language Plurality as Power Struggle, or: Translating Politics in Canada". *Target* 18:1, 69-90.

Geser, Hans (1992) "'Links und rechts, gauche et droite, sinistra e destra': Eine unverwüstliche Begriffspolarität im intersprachlichen Vergleich". In Eisner, Manuel/Fux, Beat *Politische Sprache in der Schweiz. Konflikt und Konsens.* Zurich/Cologne: Orell Füssli, 285-323.

Kriesi, Hanspeter et al. (1996) *Le clivage linguistique: Problèmes de compréhension entre les communautés linguistiques en Suisse.* Berne: Office fédéral de la statistique.

Kriesi, Hanspeter/Bernhard, Laurent/Hänggli, Regula (2009) "The Politics of Campaigning: Dimensions of Strategic Action". In Marcinkowski, Frank/Pfetsch, Barbara (eds.) *Politik in der Mediendemokratie.* Wiesbaden: VS Verlag, 345-365.

Ladner, Andreas (2007) "Political Parties". In Klöti, Ulrich et al. (eds.) *Handbook of Swiss Politics*. Zurich: NZZ Libro, 309-334.

Meylaerts, Reine (2011) "Translational Justice in a Multilingual World: An Overview of Translational Regimes". *Meta* 56:4, 743-757.

Nørholm Just, Sine (2009) "No Place like Home? The Role of the Media in the Framing of Europe". *Journal of Language and Politics* 8:2, 223-248.

Schäffner, Christina (2004) "Political Discourse Analysis from the Point of View of Translation Studies". *Journal of Language and Politics* 31:4, 117-150.

Schäffner, Christina (2007) "Politics and Translation". In Kuhiwczak, Piotr/Littau, Karin (eds.) *A Companion to Translation Studies*. Clevedon/Buffalo/Toronto: Multilingual Matters, 134-147.

Späti, Christina (2012) "Sprache, Ethnizität, Identität. Die schweizerische Sprachenpolitik zwischen Ethnisierung und nationaler Kohäsion". In Engler, Balz (ed.) *Wir und die Anderen. Stereotypen in der Schweiz – Nous et les autres. Stéréotypes en Suisse*. Freiburg: Academic Press Fribourg, 140-155

Tresch, Anke (2008) *Öffentlichkeit und Sprachenvielfalt: Medienvermittelte Kommunikation zur Europapolitik in der Deutsch- und Westschweiz*. Baden-Baden: Nomos Verlag.

Widmer, Jean (2004a) "Ordre des langues et ordre du politique. Plurilinguisme et démocratie en Suisse". In Archives fédérales suisses (eds.) *Die Erfindung der Demokratie in der Schweiz/L'invention de la démocratie en Suisse*. Zurich: Chronos Verlag, 157-181.

Widmer, Jean (2004b) "Constitutions d'une Suisse plurilingue: Une introduction". In Widmer, Jean et al. (eds.) *Die Schweizer Sprachenvielfalt im Öffentlichen Diskurs/La diversité des langues en Suisse dans le débat public*. Berne: Peter Lang, 1-30.

Appendix

List of abbreviations used

The codes are made of two parts. The first one corresponds to the political party; the second one represents the multilingual territory. Thus, PS BE means the Socialist Democratic Party (PS) of the canton of Bern (BE).

Code territory

BE: Canton of Bern
CH: Federal level
FR: Canton of Freiburg
GR: Canton of Graubünden
VS: Canton of Wallis

Code political party

JCS: Jeunesse Communiste; Kommunistische Jugend; Communist Youth.
JUSO: Jeunesse Socialiste; JungsozialistInnen; Young Socialists.
JUDC: Jeunes UDC (Union Démocratique du Centre); Junge SVP (Schweizerische Volkspartei); Youth of the Swiss People's Party.
Green: Les Verts; Die Grüne; Green Party.
PDC: Parti Démocrate-Chrétien; Christlichdemokratische Volkspartei; Christian Democratic People's Party.
PEV: Parti évangélique; Evangelische Volkspartei; Evangelical People's Party.
PLR: PLR.Les libéraux-Radicaux; FDP.Die Liberalen; Liberal Party.
PS: Parti Socialiste; Sozialdemokratische Partei; Socialist Democratic Party.
PST: Parti Suisse du Travail; Partei der Arbeit; Swiss Party of Labour.
UDC: Union Démocratique du Centre; Schweizerische Volkspartei; Swiss People's Party.
UDF: Union Démocratique Fédérale; Eidgenössisch-Demokratische Union; Federal Democratic Union.

For the Socialist Democratic Party at the federal level (PS CH), the code is completed by a further indication, as this party publishes two different periodicals in each language (gen. for the publication on general topics; en. for the publication on energy-related issues).

ELENA VOELLMER

Universitat Pompeu Fabra, Spain

When *Herman the German* becomes *Erik der Wikinger*: Heterolingualism in US Sitcoms and Their German Dubbed Versions

This paper deals with heterolingualism in US sitcoms, in particular the use of German and the appearance of German characters, how they are stereotyped and how certain characters are portrayed in the German dubbed versions of the series. A general introduction into the research topic of heterolingual texts is given, including the concept of L3 (a language or language variety, other than the prevalent one, that may appear in a (audiovisual) text), and the case of language coincidence (Corrius 2008) in translating a heterolingual text is explained. By analysing scenes from four different US sitcoms, and referring to further examples, possible translation patterns in the target texts are described and potential reasons for them explored. Decisive factors that may play a key role in dubbing decisions are explained, based on the examples found in this study.

Keywords: German dubbing; heterolingualism; L3; language coincidence; US sitcoms

Introduction

US films and television series often feature inter- and intralingual variation, i.e., they include characters that speak a foreign language, with a foreign accent or in different varieties of a language, for example, British and American English. This can be due to an attempt at reflecting certain historical periods in the settings of the plots and thus an intention to reflect real-life polylectal encounters or a means of portraying characters as belonging to a certain social, professional or ethnic group by the use of slangs, jargons and accents.

A heterolingual text, audiovisual or otherwise, fictional or non-fictional, is one that combines different languages (e.g., English, French, and Italian) or that displays intralingual variation (diatopical, diastratical and diaphasical), or both.[1] This can be and often is combined with visual differentiation of a character. For example, a character may speak differently from the others, s/he may speak in his or her distinct stylistic way (e.g., with an unusual pronunciation), with a foreign accent or in a foreign language combined with (stereo)typical gestures, physical appearance, etc. Foreignism may appear only in a few sentences or a different language may have such an important presence throughout a text that, for a mainly monolingual audience, it becomes difficult to understand the entire film if there are no subtitles provided within the source text (ST) – also called *part-subtitling* (O'Sullivan 2007:81). However, their presence is often qualitatively important as opposed to quantitatively, as language variation is an important functional element in fiction and there is usually a reason for its deployment (O'Sullivan 2011:20). One of these functions of heterolingualism is representing "the richness and complexity of real-life multilingual realities" (Bleichenbacher 2008:21), for example, a representation of the place of action or an indication of the nationality of a character. This can be described as "intended realism". Heterolingualism can also express some form of social criticism (ibid.) or it can provide an effect of suspense. It can also be used in a rather distorted, artificial way in order to make a linguistic or social statement. Often, heterolingualism is used to expose certain features of a language for the pursuance of a comic effect.

This paper focuses on heterolingualism within the genre of television comedy, with the use of German in US sitcoms and their dubbed versions into German. The latter is a highly interesting case as communication problems or polylectal encounters of any kind that are part of the ST disappear by dubbing the English parts into German. Different solutions can be found for these cases, such as rewriting the script and changing the entire communicative situation, as can be witnessed in certain scenes of *Inglourious Basterds* (Voellmer 2012:53-57), or even using a different language and thus changing the identity of the ST character, as seen in the case study

[1] I use the term "heterolingualism" because it is one of the prevalent terms in this research area. I likewise favour the use of "polylingual" and "polylectal", if one is particularly dealing with texts that also include diatopic, diastratic and/or diaphasic varieties or simply uses the term because it is neutral and conceptually very open, also including standard varieties. The other widely used term is "multilingual", which, in my opinion, is exclusive to societies and individuals (although many studies in this field favour the use of plurilingual) or used to refer to real-life multilingualism that is reflected in fiction, but not to fictional texts themselves (see Sternberg 1981).

of Gunnar, the German fencing instructor in *Frasier* (Angell, Casey and Lee 1993-2004).

Diatopic varieties, foreign languages and accents, or some form of mock language (a faked foreign language by the use of some of its stereotypical features), are often employed for the sake of creating a comic effect. Due to historical and narrative reasons (e.g., movies about World War II), German has been one of the most popular foreign languages to be included in films and television series. In television sitcoms, the German language and German characters are used as a basis for creating jokes – verbal, non-verbal, or both – that usually target some stereotypical features of the German language or culture, or the image of a native speaker with his or her likes, dislikes, beliefs and habits.

In this paper, the following section introduces the concept of L3 – a language or language variety, other than the prevalent one, that may appear in a (audiovisual) text – and language coincidence, as well as transfer options in translating heterolingual texts. The subsequent section presents the source texts and fragments of dialogue alongside the corresponding TT remarks. The succeeding section resumes the results and discusses them, comparing with further cases, while the last section provides a short conclusion.

The concept of L3 and language coincidence

The concept of L3 was proposed by Corrius and Zabalbeascoa (2011) and is an attempt to define a finer point from the traditional assumption of L1 being the language of the ST and L2 being the language of its corresponding target text (TT). Interlingual translation, or "translation proper" as Roman Jakobson (1959:232) calls it, supposedly happens between L1 and L2 and assumes that both ST and TT are each in a different language and that they both have only one language, preferably of a standard variety (high register as, e.g., in canonical texts). Within this concept, non-verbal and paralinguistic items are only considered contextual features. Grutman poises, for the translation of heterolingual literature, "a theory of translation cannot limit itself to the most common or plausible scenarios" (2006:17) if we really can assume that a purely unilingual text can be regarded as common. L3 allows for all possible language combinations and scenarios. In this paper, the following abbreviations will be used:

Abbreviation	Definition
L1	The predominant language of a source text (ST), for this case study L1 is English
L2	The predominant language of a target text (TT), for this case study L2 is German
L3	A "distinct, independent language or an instance of relevant language variation, sufficient to signal more than one identifiable speech community being portrayed or represented within a text" (Corrius and Zabalbeascoa 2011:115)
$L3^{ST}$	A further language in a source text (ST), which is not L1, for this case study $L3^{ST}$ is German (and in one case there is a second $L3^{ST}$, which is Spanish)
$L3^{TT}$	A further language in a target text (TT), which is not L2

Challenges arise when (one of) the L3(s) of a source text coincides with L2 ($L3^{ST}$=L2), which is the focus of this paper. This language coincidence is described by Zabalbeascoa and Corrius (2012) for the case of *Butch Cassidy and the Sundance Kid* (Hill 1969) and its Spanish dubbed version, as well as by Labate (2012) in a paper on the translation of French scenes in *Close Encounters of the Third Kind* (Spielberg 1977) into French, and Voellmer (2012) for the translation of German scenes in *Inglourious Basterds* (Tarantino 2009) into German. Case studies in audiovisual translation show that there are different solutions for the $L3^{ST}$=L2 scenario and they seem to be linked to national dubbing traditions, some sort of translation norm. Parini (2009) and Ferrari (2010) show, for example, that in Italian dubbing, there seems to be a tendency to adapting $L3^{ST}$ to a regional variety. Thus, when a ST includes an Italian character speaking Italian or some other representation of the Italian language, such as an Italian accent, this is often adapted to Sicilian, Sardinian, Neapolitan or other diatopic varieties. This is not only the case for a $L3^{ST}$=L2 coincidence. It is also apparent for different $L3^{ST}$ that are not Italian but varieties of L1 (mainly English). In German dubbed versions it seems that rather than the L3 the dialogue is adapted and the communicative situation changed, so the communicative problem, if, for example, the character of an interpreter is present, disappears. Nevertheless, this has mainly been shown for movies in which $L3^{ST}$-German is a component of intended realism, i.e. when a movie takes place in Berlin, the inhabitants should logically speak German (Zabalbeascoa and Voellmer 2014). The question posed in this research is thus: how $L3^{ST}$-German is adapted when there is no such situation as intended realism, when the series or episode is not set in Germany but rather German characters or their language are used to create comic effect.

L3 variables in the analysis of ST and TT and transfer options for L3

This subsection and the one that follows are drawn from Zabalbeascoa (2012:327-328), in what he calls variables for L3, further illustrated with examples and case studies in Zabalbeascoa and Voellmer (2014). When analysing L3 in a ST and its corresponding TT, it might be important to pose the following questions: Is L3 made-up or real? Is L3 coincidentally the same language as L2? How exotic or familiar is L3 for the intended audience? Is the L3 message comprehensible and is the language identifiable? Are the words in L3 meant to communicate information? Is L3 spoken or is it just talked about/hinted at in another way without being present?

If L3 is a made-up invented language by the writer, it can be strongly L1-based or weakly L1-based (to be imagined on a continuum), which influences comprehensibility. If L3 is a real language, it can be a real/faithful presentation of an existing language (e.g., French, Russian, Polish) or a language that existed in the past (e.g. Latin), or it can be a parody, and/or a pseudo-language.

L3 can coincide with L2 ($L3^{ST}$=L2), as mentioned before, or not ($L3^{ST}$≠L2). There are different transfer options for both cases, explained below.

L3 can sound rather exotic or more familiar to an intended audience. This degree of familiarity, also to be imagined on a continuum, can vary greatly between ST audience and TT audience and is certainly of interest for the translator. In addition, it is strongly connected to comprehensibility and communicative content.

Comprehensibility of L3 is a very important variable in L3 analysis. L3 may only appear in short utterances, such as military orders or announcements at a train station, and may be comprehensible due to the visuals, context or the general knowledge of the audience. L3 can also appear in more complex and probably longer conversations and therefore not be comprehensible (unless one is dealing with a bi- or plurilingual audience). L3 can then be identifiable by the audience because of greater familiarity of a certain linguistic landscape, through explicit naming of the language by characters or a narrator, or it cannot be identifiable because it is too unfamiliar or too similar to another related language, for example, certain Scandinavian languages or Slavic languages for a Spanish, French or German audience.

When L3 communicates information or content, a translation can be provided diegetically (by a third person, e.g., the character of an interpreter) or non-diegetically (e.g., subtitles). If L3 carries no real information, such as in short orders or announcements as mentioned above, no translation is required as the messages do not need to be completely understood and their meaning can be inferred. Nevertheless, a translation can be provided and even be used as a means of misleading the audience into believing something is happening on the screen that is not actually the case.

L3 can be clearly visible and noticeable or just hinted at. Diastratic, diaphasic and diatopic variations are usually hardly distinguishable from the main language of a text (some more than others), similar to instances of conspicuous pronunciation as compensation strategy. L3 can be only referenced through hints, indirectly represented through different strategies, such as linguistic (e.g., vocabulary), paralinguistic (e.g., voice pitch) and non-verbal strategies (e.g., costume or mannerisms).

Transfer options for $L3^{TT}$

Presumably influenced by the variables presented above, there are different transfer options for $L3^{TT}$. A principal distinction into four transfer options can be made: (1) $L3^{TT}$=L2; (2) $L3^{TT}$=L1; (3) $L3^{TT}$=$L3^{ST}$; and (4) $L3^{TT}$=any other language.

(1) If $L3^{TT}$ and L2 are the same, there are several options: (a) ST language variation became invisible by either leaving $L3^{ST}$ unchanged (if $L3^{ST}$=$L3^{TT}$=L2), by translating it into L2, or by deleting the $L3^{ST}$ segments; (b) some degree of awareness of language variation by compensation within L2, for example, conspicuous pronunciation, accents or vocabulary; (c) signalling that a character has a certain ethnic profile or nationality by compensation within L2, regardless of the language spoken by them in the ST. (a) and (b) are cases of *neutralisation*.

(2) If $L3^{TT}$ and L1 are the same, given that L1 and L2 are different, L1 is used as $L3^{TT}$. This would be a case of *adaptation* and, although highly unlikely, has been observed (see Valdeón 2005).

(3) If $L3^{TT}$ is $L3^{ST}$ there are several options: (a) it is a verbatim transcription, or different words in the same L3 are used. Features of L3 change with the L1 to L2 change of scenarios and are important to take into account, for example, different prejudices and stereotypes of the new audience with a different mother tongue and possible command of other languages. The L1-$L3^{ST}$ intratextual relationships and connotations may differ from L2-$L3^{TT}$. Another option is a (b) conveyed accent, stronger or weaker, but recognisable. For example, one whose mother tongue is Spanish can speak English with a non-native accent and this may be conveyed in German dubbing as German with a Spanish accent. (a) and (b) are both cases of *transfer unchanged.*

(4) $L3^{TT}$ is any other language. This would also be a case of *adaptation.* Important to take into account are the connotations by the ST audience with $L3^{ST}$ and possible connotations by the TT audience with a different L3.

Indubitably, other factors may influence decisions for L3 transfer such as ideological constraints (including prejudice) of the translator and/or the audience that cannot be taken into account in a formal approach. The focus of such an analysis using the L3 variables and $L3^{TT}$ transfer options is solely on the textual result, not on the process or motivations behind the TT solutions provided. The obtained data can, however, be perfectly used as a basis for further investigation, looking at precisely these extratextual factors and influences.

In this paper, I look at some heterolingual scenes from episodes taken from two US sitcoms, namely *Frasier* and *Scrubs* (Lawrence 2001-2010), and their corresponding dubbed fragments in German. I will briefly compare my findings with excerpts from *How I Met Your Mother* (henceforth *HIMYM*) (Bays and Craig 2005-ongoing) and *The Big Bang Theory* (henceforth *BBT*) (Lorre and Prady 2007-ongoing) in which Germans or the German language is thematised. I chose these series because they evidence different instances of the use of native and non-native German, with the main objective of provoking laughter through different means. I look at several series in order to make a statement on possible tendencies.

The goal of this research is to see if the predominant use of *transfer unchanged* of L3 German for cases of language coincidence in movies with intended linguistic realism and other L3 functions (Zabalbeascoa and Voellmer 2014) apply for the function of comedy too. The list of transfer options elaborated above will therefore be applied to the findings and results discussed in the conclusion, mentioning important factors in L3 dubbing.

L3-German in US sitcoms

Frasier

After a divorce from his wife, psychiatrist Dr. Frasier Crane returns to his hometown of Seattle where he starts to work as the host of the *Dr. Frasier Crane Show* on talk radio station *KACL*. Frasier has to take care of his father, a former police detective who was injured during a robbery. He has a younger brother, Niles, who also works as a psychiatrist and frequently visits the two. One of the recurring themes of the series is based around the problems of Niles' marriage and its eventual breakdown. His (ex)wife Maris is never seen in the series, an aspect used as one of the running gags in the show.

In *An Affair to forget*, episode twenty-one of season two, Frasier receives a call on air by a woman called Gretchen who talks with a slight German accent mixed with a medley of some stereotypical German or German-sounding words. She is concerned that her husband, a fencing instructor, is having an affair with a new client. Later, Frasier learns from Niles that Maris has taken up fencing, with a German fencing instructor called Gunnar. Frasier is convinced that his brother's wife is having an affair. The situation culminates when Niles storms off to talk to Gunnar, which results in one of the most popular moments of the show: a three-way interpreting scene between Marta (Niles' and Maris' Guatemalan maid who speaks a little bit of German), Frasier (who speaks a little bit of Spanish) and the two monolingual "opponents" Niles and Gunnar.

German as a native language

Both Gretchen and Gunnar are native speakers of German. Whereas Gretchen, besides borrowing two (for an American audience) stereotypical expressions and using a made-up German compound, speaks English, Gunnar can only communicate with Niles using two interpreters (Marta, who speaks Spanish and German, and Frasier, who speaks English and

Spanish). This culminates in an awkward but hilarious conversation between the four of them, riddled with many misunderstandings and misinterpretations, as seen in (1). Niles wants to discuss the situation with Gunnar and tells him to stay away from his wife. Gunnar does not understand what he is saying, so Marta and Frasier are trying to help.

(1) GUNNAR: [to Marta] *Wieso ist er so böse?*

'Why is he so mad?'

MARTA: *Ich weiß nicht.*

'I don't know.'

NILES: *Marta! You speak German?*

MARTA: *¿Qué?*

'What?'

FRASIER: *Uh, ¿habla alemán?*

MARTA: *Sí, yo trabajo para una familia alemana que llegó a Guatemala después de la Guerra.*

FRASIER: *Apparently she worked for a German family that turned up in Guatemala...* [deep voice] *just after the war.*

English as a native language, the main language of the source text (L1), is rendered as native German – the main language of the TT (L2). This is certainly the standard transfer in dubbing. German as a native language ($L3^{ST}$-German) spoken by Gunnar is rendered as Danish ($L3^{TT}$-Danish), as seen in (2).

(2) GUNNAR: [to Marta] *Hvorfor er han så vred?*

'Why is he so mad?'

MARTA: *Det ved jeg ikke.*

'I don't know.'

NILES: *Marta! Sie sprechen Dänisch?*

'Marta, you speak Danish?'

MARTA: *¿Qué?*

'What?'

FRASIER: *Äh... ¿habla danmarca* [sic]*?*

MARTA: *Sí, yo trabajo para una familia dinamarquesa que cultiva cáñamo en Guatemala.*

FRASIER: *Marta hat für einen dänischen Einwanderer gearbeitet, der in Guatemala* [deep voice] *Hanf angebaut hat.*

'Marta worked for a Danish immigrant who cultivated hemp in Guatemala.'

German as a foreign language

Marta is the only person who speaks German as a foreign language, but she seems to have problems with the pronouns, which is thematised twice in the episode. This leads to a fatal misunderstanding at the end when Niles has left the scene to see Maris and Frasier tells Gunnar that his wife Gretchen loves him. Both in L3ST-German as well as in L3^{TT}-Danish, Marta has a foreign (not necessarily Spanish or Latin) accent to more or less the same degree. Since her pronoun problem is thematised and the key sentence of (3) can be rendered accordingly into Danish (4), it does not pose a challenge for the translator.

(3) GUNNAR: [looking up] *Gretchen?*

FRASIER: *Ja, ja, uh...* [to Marta] *Tell him that his wife loves him very much. Uh, I mean, diga a Gunnar que su esposa le ama mucho.*

MARTA: *Dein* [sic] *Frau* [points at Frasier] *liebt ihn sehr.*

'Your wife loves him very much.'

[Frasier smiles. Gunnar draws his sword.]

GUNNAR: Schweinehund!

'Bastard!'

FRASIER: *No, no, not me! You, you! Marta, damn your pronoun problems! All right, then, you hapless wretch!*

[Frasier grabs the other sword and starts to fight.]

(4) GUNNAR: *Greta?*

FRASIER: *Ja ja, ähm... Sagen Sie ihm, dass seine Frau ihn sehr liebt. Ich meine, diga a Gunnar, que su esposa le ama mucho.*

MARTA: *Din kone elsker ham meget.*

GUNNAR: *Svinehund!*

> FRASIER: *Nein, nein, nicht mich! Sie, Sie! Marta, ihre verdammten Probleme mit den Pronomen! Na dann, wie du willst, du Fischkopf!*[2]
>
> 'No, no, not me! You, you! Marta, damn your pronoun problems! All right, then, you fish head [lit.]!'

English as a foreign language

For both Gunnar and Gretchen, English is a foreign language. Gunnar does not speak or understand a word, while Gretchen has a good level of English which she speaks with a German accent. Gretchen's German accent is mainly rendered through grammatical inaccuracy, although she does not commit any grammatical errors in English in the ST. In the TT, the accent is rendered through incorrect gender use in German, for example, in "Ich hab das [sic] Rat von Roz befolgt" ['I took Roz's advice'], "das [sic] Teller" ['the plate'] and "das [sic] Liebesbrief" ['love letter'], as well as morphosyntactic incorrectness "Ich hab' […] meinem Mann zwei verschiedenen [sic] Essen hingestellt" ['I […] gave my husband two choices for dinner']. Greta, as she is called in the German dubbed version, also speaks with a Danish accent mainly mispronouncing 'sch' [ʃ] as 's' [z].

Cultural references and stereotypes

Gretchen and Gunnar are stereotyped by different means. Gretchen, who is never seen on the screen and only has her voice heard over the phone, is linguistically stereotyped, while Gunnar is both linguistically and visually stereotyped. Gretchen uses borrowings or German-sounding expressions such as *bumsen* [to hump], the aforementioned non-existent compound *Nichteinmenschlichfrau*, and realia such as *Leberknödel* [liver dumplings]. Niles calls Gunnar "strudel boy", which becomes "Knäckeboy" [crisp bread boy] in the TT, since the word "boy" is perfectly understandable for a German audience and crisp bread a well-known and stereotypical food that is associated with Scandinavian countries. When Frasier refers to Gunnar as "this man", telling Niles that he "can't possibly fight this man", a cultural reference is introduced in the German dubbed version, namely "diesen Wikinger" [this viking]. Gretchen borrows the rather vulgar expression *bumsen* [to hump], which is actually understood by many Americans and, if

---

2 *Fischkopf* or *Fischkopp* [lit. fish head] is used as an insult to the Northern Germans living by the coast. Their mentality and sense of humour is considered as different from the rest of Germany. Since Denmark is close and shares the coast, the expression is easily applicable to the Danish too.

not, its meaning is easily deduced from the context it is used. It is rendered as *rømmeln* (6), a non-existent Danish word that uses stereotypical Danish sounds (for a German audience) and shows a resemblance to the word *rammeln*, a German synonym for *bumsen*. Danish and the Danish foreign accent are usually seen by Germans (and likewise represented in fiction) as including many umlauted o's [œ] – the Dano-Norwegian "ø" – and, as happens with Greta's foreign accent, leads to mispronouncing the German *sch-Laut* [ʃ], using a voiced s [z] instead.

The image of the German language as harsh and cold is thematised when Martin asks if Maris is learning the language: "[She] is learning German, huh? Just when you thought she couldn't get any cuddlier". This sarcastic utterance is weakened and generalised in the dubbed version. Martin's utterance is consequently rendered "Und da denkst du, dass sie einem nicht mehr überraschen kann" [Just when you thought she couldn't surprise you anymore].

The reference to the German family coming to Guatemala (1) right after the war is translated as a reference to a Danish immigrant cultivating hemp (2) in Guatemala, possibly hinting at the fact that cannabis is more tolerated in Denmark than in any other Scandinavian country. It is well known among German citizens that cannabis can be purchased in some underground nightclubs in Copenhagen as well as openly in Freetown Christiania for its citizens, and thus creates a certain Danish and typical Denmark traveller stereotype.

German as L3 is adapted to Danish in order to maintain the comic effect. References are changed accordingly. The German as a foreign accent in English is reflected as a Danish accent in German but also compensated for on a grammatical level.

Scrubs

John Dorian "J.D." and his friends work as medical assistants and aspiring physicians at the fictional hospital *Sacred Heart*. The series follows their professional and private lives, featuring slapstick and surreal vignettes, often accompanied by music and mostly depicted as daydreams of the central character J.D. The screenplay is fast-paced and as a consequence some references are hard to catch, even for native speakers. The series frequently includes dialogues in languages other than English. The Dominican nurse often speaks in Spanish and Elliot, one of the interns and J.D.'s on-and-off girlfriend, speaks German in a few episodes.

In *My Interpretation*, episode twenty of season two, J.D. is treating a German patient, Rolf Mueller, and struggles with informing him that he may be suffering as a result of pancreatic cancer. Rolfs' brother Hermann acts as an interpreter but, as later turns out, withholds information from his brother in the process. Elliot, who speaks German fluently, helps J.D. out, eventually clearing up the confusion.

English as a foreign language

Hermann is the only person to speak English as a foreign language and since his brother does not understand a word, he needs Hermann to translate for him. Interestingly, the actor's German is non-native and is hardly understood from a German perspective. This is probably not noticed by the ST audience, unless they are bi- or plurilingual (which, throughout the States is plausible, but the vast majority would not notice it). A key scene for the episode is when J.D. tells Rolf that his prognosis does not look good and his brother tells him that everything is going to be fine. English as a foreign language is rendered as German as a foreign language with a Danish accent in the way described for *Frasier* above.

German as a second language

Elliot speaks German as a second, near native language and actually better than at least one of the actors that is supposed to be German, if not both. When she tells J.D. that she speaks German (5), she says two sentences filled with stereotypes (milkmaid and *Schnitzel*).

(5) ELLIOT: *Hey! I just met your patient, Mr. Mueller; we had such a nice chat.*

J.D.: *You speak German?*

ELLIOT: *Yeah! I can do a sweet little milkmaid: "Guten Morgen, möchten Sie die Kühe melken?"* ['Good morning, do you want to milk the cows?'] *I can do an evil old Hausfrau: "Iss dein Schnitzel auf, sonst kriegst du keinen Nachtisch!"* ['Eat your Schnitzel, or you won't get dessert!']

J.D.: *German is such a beautiful language ... Anyway, I think Mr. Mueller is so amazing. I mean, yesterday, I pretty much told him he was gonna die and his brother turned to him and he said, "Es wird alles wieder gut" and*

Mr. Mueller just accepted it.

ELLIOT: *Well, why wouldn't he? "Es wird alles wieder gut" means "You're going to be fine".*

J.D.: *Germans!*

Elliot's German is rendered as native or second language Danish, without a noticeable accent. The sentences are rendered accordingly and no reference is changed to the Danish language or culture ("Godmorgen. Vil du gerne malke køerne?" and "Spis din Schnitzel, ellers får du ingen dessert!"). The only change occurs when J.D. says "Germans!" which is rendered "Die spinnen doch!" [They are crazy!].

Cultural references and stereotypes

As is the case in Frasier, this Scrubs episode is also full of references and stereotypes, for example, the German language being regarded as harsh, shown by Elliot almost screaming two sentences (5) in German and J.D. commenting on it. J.D. calls Rolf's brother Hermann "Hermann the German" (6) which is a very stereotypical and often used name for Germans in American shows, also being used for a character in the film *Death Race 2000* (Bartel 1975) and for the album *Herman ze German* by the Scorpions drummer Herman Rarebell, as well as for other personalities and cultural products.

(6) HERMANN: *Hey, you must be Dr. Dorian. I am -uh- Rolf's brother, Hermann.*

J.D.: *Hermann the German! You must get that all the time!*

HERMANN: *No, first time.*

J.D.'s nickname for Hermann is rendered as *Erik der Wikinger* [Eric the Viking] in the dubbed version and makes use of the stereotypical Scandinavian image. The brothers' typical family name Müller/Mueller is changed into the typical Danish name Olsen.

The translator's job becomes more difficult when the cultural reference is purely or partly visual and can thus not or hardly be modified. When J.D. is desperate because he cannot speak German and says how much he wishes to "communicate with [Rolf]", one of his daydream sequences sets in. He is in a room full of red balloons dancing with Rolf to *Nena*'s song *99 Red Balloons*. One could choose a different song in the dubbed version that would make the red balloons lose their intended meaning, perhaps being perceived as being part of a decoration of a dancing party. This would probably not come with a gain in comedy or anything else, unless the song makes perfect sense within the TT and the target culture. In the actual translation, the song is not changed and there is no explanation, except J.D.'s comment after the sequence finishes. His comment in the ST ("Probably won't work") is rendered as "*Dänen lügen nicht* wäre besser" [Danes don't lie would be better], which refers to a song by a German comedian. Discrepancies like these are often not noticed as problematic by the target audiences, if noticed at all. They are accepted as a "by-product" of the more comfortable modality of dubbing. The audience knows that they are watching a US sitcom and they know that the actors are not actually speaking German.

Here again, L3-German is adapted to Danish in order to maintain the comic effect. References to the German culture are not necessarily adapted (e.g., Elliot's typical sentences) and visual references to the ST L3 are briefly commented on in order to hint at the Danish culture.

The Big Bang Theory and *How I Met Your Mother*

BBT is a television comedy about the life of two brilliant but strange and socially awkward physicians Sheldon Cooper and Leonard Hofstadter and their equally awkward friends and co-workers. Their strangeness is combined with the common sense and down to earth personality of waitress Penny, who moves in next door and eventually falls in love with Leonard.

A first reference to the German language is made in the first season, episode eleven, *The Pancake Batter Anomaly* (2008), when Sheldon is ill and his friends leave him alone because they cannot stand him being more demanding than usual. When Penny takes him home and takes care of him, she asks if he has never been ill before (9).

(7) SHELDON: *Well, once. When I was fifteen, and spending the summer at the Heidelberg Institute in Germany. […] Anyway, the housekeeper in the faculty residence didn't speak any English, when I finally managed to convince her I was sick, she said "Möchtest Du eine Darmspülung?"*

PENNY: *What does that mean?*

SHELDON: *Based on what happened next, I assume it means "would you like an enema?"*

Sheldon's remark is rendered in *Badisch* dialect, the dialect of the South Western region of Baden. It also uses a more colloquial expression for *Darmspülung* [enema], namely *Einlauf*. Combined with the different pronunciation, this sentence is probably easier to understand by Germans from the region of Baden and more complicated for Germans from other parts of the country. Sheldon's explanation of what happens afterwards is therefore necessary, both in the ST and the TT.

In episode fourteen of season five, *The Beta Test Initiation*, when Sheldon records a clip for his *YouTube* series *Fun With Flags* presenting the Bavarian flag, he wears *Lederhosen* and his girlfriend Amy a pretzel costume. They anchor the introduction to his show in German. Due to this visual restriction, L3ST-German is rendered as Bavarian in the dubbed version.

HIMYM is a television comedy about Ted and his friends in Manhattan. In the first episode of season eight, *Farhampton*, the secondary character Klaus rushes away from his wedding and in the process runs into Ted at the nearby train station. They start talking about love and fate. Besides some native German utterances by Klaus (8), the German language is stereotyped by forming non-existing overly long compounds that are understood by German speakers but noticeably a little bit over the top. To native English speakers these words may sound typical German. The two words that are most used are *Lebenslangerschicksalsschatz* [lifelong treasure of destiny] and *Beinaheleidenschaftsgegenstand* [almost object of passion].

(8) KLAUS: *Ach, okay, Victoria is wunderbar. I'm sorry,* wunderbar *is the German word for wonderful.*

TED: *Yeah, no, I know.*

KLAUS: *Oh, you speak German? Sie sprechen Deutsch?! Ich habe keine Freunde, die Deutsch sprechen in Amerika! Das macht mich so einsam, so einsam!*

'You speak German? I have no friends in America that speak German. It makes me so lonesome, so lonesome!'

TED: *No... No, no, no... No, just-just-just the one word.*

The native German utterances are rendered in Saxonian dialect and the fictitious compounds are rendered as "Lebensschicksalsschatz" [life's treasure of destiny] and "Beinahe-Ein und Alles" [almost one and only]. They are toned down and made more realistic, as the compounds in the ST are too exaggerated and could be perceived as highly ridiculous by the target audience. A different language might have been opted for; Klaus could have been, if considering what seems to be some sort of norm, Erik from Denmark or maybe Ole from Sweden. However, in an earlier season, when Ted meets Victoria, she tells him that she is going to live in Germany for a while. By that time, the dubbing studio probably had no idea that a German character would eventually appear in the series and rendered accordingly. In order not to be incongruent, Klaus had to be German in the dubbed version, too. Klaus' sister is depicted as a tall and strong woman who competes as a ringer, a typical prejudice and stereotype of German women in US film and television, as exemplified in *Top Secret!* (Abrahams, Zucker and Zucker 1984), where a women's sports team of the German Democratic Republic is portrayed by an all-male cast.

In these two series, L3-German plays a less important role, at least quantitatively. The joke rests more on a linguistic misunderstanding or a linguistic mocking than a general depiction of Germans throughout the episode. L3-German is adapted to regional varieties in order to maintain the linguistic difference and (the success of it is, by all means, debatable) the comic effect.

Discussion of the results

The examples above show that Danish seems to be a frequent solution in the German dubbing of US television comedy when L3ST and L2 coincide (*Frasier*, *Scrubs*). When comedy is purely based on a linguistic joke – a couple of words that might or are supposed to be (partly) understood and sound funny or ambiguous – the preferred solution seems to be the use of a regiolect (*BBT*, *HIMYM*). However, all cases in which a regiolect has been used have narrative or visual restrictions which complicate the use of any other language and culture than German – except *BBT* 1 (11), where theoretically the script could have been adapted to refer to any other university or country. Another conspicuous correlation is that wherever regiolects are used, the instances of L3ST-German are rather short. The use of a regiolect in German dubbing throughout an episode or even the entire series might be unnatural for a target audience or become somewhat ridiculous in the case where they are used to hearing High German on screen.

Looking at further series, Danish is also the preferred solution for the dubbing translators of *Malcolm in the Middle* (Boomer 2000-2006), where

Otto and Gretchen in season four and five become Danish in the dubbed version (their names, however, are not changed). French is used for the German dubbing of *Lust in Translation*, episode ten of the second season of the series *Better Off Ted* (Fresco 2009-2010), in which the research department of a fictional company invents a translating machine that allows speech into a mouthpiece in one language and subsequently its translation can be heard out of a loudspeaker in another language. The company's boss uses the invention in order to date a German business partner. In *King of Queens* (Litt and Weithorn 1998-2007), season five of episode twenty-one, when Doug wants to return a pair of shoes for his wife and the saleswoman starts talking German with her colleague, the German dubbed version shows $L3^{ST}$-German rendered as $L3^{TT}$-Turkish.

Series	Season and Episode	L1	$L3^{ST}$	L2	$L3^{TT}$	Transfer option
BBT	1 (11)	English	German	German	Badisch	adaptation
	5 (14)	English	German	German	Bavarian	adaptation
BoT	2 (10)	English	German	German	French	adaptation
Frasier	2 (21)	English	German	German	Danish	adaptation
HIMYM	8 (1)	English	German	German	Saxonian	adaptation
KoQ	5 (21)	English	German	German	Turkish	adaptation
MitM	4	English	German	German	Danish	adaptation
Scrubs	2 (20)	English	German	German	Danish	adaptation

BBT: The Big Bang Theory
BoT: Better off Ted
HIMYM: How I Met your Mother
KoQ: King of Queens
MitM: Malcolm in the Middle

Table 1: Overview of L3 transfers in the selected series

The overview of the analysed material in table 1 above shows that *adaptation* is a popular transfer option for when $L3^{ST}$ has a comic function as opposed to *transfer unchanged* for other functions of L3, such as intended realism (Zabalbeascoa and Voellmer 2014).

Conclusions

Both on a theoretical and a practical level, it is crucial to take into account features that Zabalbeascoa (2012) calls L3 variables, as they may be important restrictions imposed by the ST (besides the visual and narrative ones mentioned). For the case of language coincidence, the key variables to look at are *visibility* (how visible is L3ST within the ST? Can it be easily recognised?), *familiarity* (how familiar is the ST audience with L3ST?), and *information content* (what information is communicated in L3ST?). I would like to add *quantity/frequency* to this list as well as *joke-type* as a specific variable for the context of television comedy (Zabalbeascoa 2005:189-196). Usually, jokes have some sort of victim or target (ibid.:193), like individuals, groups, authorities, institutions, habits, beliefs, etc. When heterolingualism is used in comedy, the typical situation is the "other" person represents the victim, or the language and culture that they represent. Indeed, it can also be the L1 culture, for example, if a character as representative of the source culture is not able to memorise a single word of a foreign language. In the usual case of the "other" being mocked, it can be distinguished between two basic "subtargets": (1) the image and stereotype of the person (as representative of a certain ethnic group), their habits, beliefs, the way they behave, how they say something (tone that makes the audience deduce certain characteristics, e.g., nasal tone for arrogance), or what they say (content); and (2) the language of the ethnic group of the character itself (prosody, phonetics), for example, the excessive use of certain features of a language like the non-existing but impressively long and harsh-sounding compounds found in *HIMYM* for the case of German.

As this particular study regards, as mentioned before, the preferred solution in the German dubbing of US sitcoms seems to be to adapt L3 in order to maintain the comic effect. This can be strived for through adapting to a different standard or a regional variety. Accents and peculiarities of speech can be and are often adapted to an accent of the standard variety. L3-German is adapted with some form of compensation on a grammatical, lexical or phonetical level – or all three. In my regard, it is worthwhile looking at further examples of this particular case of L3 for different texts, as well as other L3 and their corresponding cases of language coincidence in translation.

References

Bleichenbacher, Lukas (2008) *Multilingualism in the Movies: Hollywood Characters and their Language Choices.* Tübingen: Francke.

Corrius, Montse (2008) *Translating Multilingual Audiovisual Texts: Priorities and Restrictions, Implications and Applications.* Barcelona: Universitat Autònoma de Barcelona: PhD Dissertation.

Corrius, Montse/Zabalbeascoa, Patrick (2011) "Language Variation in Source Texts and their Translations: The Case of L3 in Film Translation". *Target* 23:1, 113-130.

Ferrari, Chiara Francesca (2010) *Since When is Fran Drescher Jewish? Dubbing Stereotypes in the Nanny, the Simpsons, and the Sopranos.* Austin: University of Texas Press.

Grutman, Rainier (2006) "Refraction and Recognition: Literary Multilingualism in Translation". *Target* 18:1, 17-47.

Jakobson, Roman (1959) "On Linguistic Aspects of Translation". In Brower, Reuben A. (ed.) *On Translation.* Cambridge: Harvard University Press, 232-239.

Labate, Simon (2012) "Translating French into French: The Case of Close Encounters of the Third Kind". Paper presented at the conference *The Translation and Reception of Multilingual Films/La traduction et réception de films multilingues*, 3 June 2012. France: Université Montpellier.

O'Sullivan, Carol (2007) "Multilingualism at the Multiplex: A New Audience for Screen Translation?". *Linguistica Antverpiensia* 6, 153-166.

O'Sullivan, Carol (2011) *Translating Popular Film.* Basingstoke: Palgrave Macmillan.

Parini, Ilaria (2009) "The Changing Face of Audiovisual Translation in Italy". In Kemble, Ian (ed.) *The Changing Face of Translation.* Portsmouth: University of Portsmouth, 19-27.

Sternberg, Meir (1981) "Polylingualism as Reality and Translation as Mimesis". *Poetics Today* 2:4, 221-239.

Valdeón, Roberto A. (2005) "Asymmetric Representations of Languages in Contact: Uses and Translations of French and Spanish in Frasier". *Linguistica Antverpiensia* 4, 279-294.

Voellmer, Elena (2012) *Excuse me, but your Accent is Very Unusual. The Complexity of Establishing Third Languages in* Inglourious Basterds. Barcelona: Universitat Pompeu Fabra, MA Dissertation.

Zabalbeascoa, Patrick (2005) "Humor and Translation, an Interdiscipline". *Humor* 18:2, 185-207.

Zabalbeascoa, Patrick (2012) "Translating Heterolingual Audiovisual Humor: Beyond the Blinkers of Traditional Thinking". In Muñoz-Basols, Javier et al. (eds.) *The Limits of Literary Translation: Expanding Frontiers in Iberian Languages.* Kassel: Reichenberger, 317-338.

Zabalbeascoa, Patrick/Corrius, Montse (2012) "How Spanish in an American Film is Rendered in Translation: Dubbing Butch Cassidy and the Sundance Kid in Spain". *Perspectives* 22:2, 1-16.

Zabalbeascoa, Patrick/Voellmer, Elena (2014) "Accounting for Multilingual Films in Translation Studies: Intratextual Translation in Dubbing". In Abend-David, Dror (ed.) *Media and Translation: An Interdisciplinary Approach*. New York: Bloomsbury Academic, 25-52.

Audiovisual References

Abrahams, Jim/Zucker, David/Zucker, Jerry (1984) *Top Secret!*. Los Angeles, CA: Paramount Pictures/Kingsmere Properties.

Angell, David L./Casey, Peter/Lee, David (1993-2004) *Frasier*. Los Angeles, CA: Paramount Network Television.

Bartel, Paul (1975) *Death Race 2000*. Atlanta, GA: New World Pictures.

Bays, Carter F./Craig, Thomas (2005-ongoing) *How I Met Your Mother*. Los Angeles, CA: 20th Century Fox Television.

Boomer, Linwood (2000-2006) *Malcolm in the Middle*. Los Angeles, CA: Regency Television.

Fresco, Victor (2009-2010) *Better Off Ted*. Los Angeles, CA: 20th Century Fox Television.

Hill, George R. (1969) *Butch Cassidy and the Sundance Kid*. Los Angeles, CA: 20th Century Fox.

Lawrence, Bill (2001-2010) *Scrubs*. Burbank, CA: Doozer/ABC Studios.

Litt, David/Weithorn, Michael J. (1998-2007) *King of Queens*. Los Angeles, CA: CBS Productions.

Lorre, Chuck/Prady, Bill (2007-ongoing) *Big Bang Theory*. Burbank, CA: Warner Bros. Television.

Spielberg, Steven (1977) *Close Encounters of the Third Kind*. Culver City, CA: Columbia Pictures.

Tarantino, Quentin (2009) *Inglourious Basterds*. New York: The Weinstein Company

ZANE VEIDENBERGA

Ekonomikas un Kultūras Augstskola/Ventspils Augstskola, Latvia

Transfer of Implied Values of the Latvian Diminutives into Their English Language Counterparts

Latvian is replete with diminutives that express a spectrum of emotional connotations. This paper is part of on-going research into the English translations of Latvian literary texts, which aims to identify the patterns of transferring the implied values of the source text diminutives into their target text counterparts. The object of the research is represented by two anthologies of Latvian literature published in English – *Bear's Ears. An Anthology of Latvian Literature* (2003) and *Latvian Fiction. The Review of Contemporary Fiction* (1998). The results of contrastive and quantitative analysis have identified a negative tendency to lose more than a half (59%-78%) of the implied values of diminutives in target texts, the loss occurring mainly at the expense of emotional connotations.

Keywords: diminutive, implied value, diminutive formation types, translation, transfer

Introduction

In the Latvian language, diminutives are synthetically derived from nouns, adjectives, verbs and other word classes and are widely used to convey not only the objective denotation of smallness, but also affectionate and pejorative values ranging from endearment, love and joy, to pity, scorn or disdain (Rūķe-Draviņa 1959; Vulāne 2002). Latvian folklorist Janīna Kursīte[1] maintains that the extensive use of diminutives is rooted in the Latvian folklore. Thus, for a small nation to protect itself and co-exist with the others, it was essential to adopt a kind of sacral tactics in front of the *almighty* and the others. This was done by dividing the world into *ours* and *theirs*. Diminutives served this function to express love and endearment towards the *ours*, address the unknown and connote various nuances of positive and negative emotions and attitudes. A similar opinion is expressed by Anna Vulāne (2002:12) who claims that the derivative structures of

---

[1] See Iveta Aizpura's (1998) and Ieva Alberte's (2009) interviews with Janīna Kursīte.

lexemes have accommodated the ethical code of our ancestors – living in harmony with oneself and the surrounding world, and demonstrating awe, love and respect towards both the tiny and the grand.

Various dictionaries, including Latvian, English, German, etc. (Bußmann 2002; Brown 2006; Skujiņa et al. 2007 etc.) and researchers of the phenomenon of diminutives (among others, Rūķe-Draviņa 1959; Jurafsky 1993, 1996; Schneider 2003; Chamonikolasová and Rambousek 2007, Bagasheva-Koleva 2010), agree upon two main aspects the diminutives express: smallness (small size, dimension etc.) and emotional colouring (personal attitude or evaluation, e.g. endearment or some other positive evaluation, or derogatory attitude, e.g. scorn, disdain, etc.).

The aim of the present research is to identify the patterns in transfer of the implied values of the source diminutives into their target text counterparts. For this purpose, the translations of prose texts included in two anthologies of Latvian literature have been chosen to answer the research question: What means have translators used to transfer the meaning of smallness and/or emotional connotations expressed by diminutives in Latvian source texts to English target texts on word, collocation and sentence level?

Anna Wierzbicka (1992:3) suggests that "if language is a tool for expressing meaning, then meaning, at least to some extent, must be independent of language and transferable from one language to another". But the problem is to what extent the meaning can be transferred to another language and what role is played by culture differences or "to put it differently, to what extent languages are shaped by "human nature" and to what extent they are shaped by culture" (ibid.:7). In view of the fact that in Latvian the diminutive is a part of the lexical layer that conveys culture-specific information and thus reflects the Latvian world view (Vulāne 2002:12), and bearing in mind that English and Latvian represent different language types (analytical and synthetic respectively) with different traditions of using the diminutive, the translator, undoubtedly, faces a challenge to transfer the culture-bound implied values of diminutives from the Latvian source texts into English.

In Latvian, the use of diminutives is integral to a writer's individual style. As such, if the writer's style is defined as a "motivated choice" (Verdonk 2002:5) and "a distinctive way of using language for some purpose and to some effect" (ibid.), diminutives should be transferred to the target readers as, "awareness of style is essential for the understanding and appreciation of literary texts" (Načiščione 1996:30).

Intralinguistic variability of diminutives makes the interlinguistic and intercultural study of the same a challenge and problems related to this research:

> [A]t least in part, stem from the fact that "diminutive" is a category derived from traditional grammar, originally used in the description of Latin, with a typical mélange of structural and semantic aspects. Thus, as traditional definitions tend to be circular, and as it is neither clear what exactly diminutive formation is, nor what diminutive meaning is, diminutives pose a two-fold challenge. (Schneider 2013:137)

The problem mentioned above is topical for the Latvian-English language pair. In Latvian, the diminutive is a morphological category – a derivation (noun, adjective, verb etc.) formed by the addition of one or several suffixes (e.g., *-iņ-*, *-īt-*, *-uk-* etc.) expressing smallness (*mājiņa, celiņš*) and also positive (*mīlulītis, mammīte*) or negative (*amatnieķelis*) emotional connotations (Saule-Sleine 1955; Rūķe-Draviņa 1959; Skujiņa et.al. 2007). The above is chosen as the working definition of the diminutive for the present research, as diminutives will be considered in terms of their semantic and pragmatic component.

In the English language, diminutives are more an onomasiological than morphological category (Schneider and Strubel-Burgdorf 2012:15) and, according to Schneider (2003), they are marked by analytical and synthetic diminutive markers, i.e., two types of diminutive formation are used: the morphological (also called the synthetic) and syntactic (or analytical). The synthetic type includes prefixation (*minivan*), suffixation (*ringlet*), reduplication (*goody-goody*), compounding (*baby tree*) and truncation (e.g., diminutive forms of proper names *Billy, Kitty*), while adjectives like *little, tiny, petite* are listed as analytic diminutive markers (ibid.:73). The traditions of diminutive use in modern English are different from Latvian (Rūķe-Draviņa 1953:452). English is less replete with diminutives (Schneider and Strubel-Burgdorf 2012:15), therefore, to transfer not only the explicitly expressed information, but also the implied meaning (see Hatim 2001:181-182), translators should resort to various means of expression. To be able to do that, they should recognise the implications and the signals sent by the author of the source text.

As mentioned above, the present research focuses on the implied values of diminutives, but is challenged by a lack of, as Wierzbicka (1992) maintains, appropriate methodology for profound studies of the semantics of diminutives, especially when they are analysed within interlinguistic and intercultural context. The existent attempts to identify common tendencies in the semantics of the diminutive (e.g., Jurafsky 1993, 1996 etc.) still have to be elaborated and adapted for comparative analysis. Several researchers on the translation of diminutives into English (for example Chamonikolasová and Rambousek 2007; Al-Ghazalli 2012) focus more on the transfer of the denotative meaning of smallness than emotional connotations; hence centring more on formal and semantic studies.

Schneider (2013) suggests analysing not only the meaning of diminutives but also their function, thus specifying two components of diminutives, viz. semantic and pragmatic in his formal-functional model. In view of the interlinguistic perspective of the present research, the major interest is, undeniably, the communicative or social function of the diminutives, however, the semantic component is also considered.

Methodology of contrastive and quantitative analysis: a brief outline

The language material for analysis is excerpted from two collections or anthologies of Latvian literature published in English. *Bear's Ears. An Anthology of Latvian Literature* (henceforth – *Bear's Ears*) is intended "to create a representative picture of Latvian literature up to 1940" (Zauberga 2003a:14), while a literary journal *The Review of Contemporary Fiction: New Latvian Fiction* (henceforth – *New Latvian Fiction*) represents the Latvian short prose of the 1980s and 1990s (Dumbere 1998). Though the source texts of the two anthologies are created in different time periods – at the beginning and at the end of the twentieth century – their translations have been made at the very end of the twentieth and beginning of the twenty-first centuries.

For the purpose of analysis, the cases of diminutive use have been excerpted from the selected source texts, coded indicating whether they express smallness and/or any emotional connotation in the given context and entered into a MS Excel table. The functions of the source text diminutives have been grouped following the framework of categories set by

Latvian linguist Velta Rūķe-Draviņa[2] in *Diminutive im Lettischen* (1959), which includes 17 meanings and connotations of Latvian diminutives (smallness, love, endearment, scorn etc.).

Further, the respective target texts have been examined to excerpt the matching translation segments. The contrastive analysis helped to identify whether different translators of the two anthologies have successfully used morphological or syntactic means to transfer to the target language the meaning and/or emotional connotation expressed by the diminutive. The information obtained was entered into a MS Excel table for further data filtering and processing to achieve the aim of the present research.

At this stage of the research, all source text diminutives (nouns, verbs, adverbs etc.) have been included in the corpus for analysis, as the purpose is to identify general tendencies of rendering the meanings and connotations (i.e. the implied values) in translations, irrespective of the time the texts and translations have been created.

It should be noted that quantitative data analysis has been used in this research in order to identify the patterns, but it does not offer comprehensive findings. Quantitative data processing requires grouping data into fixed categories, which levels out the high variety of diminutive connotations and their context-dependency. Therefore, in future, quantitative data analysis has to be linked with an in-depth qualitative analysis.

Translations of Latvian prose texts for the purpose of the two anthologies

When discussing the specificity of translation, Theo Hermans (1996:12) claims that it "refers, expressly or tacitly, to an anterior discourse in another sign system which it claims to represent in one way or another". He maintains that "the systemic 'otherness' of the source is unlikely to be wiped out altogether in translation. Translated texts, we can say, always signal to textual models of at least two cultures" (ibid.:12). The usage of diminutives in Latvian is a way to express this "otherness" – the culture-specific values and perception of the world as well as attitudes towards it (Vulāne 2002:12)

---

[2] Velta Rūķe-Draviņa's research *Diminutive im Lettischen* (Diminutives in Latvian) (1959) is the most profound study of Latvian diminutives up to the present time. In later research and publications of other scholars, *Diminutive im Lettischen* has been used as a foundation or framework, by adding more detailed, descriptive or normative aspects.

that are rooted in the mythologies of the nation. The implied values of diminutives are bound with the national identity, as discussed above by Janīna Kursīte, therefore translators should raise their culture and language awareness to minimise the loss and transfer diminutives to other linguistic and cultural settings for the benefit of target readership.

Ieva Zauberga[3] (2003a:14), one of the compilers of the anthology *Bear's Ears*, claims that the anthology has quite an ambitious purpose: "This anthology is an attempt to give an insight into the historical evolution of Latvian literature [...] to create a representative picture of Latvian literature up to 1940". Some translations included in this anthology have been prepared earlier, while others were prepared specifically for this collection and still "all translations are fairly close ones, aimed at both recreating the atmosphere of the original texts and highlighting Latvian culture." (ibid.:14). As mentioned above, the Latvian language is replete with diminutives, the implied values of which are bound with the national identity, and thus it is worth analysing whether and how the implied values of diminutives in Latvian are transferred to the target setting.

New Latvian Fiction has a slightly different purpose – it contains contemporary short prose of modern Latvian writers, which is "stylistically diverse" (Ikstena 1998a:9), where "the authors use dreams and streams of consciousness to express themselves, often merging reality with the world of the irrational, the mundane with the metaphysical" (ibid.:9). All the translations have been made for the purpose of this publication. This collection introduces the reader to the patterns of short prose of the end of the twentieth century but largely ignores its historical context. Nora Ikstena,[4] a writer and the compiler of the anthology *New Latvian Fiction*, comments on this by stating that as U.S. Americans were interested in the New Latvian Fiction only, and not its context, the publishers were interested in the text itself, not in Latvia, hence, the history of the nation or its literature has been basically disregarded. At the same time she indicates that the editor of *The Review of Contemporary Fiction* journal has admitted that the sense of national identity and the expression of the Latvian view of the world within the

3 Ieva Zauberga is one of the leading Latvian translatologists interested in the impact of Europeanisation of Latvian on translation and lexicography processes and the role of conventions in cross-cultural communication (see Zauberga 2002).

4 See Laura Dumbere's (1998) interview with Nora Ikstena.

confines of modern times and stance are the most attractive features in the Latvian prose.

In a nutshell, the two anthologies differ in terms of historic perspective – *Bear's Ears* aims to offer an insight into the historical development of Latvian literature in the first half of the twentieth century, while *New Latvian Fiction* focuses on short prose of the end of the twentieth century as such, without its particular context. The common task of both anthologies is to familiarise their readers with the Latvian worldview as reflected in Latvian literature (Dumbere 1998), and diminutives, undeniably, are one of the definitive elements of this Latvianness.

Latvian diminutives and their implied values

The phenomenon of diminutiveness is interesting for research not only in Translation Studies, but also in linguistics, especially in contrastive linguistics. This is because different languages have different ways and means of expressing diminutiveness and an interlinguistic research may help in gaining an insight into the choices at the translator's disposal. In Latvian linguistics, the phenomenon of diminutives has mainly been studied within the framework of morphology (see e.g., Saule-Sleine 1955, Sokols 1959), but the main contribution to the research of the meanings conveyed by diminutives was paid by Velta Rūķe-Draviņa (1953, 1959). In *Diminutive im Lettischen* (1959) Rūķe-Draviņa lists 17 meanings and connotations of Latvian diminutives, emphasising that the implied values are revealed only in context. In Latvian diminutives can denote the meaning of small, little and young, convey the nuances of love, endearment, flattering undertone; connote enjoyment, pleasure, homage, humility, pity, compassion, derogatory attitude, irony etc. (ibid.:125-165).

In Latvian, the diminutive may often become the only marker of the speaker's attitude towards a person, character, event or phenomenon in a given context (Saule-Sleine 1955:90; Rūķe-Draviņa 1953:454; Rūķe-Draviņa 1959:120; Kvašytė 2012:250). The loss of implied value may lead to identity misrepresentation in translation. Though the diminutive is not the only marker, it is a well-represented marker of Latvian identity and should be granted a good share of attention, so not to fail the expectations set for the translation representative of a nation at a particular moment, as is the case of both anthologies discussed here.

Wierzbicka (1997:4) believes that "meanings of words from different languages do not match (even if they are artificially matched, *faute de mieux*, by the dictionaries)" due to cultural differences, because "they reflect and pass on ways of living and ways of thinking characteristic of a given society (or speech community) and that they provide priceless clues to the understanding of culture" (ibid.). Therefore, the use of diminutives makes the translator's task even more complicated. The transfer of the meaning conveyed by a diminutive to the target language proposes a challenge because the discrepancies between the source and target languages and cultures conventions are accompanied by the subjectivity factor – as the perception of the meaning conveyed by diminutives in a particular context depends on the translator's language and cultural awareness.

Translators' choices: results of data analysis

Translation scholars, for example, Toury (1995), Hermans (1996) among others, state that the decision-making process during translation is hidden because it takes place in the translator's head and researchers have no direct access to it. One of the ways to move closer to understanding it is "through confronting the input of the process with its output, i.e. the source text with the target text, and then make retrospective inferences" (Hermans 1996:4). At this stage of the research it is too premature to draw any conclusions concerning the actual reasons and arguments behind translators' decisions, whether or not and how to render the implied values of source text diminutives. More evidence is required either from interviews with translators or an in-depth qualitative analysis of the "input" and "output". Moreover, taking into account the fact that the function of diminutives is very context-bound, further analysis not only on word, collocation and sentence level, but also on text level is essential.

The fact that there have not been any strict rules or norms set for the translators[5] of the prose texts included in *New Latvian Fiction* is acknowl-

[5] The prose texts of both anthologies have been translated by different translators (*Bear's Ears* – 5, *New Latvian Fiction* – 8) with Latvian as their mother tongue. The translators of *Bear's Ears* (e.g., T.Zalīte; Z.Šteins) have longer or shorter experience in literary translation, while the translators of *New Latvian fiction* have a more diverse background – though their mother tongue is Latvian, at least 5 of them have lived in English speaking countries for long time periods and some of them have quite little experience of literary translation. There is also one case when the author has made a self-translation (M. Zelmenis).

edged by the editor of the translations, Rita Laima Krieviņa, who has been "struggling to refrain from meddling with their interpretations of the prose" (Krieviņa 1998:10). For instance, Krieviņa mentions Latvian names – some of them have been kept in the translations with all diacritical marks that are so characteristic of the Latvian language, but some have been anglicised and she has chosen to leave them that way (ibid.). The angliciastion has actually influenced the transfer of the connotations expressed by diminutives, for example, *Kārlītis* (a diminutive form of *Kārlis*) (Einfelds 1995) has been replaced by the English diminutive form *Charlie* (Einfelds 1998) and *Jānītis* (a diminutive form of *Jānis*) (Repše 1999) has been replaced by *Johnny* (Repše 1998). In both above-mentioned cases, the diminutive forms in the source texts are used as children's names – either describing or addressing them. As mentioned above, the task of this anthology (Dumbere 1998) is to offer the readers the text as such, not the Latvian context, and from this perspective, this replacement of the diminutive forms by their English counterparts seems appropriate, as in both languages they express such emotional connotation as endearment. However, it should be admitted that this replacement leads to the loss of the culture-specific element.

The translations in *Bear's Ears* aim to retain the Latvianness and the attempt is acknowledged by Zauberga (2003a:14). A case in point is the transfer of the diminutive forms of names: none of them have been anglicised and in most cases they are transcribed (e.g., *Kvēpiņš*, *Krustiņš* (Blaumanis 2003a), *Kārlēns* (Blaumanis 2003b) or replaced with the full name by adding an adjective, sometimes reduplicating it to at least partially transfer the connotation of the diminutive in the source text, for example, *Matīsiņš* (Blaumanis 1955a) – *little Matīss* (Blaumanis 2003a) or, when addressing a person with affection, "Mīļo Kārlīt!" (Blaumanis 1955a:76) "My dear, dear Kārlis" (Blaumanis 2003a:78). In the case of *Matīsiņš* – *little Matīss* some connotations have been lost in the translation. For example, in the source text the diminutive form has often been used, including in cases when the writer wants to stir the reader's compassion for the little child who has recently lost his father and who suffers from a physical disability. The replacement of *Matīsiņš* by *little Matīss* does not fully render the nuance of compassion to the target text.

When discussing "the extent to which features of a source text are retained in its translation (or even regarded as requiring retention, in the first place)", Toury (1995:12) emphasises that such a retention is not only in the interest of the source culture or even the source text, but also in the interest of the recipient side. He states that "features are retained, and reconstructed in the target-language material, not because they are 'important' in any *inherent* sense, but because they are *assigned* importance, from the recipient vantage point" (ibid.:12,original emphasis). It means that the successful transfer of the implied values from the source text to the target setting is dependent not only on the ability of the translator to use efficient translation means but also on the reader's will to explore the otherness of the text.

The analysis of the excerpted language material shows that in the short prose texts of the anthology *Bear's Ears* – in 223 out of 325 cases (see Table 1 below), and in *New Latvian Fiction* – in at least 235 out of 535 cases (see Table 2 below), diminutives in the source text convey emotional connotations together with or without the denotation of the meaning *small* or *little*. For instance, as seen in Example 1, when a widow of a rich farmer (story *Raudup's Widow*) wants to marry a young farmhand and he rejects her proposal. As a result, the insulted widow feels irritated and, addressing the young man with a diminutive form, with a hint of irony and scorn says:

(1) *Smuks tu gan esi,* ***puisīt,*** *bet lielkunga meitas jau nu tevis tikpat neņems iegātņos …* (Blaumanis 1955a:71)

You may be handsome, **my lad**, but no daughter of a rich landowner would marry you for all that! (Blaumanis 2003a:72)

In the target text given in Example 1, the translator has chosen a colloquial word *lad* and has added the possessive pronoun *my* to transfer the emotional nuance of the source text diminutive. In addition to that, she has resorted to graphical means, i.e. an exclamation mark at the end of the sentence to convey the intenseness of emotions.

In the fairy-tale *Hangman's Daughter*, the diminutive form of the word daughter – *meitiņa* – is constantly used in the Latvian source text to convey not only the message that the girl is still a little child, but also to symbolise the pure and sincere soul of the little girl and the love of her father, his sincere attitude towards her.

(2) *Reiz bija viens bende un tam bija* ***meitiņa.*** (Skalbe 1979a:111)

Once there lived a hangman and he had **a daughter**. (Skalbe 2003a:137)

(3) *Bet reizēm, kad viņš bij izgulējis grūto dzērumu, kādā tas pavadīja savas dienas, tas ņēma uz ceļiem savu* ***meitiņu,*** *un kāda skaņa viņa kaklā meklēja vārdus.* (Skalbe 1979a:111)

> But sometimes when he had sobered up after boozy days he took **his little daughter** in his lap and a strange sound would struggle in his throat for words. (Skalbe 2003a:137)

This fairy tale has been written in the period starting around 1910 and called lyricism, where

> [A] lyric is not distinguished by its verse form but by its portrayal of the world as conceived by the human heart. In lyricism the subjective, the experience of the individual comes to the foreground; the universe, social problems fade away. (Zauberga 2003a:11)

The writer Kārlis Skalbe, as a representative of this trend, has an expressive language containing a very rich and diverse use of various expressive language means, diminutive being one of them.

In Examples 2 and 3, the English translation is definitely more neutral; it has lost the contrast conveyed in the source text *bende* vs *meitiņa* (*hangman* vs (little, dear, innocent) *daughter*). In the translation of Example 2, there is no information whether his daughter is a child or adult. It should be noted that on a sentence level the implied values thinned out, but the translator has made an attempt to compensate for them on a textual level, as can be seen in Example 4 below. For the sake of analysing the use of diminutives in the source text and their corresponding translations in the target text, in Example 4 they have been numbered within the text.

(4) ***Meitiņa*** *[1] izgāja ziedošā pļavā. Un katra* ***zālīte*** *[2] tai bij tik laba kā zaļa* ***māmuliņa*** *[3]. Viņa bij nogurusi un gribēja gulēt, un viņai nebij ne segas, ne* ***spilventiņa*** *[4]. Bet puķes tai sniedza savas bārkstainās villaines un sūnas savus brūnos* ***spilventiņus*** *[5]. „Vai te jau gulta zem katras* ***zālītes*** *[6]," **meitiņa** [7] brīnījās. Viņa staigāja pa pļavu, un nevienam puķes nav smaržojušas tā, kā tai rītā bendes* ***meitiņai*** *[8]. Un nevienam* ***zālītes*** *[9] nav palocījušās tik laipni, ne pašam ķēniņam.* (Skalbe 1979a:113)

Our little girl [1] went into a blooming meadow. And every **grass stalk** [2] seemed to her as kind as **mother** [3]. She felt tired and wanted to sleep but she had neither blankets nor **pillows** [4]. But flowers offered her their fringed petal sheets and moss its **little velvet cushions** [5]. "There seems to be a bed under every **grass stalk** [6]," **the little girl** [7] wondered. She walked in the meadow and no flower had ever smelled so sweetly as on that morning for the hangman's **daughter** [8]. Never had the **little grass stalks** [9] bent so readily, not even for the king himself. (Skalbe 2003a:139)

Example 4 explicitly demonstrates the use of stylistic means and the syntactic type of English diminutive formation, as well as an attempt to transfer the poetic style and the positive, sincere atmosphere which is expressed in Latvian with the help of diminutives – by adding some extra information. At first sight, the translator has chosen neutral target language words for diminutives 3, 4 and 8, but in case of diminutive 1 (*our little girl*), the possessive pronoun *our* has been used, thus creating the sense of belonging and adding some personal colouring involving the reader. In case of diminutive 5 (*little velvet cushions*), adjectives *little* and *velvet* have been used, thus adding an extra connotation of sincerity and warm feelings.

Example 5 demonstrates that the translator has chosen lexical means to express a very sincere attitude of the main character Maria, of the story *Storm Approaching,* towards nature and the neighbourhood where she lives. Maria is a lonely elderly woman, whose whole world is her cattle in the shed and the nature around her small, old house.

(5) *Pareizi, jā, vēl putni mēro balsis un ūdens* ***klusklusītiņām murd*** *turpat viņpus* ***pļaviņai.*** (Zelmenis 1999:219)

It's true, the birds are still comparing their voices, and water **murmurs** on the other side of the meadow. (Zelmenis 1998:154)

In Example 5, the translator has used the verb *murmur* which quite precisely conveys the message expressed by an adverb in diminutive form *klusklusītiņām* (where the stem denoting *quiet* is repeated twice and two diminutive suffixes *–īt–* and *–iņ–* are added) and the verb *murd* – Maria hears a very soft, even delicate sound of the water. The addition of an adverb – *murmurs softly* – would have rendered the implied meaning even closer and at least partially compensated the loss of the connotation of the other diminutive – *pļaviņa.* The latter has been replaced by a neutral noun *meadow*, which in the target text does not connote the sincerity of the elderly women towards what she sees around her.

The above-mentioned five examples have demonstrated some of the means used by translators to retain the implied values expressed via the diminutive in the source text. Table 1 and Table 2 offer a summary of the statistics of the number of diminutives in the analysed source texts and their transfer to the target texts, indicating whether in translation the connotation has been expressed with the help of a diminutive, i.e. morphological (synthetic) type (in both tables, the abbreviation *morph. type* has been used) of diminutive formation, syntactic (analytical) (in both tables the abbreviation *synt. type* has been used) means or lost.

Title ST	Title TT	Total No.of diminutives in ST	No.of diminutives with emotional connotation in ST	Lost or partially lost emotional connotation in TT	Transfer to the TT with		
					morph. type	synt. type	lost
Skalbe 1979a	Skalbe 2003a	45	42	9	0	34	11
Skalbe 1979b	Skalbe 2003b	13	8	1	0	10	3
Skalbe 1979c	Skalbe 2003c	3	2	2	0	1	2
Blaumanis 1955a	Blaumanis 2003a	128	110	86	7	34	87
Blaumanis 1955b	Blaumanis 2003b	64	28	27	0	25	39
Jaunsudrabiņš 1982	Jaunsudrabiņš 2003	14	4	3	0	0	14
Virza 1989	Virza 2003	21	7	1	0	10	11
Mauriņa 1990	Mauriņa 2003	12	9	7	2	2	8
Upīts 1949	Upīts 2003	25	13	6	0	8	17
	Total	325	223	173	9	124	192

Table 1: Diminutives in the source texts and transfer of their meaning to the target texts / Anthology: *The Bear's Ears*

Table 1 shows that in *Bear's Ears*, in almost 59% of the cases of the diminutive use in the source text, the implied value has been lost in translation on word, collocation or sentence level. The loss has mainly occurred in those instances where diminutives in the source text have been used to convey additional emotional connotations (173 out of 223 lost, i.e. almost 76%). There are very few cases when translators have used the morphological diminutive formation type – an English diminutive, for example *memmiņa* (Blaumanis 1955a) – *mummy* (Blaumanis 2003a) or *vecmāmiņa* (Mauriņa 1990) – *granny* (Mauriņa 2003). The most widely used tool for transferring the emotional connotations are lexical means – emotionally coloured lexical choices, including adjectives, nouns, verbs etc.

Title ST	Title TT	Total No.of diminutives in ST	No.of diminutives with emotional connotation in ST	Lost emotional connotation in TT	Transfer to the target text with		
					morph. type	synt. Type	lost
Bankovskis 1995	Bankovskis 1998	17	6	2	0	4	13
Berelis 1999	Berelis 1998	65	27	7	0	29	75
Einfelds 1995	Einfelds 1998	62	55	13	20	12	30
Ikstena 1995	Ikstena 1998b	14	3	3	0	0	14
Kolmanis 1995	Kolmanis 1998	32	5	3	0	7	25
Lāce 1992	Lāce 1998	18	3	3	0	3	15
Neiburga 2004	Neiburga 1998	53	23	15	0	11	42
Ozoliņš 1991	Ozoliņš 1998	7	3	3	0	0	7
Repše 1999	Repše 1998	75	30	9	14	15	46
Zelmenis 1999	Zelmenis 1998	55	28	21	1	4	50
Ziedonis 1992	Ziedonis 1998	137	52	32	0	37	100
	Total	535	235	111	35	122	417

Table 2: Diminutives in the source texts and transfer of their meaning to the target texts. *New Latvian Fiction*

Table 2 shows that in the translations in *New Latvian Fiction*, in almost in 78% of the cases, the implied value has been lost, a large number of them again being constituted by the diminutives with emotional connotation (111 out of 235 lost, i.e. around 47%). It might be due to the subjective interpretations of the translators (Krieviņa 1998:10) or their attempt to avoid too much "otherness" (Hermans 1996:10) for the target text readers. The cases when the diminutive is used in the target text are mainly when translators have chosen to replace the diminutive form of a Latvian name by its English counterpart. The percentage of fully or partially conveyed emotional connotation is only slightly lower than in the case of *Bear's Ears* – almost

68%. The same as in *Bear's Ears*, the most widely used means for transferring the emotional connotations are lexical means – emotionally coloured lexical choices including adjectives, nouns, verbs etc.

Conclusion

Latvian literature is not well known in other cultures, since "it is hard for a "small" literature to make inroads into "big" literatures, which are notoriously wary of translations. Such translations mostly remain marginal curiosities" (Zauberga 2003a:13). With the help of an excellent work of translators, who are able to transfer the culture-specific elements and worldview, a translation can find its way to the readers worldwide, it just "needs time and considerable effort to reach an international audience" (Ikstena 1998a:9). The results of the present analysis indicate that the culture-specific "otherness" of Latvian literature conveyed by diminutives in the source texts is only partially rendered in their English translations. At the moment – it might only be a tentative guess, the proof of which requires an in-depth qualitative analysis on textual level – the analysed data demonstrate a tendency of the translations of the prose texts studied within the framework of this research to be more target audience oriented.

This paper has attempted to offer an overview of the means used by translators of two anthologies of Latvian literature to transfer the implied meanings expressed in the source texts by a very characteristic phenomenon of the Latvian language – the diminutive, which may often be the only marker to express a particular attitude or emotional connotation. It should be noted that the present research has resulted in findings similar to some other studies on diminutive translation to English (see for example Chamonikolasová and Rambousek 2007; Al-Gazalli 2012 etc.) – the diminutive's semantic meaning of smallness is mainly rendered in the English target texts while its emotional connotations are often lost.

There is a similar density of diminutives with additional connotations in the source texts of both anthologies (223 in *Bear's Ears* and 235 in *New Latvian Fiction*). Though the prose texts included in the two anthologies have been written in different time periods – at the beginning and at the end of the twentieth century – they have all been translated at the very end of the twentieth and beginning of the twenty-first centuries and analysis of the language material shows similar patterns in the transfer of the implied values of the source text diminutive to the target text:

(1) the denotative meaning of smallness is mainly rendered by syntactic means using such analytic diminutive markers as *small, little* etc.;

(2) there is no consistent approach used by the translators of the two anthologies to transfer the emotional connotations of the source text diminutives to the target text;

(3) on word, collocation and sentence level the connotations of the source text diminutives have been often lost by the translators of both anthologies (*New Latvian Fiction* – 47% and *Bear's Ears* – almost 77%);

(4) in very few cases the translators of both anthologies have transferred the implied values of source text diminutives by morphological means, mainly when transferring the diminutive forms of proper names;

(5) the translations included in both anthologies contain examples of successful use of various syntactic means – translators have chosen emotionally coloured nouns, adjectives, adverbs and other parts of speech denoting the respective emotional attitude or connotation of the source text's diminutive, thus retaining implied values;

(6) the most widely used means is syntactic diminutive formation, i.e., adding adjectives that are diminutive by meaning or denote emotional nuances;

(7) each reading is individual and subjectivity of the translator (who primarily is a reader and responds to the text subjectively) may have influenced their understanding of the emotional nuances conveyed by a diminutive in a particular context.

The analysis of the excerpted language material shows that the translators of both anthologies have not exhausted the potential of the English morphological diminutive formation type as suggested by Schneider (2003), for example, prefixation, reduplication, compounding. There are examples illustrating the possibilities offered by the syntactic diminutive formation type, and translators of Latvian prose texts can definitely apply them more extensively to accommodate the implied values of diminutives, thus retaining a specific Latvian "otherness" in the target texts.

References

Aizpura, Iveta (1998) "'Vai būt Latvietim?' Saruna ar Janīnu Kursīti: Mitoloģijas Pētnieci, LU Filoloģijas Fakultātes Dekāni" ['Being a Latvian?' An Interview with Janīna Kursīte, Mythology Researcher and Dean of the Faculty of Philology, the University of Latvia]. *Izglītības Attīstības Centra Arhīvs [Archive of Education Development Centre]*, http://iac.edu.lv/arhivs/numuri/raksti/20_kursite.doc [19 October 2014].

Alberte, Ieva (2009) "Mīlināšanās Valoda: Par ko tā Liecina" [Language of Endearment: What It Reflects]. Interview with Linguist Janīna Kursīte. *Diena* 20:4, http://www.diena.lv/dzivesstils/attiecibas/milinasanas-valoda-par-ko-ta-liecina-662830 [19 October 2014].

Al-Ghazalli, Mehdi F. (2012) "Diminutives in Arabic-to-English Translation". *Babel* 58:4, 395–407.

Bagasheva-Koleva, Mariya (2010) "Expressing Diminutiveness in English: An Overview Based on Fairytales". *BETA-IAFTEL* 3:9, http://www.beta-iatefl.org/1609/blog-publications/expressing-diminutiveness-english-overview-based-fairytales/ [19 October 2014].

Hatim, Basil (2001) "Pragmatics and Translation". In Baker, Mona (ed.) *Routledge Encyclopaedia of Translation studies.* London/New York: Routledge.

Brown, Keith (ed.) (2006) *Encyclopaedia of Language and Linguistics.* Oxford: Elsevier.

Bußmann, Hadumod (2002) *Lexikon der Sprachwissenschaft.* Stuttgart: Alfred Kröner Verlag.

Chamonikolasová, Jana/Rambousek, Jiří (2007) "Diminutive Expressions in Translation: A Comparative Study of English and Czech". *Belgian Journal of Linguistics* 21:1, 37-52.

Dumbere, Laura (1998) "Latviešu Literatūra Amerikā un Vācijā" [Latvian Literature in the United States and Germany]. *Diena* 31:3, http://www.diena.lv/arhivs/latviesu-literatura-amerika-un-vacija-10029983 [19 October 2014].

Hermans, Theo (1996) "Norms and the Determination of Translation: A Theoretical Framework". In Álvarez, Román/Vidal, M. Carmen Africa (eds.) *Translation, Power, Subversion.* Clevedon/Philadelphia/Adelaide: Multilingual Matters, 25-51.

Ikstena, Nora (1998a) "When will Latvians Witness Those Times?". *The Review of Contemporary Fiction: New Latvian Fiction* 18:1, 7-10.

Jurafsky, Daniel (1993) "Universals in the Semantics of the Diminutive". *Proceedings of the Nineteenth Annual Meeting of the Berkeley Linguistics Society: General Session and Parasession on Semantic Typology and Semantic Universals.* Berkeley: Berkeley Linguistics Society, 423-436.

Jurafsky, Daniel (1996) "Universal Tendencies in the Semantics of the Diminutive". *Language* 72:3, 533-578.

Krieviņa, Rita Laima (1998) "Note from Rita Laima Krieviņa". *The Review of Contemporary Fiction: New Latvian Fiction* 18:1, 10.

Kvašytė, Regina (2012) "Latviešu Tautasdziesmas Lietuviski: Valodnieciskais Aspekts" [Latvian Folk Songs in Lithuanian: the Linguistic Aspect]. In *Starp Lietuvu un Latviju: lingvistiskās paralēles [Between Lithuania and Latvia: Linguistic Parallels]*. Šiauliai: Šiaulių universitetas, 239-253.

Načisčione, Anita (1996) "The Diminutive in Lewis Carroll's Poem *The Little Man that Had a Little Gun*: A Study in Practical Stylistics". *Sastatāmā un Lietišķā Valodniecība. Kontrastīvie Pētījumi* 5:603, 30-35.

Rūķe-Draviņa, Velta (1953) "Adjectival Diminutives in Latvian". *The Slavonic and East European Review* 31:77, 452-465.

Rūķe-Draviņa, Velta (1959) *Diminutive im Lettischen. Acta Universitatis Stockholmiensis, No. 8*. Lund: Hakan Ohlssons Boktryckeri.

Saule-Sleine, Mērija (1955) "Par Substantīvu un Adjektīvu Atvasinājumiem ar -iņš, -iņa- Mūsdienu Latviešu Literārajā Valodā" [On the Derivatives of Substantives and Adjectives with -iņš-, -iņa- in Modern Latvian]. In *LPSR ZA Valodas un literatūras institūta Raksti [Papers of the LSSR Academy of Science Institute of Language and Literature]*. Rīga: LPSR ZA izdevniecība, 87-116.

Schneider, Klaus P. (2003) Diminutives in English. Berlin: Max Niemeyer Verlag.

Schneider, Klaus P. (2013) "The Truth About Diminutives, and How we Can Find it: Some Theoretical and Methodological Considerations", *SKASE Journal of Theoretical Linguistics* 10:2.

Schneider, Klaus P./Strubel-Burgdorf, Susanne (2012) "Diminutive -let in English". *SKASE Journal of Theoretical Linguistics* 9:1, 15-32.

Skujiņa, Valentīna et.al. (2007) *Valodniecības Pamatterminu Skaidrojošā Vārdnīca [Dictionary of Main Linguistic Terms]*. Rīga: LU Latviešu valodas institūts.

Sokols, Ēvalds (ed.) (1959) *Mūsdienu Latviešu Literārās Valodas Gramatika I: Fonētika un Morfoloģija [Grammar of Modern Latvian Literary Language I: Phonetics and Morphology]*. Rīga: LPSR ZA izdevniecība.

Toury, Gideon (1995) *Descriptive Translation Studies and Beyond*. Amsterdam/Philadelphia: Benjamins.

Verdonk, Peter (2002) *Stylistics*. New York/Oxford: Oxford University Press.

Vulāne, Anna (2002) "Deminutīvu Konotācija Latviešu Tautasdziesmās" [Connotations of Diminutives in Latvian Folk Songs]. In: *Лексикология и лексикография балтийских языков. Материалы XXXI межвузовской научно-методической конференции. Секция балтистики. Тезисы докладов [Lexicology and Lexicography of the Baltic Languages. Materials of XXXI Interuniversity Scientific and Methodological Conference. Baltistics Section. Abstracts]*. Saint Petersburg: Faculty of Philology, Saint Petersburg State University, 11–12.

Wierzbicka, Anna (1992) *Semantics, Culture and Cognition: Universal Human Concepts in Culture Specific Configurations*. New York/Oxford: Oxford University Press.

Wierzbicka, Anna (1997) *Understanding Cultures through Their Key Words: English, Russian, Polish, German, and Japanese*. New York/Oxford: Oxford University Press.

Zauberga, Ieva (2002) "Role of Conventions in Cross-cultural Communication". *Humanities and Social Sciences in Latvia. Languages, Literatures, and Manipulations* 1:34, 126-149.

Zauberga, Ieva (2003a) "Landmarks of Latvian Literature". In Zauberga, Ieva/ Veisbergs, Andrejs/Chesterman, Andrew (eds.) *Bear's Ears: An Anthology of Latvian Literature*. Riga: University of Latvia, 5-14.

Zauberga, Ieva (2003b) "Poetics of Latvian Folksongs". In Zauberga, Ieva/Veisbergs, Andrejs/Chesterman, Andrew (eds.) *Bear's Ears: An Anthology of Latvian Literature*. Riga: University of Latvia, 15-22.

Corpus

Bankovskis, Pauls (1998) "The Week of Golden Silence" (tr. Māra Sīmanis). *The Review of Contemporary Fiction: New Latvian Fiction* 18:1, 11-16.

Bankovskis, Pauls (1995) "Zeltītās Klusēšanas Nedēļa". *Karogs* 7, 3-7.

Berelis, Guntis (1998) "Beckett is Alive". *The Review of Contemporary Fiction: New Latvian Fiction* 18:1, 17-44.

Berelis, Guntis (1999) "Bekets ir Dzīvs". In Berelis, Guntis *Mīnotaura medības*. Rīga: Atēna, 7-41.

Blaumanis, Rūdolfs (1955a) "Raudupiete". In Blaumanis, Rūdolfs *Stāsti un Noveles. Izlase*. Rīga: Latvijas Valsts izdevniecība, 60-79.

Blaumanis, Rūdolfs (1955b) "Nāves ēnā". In Blaumanis, Rūdolfs *Stāsti un Noveles. Izlase*. Rīga: Latvijas Valsts izdevniecība, 391-408.

Blaumanis, Rūdolfs (2003a) "Raudup's Widow" (tr. Tamāra Zālīte). In Zauberga, Ieva/Veisbergs, Andrejs/Chesterman, Andrew (eds.) *Bear's Ears: An Anthology of Latvian Literature*. Riga: University of Latvia, 60-81.

Blaumanis, Rūdolfs (2003b) "The Shadow of Death" (tr. Tamāra Zālīte). In Zauberga, Ieva/Veisbergs, Andrejs/Chesterman, Andrew (eds.) *Bear's Ears: An Anthology of Latvian Literature*. Riga: University of Latvia, 82-102.

Einfelds, Jānis (1995a) "Brīnišķis putns". In Einfelds, Jānis *Mēness bērns*. Rīga: Preses nams, 17-18.

Einfelds, Jānis (1995b) "Dundagas rīti". In Einfelds, Jānis *Mēness bērns*. Rīga: Preses nams, 98-99.

Einfelds, Jānis (1995c) "Etīde ar lodi". In Einfelds, Jānis *Mēness bērns*. Rīga: Preses nams, 26-27.

Einfelds, Jānis (1995d) "Gurķu ārija". In Einfelds, Jānis *Mēness bērns*. Rīga: Preses nams, 97-98.

Einfelds, Jānis (1995e) "Lāga vīrs Mēness". In Einfelds, Jānis *Mēness bērns*. Rīga: Preses nams, 31-32.

Einfelds, Jānis (1995f) "Liktenis". In Einfelds, Jānis *Mēness bērns*. Rīga: Preses nams, 22-23.

Einfelds, Jānis (1998) "Cucumber Aria", "The Wonderful Bird", "Fate", "Etude with A Bullet", "Nice Guy Moon", "Dundaga Mornings" (tr. Ilze Kļaviņa-Mueller). *The Review of Contemporary Fiction: New Latvian Fiction* 18:1, 45-54.

Ikstena, Nora (1995) "Svēto izpriecas". In Ikstena, Nora *Nieki un izpriecas*. Rīga: Karogs, 110-135.

Ikstena, Nora (1998b) "Pleasures of the Saints" (tr. Rita Laima Krieviņa). *The Review of Contemporary Fiction: New Latvian Fiction* 18:1, 55-64.

Jaunsudrabiņš, Jānis (1982) "Šupolēs". In Avotiņa, Daina et al. (eds.) *Jānis Jaunsudrabiņš. Kopoti raksti.* Vol. 8. Rīga: Liesma, 450-453.

Jaunsudrabiņš, Jānis (2003) "Swinging" (tr. Gunita Salmiņa). In Zauberga, Ieva/ Veisbergs, Andrejs/Chesterman, Andrew (eds.) *Bear's Ears: An Anthology of Latvian Literature.* Riga: University of Latvia, 152-155.

Kolmanis, Arvis (1995) "Stāsts par Skolnieci Veroniku". In Kolmanis, Arvis *Greniāna jeb Ceturtā Versija.* Rīga: Daugava, 133-159.

Kolmanis, Arvis (1998) "Veronica, the Schoolgirl" (tr. Mārtiņš Zelmenis). *The Review of Contemporary Fiction: New Latvian Fiction* 18:1, 65-83.

Lāce, Aija (1992) "Kāpnes". *Diena* 9:5 (Supplement *Sestdiena)*, 12.

Lāce, Aija (1998) "The Stairs" (tr. Ieva Lešinska). *The Review of Contemporary Fiction: New Latvian Fiction* 18:1, 84-91.

Mauriņa, Zenta (1990) "Zelta putns". In Mauriņa, Zenta *Uzdrīkstēšanās: Izlase 1929-1944.* Rīga: Liesma, 87-93.

Mauriņa, Zenta (2003) "The Golden Bird" (tr. Andrejs Veisbergs). In Zauberga, Ieva/Veisbergs, Andrejs/Chesterman, Andrew (eds.) *Bear's Ears: An Anthology of Latvian Literature.* Riga: University of Latvia, 181-187.

Neiburga Andra (1998) "Summer Log (The Zone)" (tr. Baņuta Rubess). *The Review of Contemporary Fiction: New Latvian Fiction* 18:1, 92-110.

Neiburga Andra (2004) "Vasaras pieraksti. Zona". In Neiburga, Andra *Stum, Stum.* Rīga: Valters un Rapa, 283-300.

Ozoliņš, Aivars (1991) "Pasaka Nr.13". *Grāmata* 12, 54-62.

Ozoliņš, Aivars (1998) "Tale No.13" (tr. Ieva S. Celle). *The Review of Contemporary Fiction: New Latvian Fiction* 18:1, 111-124.

Repše, Gundega (1998) *From* "Stigmata" (tr. Baņuta.Rubess). *The Review of Contemporary Fiction: New Latvian Fiction* 18:1, 125-144.

Repše, Gundega (1999) "Stigma". In Repše, Gundega/Rožkane, Anita *Septiņi Stāsti par Mīlu.* Rīga: Pētergailis, 216-234.

Skalbe, Kārlis (1979a) "Bendes Meitiņa". In Skalbe, Kārlis *Pasakas.* Rīga: Liesma, 111-115.

Skalbe, Kārlis (1979b) "Divi Draugi". In Skalbe, Kārlis *Pasakas.* Rīga: Liesma, 185-190.

Skalbe, Kārlis (2003a) "Hangman's Daughter" (tr. Ieva Zauberga). In Zauberga, Ieva/Veisbergs, Andrejs/Chesterman, Andrew (eds.) *Bear's Ears: An Anthology of Latvian Literature.* Riga: University of Latvia, 135-141.

Skalbe, Kārlis (1979c) "Pārvēršanās". In Skalbe, Kārlis *Pasakas.* Rīga: Liesma, 260-262.

Skalbe, Kārlis (2003b) "Two Friends" (tr. Zigmunds Šteins). In Zauberga, Ieva/ Veisbergs, Andrejs/Chesterman, Andrew (eds.) *Bear's Ears: An Anthology of Latvian Literature.* Riga: University of Latvia, 145-150.

Skalbe, Kārlis (2003c) "Metamorphosis" (tr. Ieva Zauberga). In Zauberga, Ieva/ Veisbergs, Andrejs/Chesterman, Andrew (eds.) *Bear's Ears: An Anthology of Latvian Literature.* Riga: University of Latvia, 142-144.

Upīts, Andrejs (1949) "Sirdsapziņa". In Upīts, Andrejs *Noveļu izlase pa četrdesmit gadiem. 1903-1943.* Rīga: Latvijas Valsts izdevniecība, 74-80.

Upīts, Andrejs (2003) "Conscience" (tr. Tamāra Zālīte). In Zauberga, Ieva/Veisbergs, Andrejs/Chesterman, Andrew (eds.) *Bear's Ears: An Anthology of Latvian Literature.* Riga: University of Latvia, 171-178.

Virza, Edvarts (1989) *Straumēni.* Rīga: Liesma.

Virza, Edvarts (2003) "Straumēni Homestead" (tr. Andrejs Veisbergs). In Zauberga, Ieva/Veisbergs, Andrejs/Chesterman, Andrew (eds.) *Bear's Ears: An Anthology of Latvian Literature.* Riga: University of Latvia, 158-168.

Zelmenis, Mārtiņš (1998) "Storm Approaching" (tr. Mārtiņš Zelmenis). *The Review of Contemporary Fiction: New Latvian Fiction* 18:1, 153-164.

Zelmenis, Mārtiņš (1999) "Negaisa Nāciens". In Zelmenis, Mārtiņš *Rokenroli un citas izmeklētas mīlasdziesmas.* Rīga: Intelekts, 219-229.

Ziedonis, Rimants (1992) "Lidojošās Zivis". In Ziedonis, Rimants *Dzīves pieredze un ziepju burbuļi.* Rīga: SIA "Latvijas Jaunatne", 29-73.

Ziedonis, Rimants (1998) "The Flying Fish" (tr. Sarma Muižnieks-Liepiņš). *The Review of Contemporary Fiction: New Latvian Fiction* 18:1, 165-192.

List of contributors

VÉRONIQUE BOHN completed a Master's degree in Translation (Specialised Translation) in 2010 at the Faculty of Translation and Interpreting (FTI) of the University of Geneva (UNIGE), for the language combination French-German-Spanish. She also achieved a Complementary Certificate in Translation in 2012 at the FTI in order to add English to her language combination. She is currently working as a research assistant at the French Unit of the FTI besides a professional activity as a freelance translator on the Swiss market. She is currently working on a PhD dissertation at the University of Geneva in which she explores the role translation plays in political communication in Switzerland.
Email: veronique.bohn@unige.ch

SILVIA COBELO is a doctoral candidate and researcher of Spanish Literature at the Department of Modern Languages, Faculty of Philosophy, Letters and Human Sciences of the University of São Paulo, Brazil. She also works as a translator. In her PhD dissertation she focuses on the history of retranslations and adaptations in Brazil from 1886 to 2012. Her main research interest is the translations and other rewritings of Cervantes, within the Translation and Adaptation Studies perspective.
Email: silvia.cobelo@usp.br

CECILIA FOGLIA received her BA in Foreign Languages, Literatures and Cultures, and her MA in Modern Euro-American Languages and Literatures from the University of Macerata, Italy. She is currently a doctoral candidate at the University of Montreal, where she also works as a research and teaching assistant of Italian. Her interests include the sociology of translation, cultural translation and migration literature in translation. Her doctoral research focuses on the literary production and trajectory of Marco Micone, an Italian writer, adapter, translator and self-translator who migrated to Québec after World War II.
Email: cecilia.foglia@umontreal.ca

WILLIAM F. HANES is a PhD candidate in the Department of Translation Studies at the Federal University of Santa Catarina, Brazil. His dissertation is

on language policy in the Brazilian interdisciplinary science journal *Memórias do Instituto Oswaldo Cruz*. His research interests include translation and the dynamics of scientific culture, authorship and the open access movement as well as lingua franca and identity.
Email: hanes.wf@gmail.com

ABDEL WAHAB KHALIFA is a double major doctoral candidate at the Centre for Translation Studies (CTS) and Centre for Arabic, Islamic and Middle Eastern Studies (AIMES) at the University of Leeds. He has a BA and a PGDip in English Language and Literature from Tanta University, Egypt, and an MPhil in Translation and Intercultural Studies from the University of Salford. He lectured at several universities, including Manchester Metropolitan University and Graz. His research interests include the sociology of translation; translation historiography; translation motivation as well as literary criticism and Arabic, Islamic and Middle Eastern cultural and literary histories.
Email: a.w.khalifa13@leeds.ac.uk

HEDINA TAHIROVIĆ-SIJERČIĆ is a PhD student in Translation Studies at Katholieke Universiteit Leuven. Besides teaching Romani language, culture and literature, she works as a translator. She is currently writing her PhD thesis on Translation, Multilingualism and Romani literature in the Balkans. Her main research interest is translation within the context of Romani Studies.
Email: hedina.sijercic@mail.com

SERENA TALENTO is a junior fellow at the Bayreuth International Graduate School of African Studies. She completed a Master's degree in Languages and Cultures of Africa from the University of Naples "L'Orientale", where she specialised in Swahili language and literature. Currently she is pursuing her PhD, working on the construction of a discourse on literary translation into Swahili in three different historical settings. Her research interests include sociology of translation, translation history, post-colonial translation theories, translation and discourse analysis. She has also a special interest in cognitive linguistics, sociolinguistics, and corpus linguistics.
Email: serena.talento@uni-bayreuth.de

ZANE VEIDENBERGA is a PhD student of Interuniversity Doctoral programme "Linguistics" at Ventspils University College, Latvia. She works as a senior lecturer and director of the bachelor study programme "Translation and Interpreting" at The University College of Economics and Culture, Latvia. Besides her experience in teaching and training, she has worked as a translator and interpreter for various organisations and international projects. Her PhD project focuses the issue of rendering the emotional connotations conveyed by diminutives in Latvian source (prose) texts to English target texts.
Email: zane_veidenberga@apollo.lv

ELENA VOELLMER is a predoctoral scholar and lecturer at Pompeu Fabra University, Spain, where she teaches in the graduate programmes of Translation and Applied Language Studies. She holds a Bachelor's degree in Translating and Interpreting from the University of Heidelberg and a Master's degree in Translation Studies from Pompeu Fabra University. She is part of the research group CEDIT, the *Center for Studies on Discourse and Translation.* She is currently working on her PhD project, which is sponsored by the Catalan government. Other fields of interest include literary translation, translation theory, the sociology of translation, wordplay and phraseology.
Email: elena.voellmer@upf.edu

Subject Index

Name Index

Repräsentation – Transformation
representation – transformation
représentation – transformation
Translating across Cultures and Societies
hrsg. von Ao. Univ. Prof. Dr. Michaela Wolf (Universität Graz)

Heike van Lawick; Brigitte E. Jirku (Hg.)
Übersetzen als Performanz
Translation und Translationswissenschaft in performativem Licht
Konzepte wie Performanz und Performativität haben im Anschluss an die kulturelle und soziologische Wende an Brisanz gewonnen. In den Kapiteln über Performanz als Rezitation, PerformerInnen und performatives Handeln, Translatorische Performanz und System sowie Probleme des performativen Handelns präzisieren, reflektieren und illustrieren die Beiträge in diesem Band unterschiedliche Ansätze des Übersetzens als Performanz und performative Praxis. Die Beiträge dieses Bandes weisen auf eine „performative Wende" hin.
Bd. 8, 2012, 320 S., 29,90 €, br., ISBN 978-3-643-50451-7

LIT Verlag Berlin – Münster – Wien – Zürich – London
Auslieferung Deutschland / Österreich / Schweiz: siehe Impressumsseite

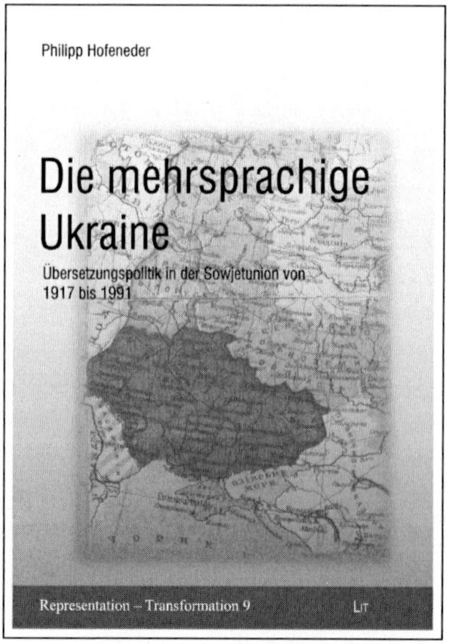

Philipp Hofeneder
Die mehrsprachige Ukraine
Übersetzungspolitik in der Sowjetunion von 1917 bis 1991

Die vorliegende Studie untersucht Übersetzungen aus und in das Ukrainische in der Zeit von 1917 bis 1991. Mit der Machtübernahme der Kommunisten einhergehend wurde ein extrem umfangreiches und vielschichtiges Übersetzungswesen aufgebaut. Es beschränkte sich nicht auf die – teilweise wechselseitige – Rezeption westeuropäischer Literaturen, sondern umfasste im Besonderen die Sprachen innerhalb der Sowjetunion und des Sozialistischen Lagers. In sechs Mikrostudien werden die Entstehungsgeschichte, die wesentlichen Merkmale sowie die kulturpolitischen Umstände dieser Translate eingehend beleuchtet.

Bd. 9, 2013, 216 S., 24,90 €, br., ISBN 978-3-643-50544-6

LIT Verlag Berlin – Münster – Wien – Zürich – London
Auslieferung Deutschland / Österreich / Schweiz: siehe Impressumsseite